Concepts of Communication: **Reading**

Ideas Module
Inferences Module

Concepts of Communication: **Reading**

IDEAS MODULE

INFERENCES MODULE

Mary Lou Conlin **Cuyahoga Community College**

Houghton Mifflin Company Boston
Dallas Geneva, Illinois Hopewell, New Jersey
Palo Alto London

To the Instructor

In the *Ideas Module,* students are taught the various skills involved in finding the main ideas and details in both general and textbook readings. They work with determining the organization of and finding the relationships among the different ideas included in a reading selection.

Many of the study skills that are often included in reading improvement courses are also incorporated within the *Ideas Module* instruction. Thus, students are taught to preread and survey essays, articles, and textbook excerpts for their controlling ideas and major points, and to find the topic sentences of paragraphs. They are also taught about close reading of sentences, about grouping the words within a sentence according to units of meaning, and about working out the meanings of several kinds of sentences that frequently create reading difficulty. In addition, students are taught how to outline, paraphrase, and summarize various kinds of reading selections. The purpose of teaching these skills is to improve students' retention of materials read and their ability to communicate their understanding of these materials.

All of the general reading skills are taught first through high-interest general readings. The skills are then transferred to the reading of textbooks. Students are shown the similarities among essays, articles, and textbook chapters. Another task shows students how to make efficient use of the various reading and study aids available in a textbook (contents, footnotes, bibliography, glossary, index, and so on . This task also includes a section on reading charts and graphs. Three other tasks further relate the *Ideas Module* instruction to textbooks in different content areas: math, chemistry, and biology; English, psychology, sociology, and history; and business, data processing, and nutrition. In these tasks students are shown the ways in which textbooks in particular subjects are generally organized and also the ways of explaining (methods of development) that will be used with great frequency in each of the subjects.

Students participate in each lesson by working examples and answering multiple-choice questions about the meaning of the examples. They can check the answers to these questions by using the Answer Key at the end of each task. A reading practice at the end of each lesson gives the instructor ample opportunity to check each student's progress. Twenty readings, ranging from fifth-grade to college level in difficulty, are included in the *Ideas Module.*

To date, most of the instructional materials used in reading improvement courses have been based on finding the main ideas and details in rhetorically and structurally perfect paragraphs. The problem with this approach is that it is unrealistic. First, rhetorically and structurally perfect paragraphs are rarely found in whole reading selections. The paragraph within a whole selection must, indeed, take on somewhat different characteristics from those of an isolated paragraph. Second, the techniques involved in finding the main ideas and details in a single paragraph generally break down when students try to apply them to a whole selection. A whole selection is, of necessity, more complex in organization and content than a single paragraph. For these reasons and because the student is required to read and understand whole selections, not just perfect paragraphs, and determine their ideas, the *Ideas Module* builds on and expands the traditional main-ideas-and-details approach into a whole-selection approach to reading.

The terminology used has been kept to a minimum. However, the terms used have been selected both for their appropriateness to a reading course geared to a whole-selection approach to reading and for their transferability to subsequent courses in composition, English literature, or other subjects.

Perhaps it is appropriate at this point to say a word about reading rate. The subject of building speed is not addressed directly in the instructional materials. For the instructor who wishes to work on rate, word counts of the supplementary readings have been included in the *Instructor's Guide*, along with the reading levels of the readings. The approach of the *Ideas Module* usually results in an increase in students' reading rates. Because students are taught to use the reading skills utilized by efficient readers, they are discouraged from the word- and phonics-bound habits that so often contribute to slow and ineffective reading. Further, as students gain confidence about their comprehension, reading rates often increase.

In the first lesson of the *Inferences Module*, students learn to determine the meanings that a writer has only implied in the stated information in reading materials. They learn about making inferences from similes, metaphors, irony, allusions, examples, facts, and cause and effect explanations.

In the second lesson of the module, students learn how to form reasoned opinions, based on the stated information in articles and textbook readings. Students are led through the reasoning process that they would use to answer the various kinds of questions that instructors ask about a reading assignment. The lesson is particularly suited to the reading that students should do to prepare for an essay examination.

In the last task of the module, students work with selecting related ideas from different sources, assessing those ideas for similarities and differences, and forming their own generalization, based on the information in the reading materials.

As in the other modules of the program, students work examples and answer multiple-choice questions about the meaning of the materials they have read. They can then check their answers in the Answer Key at the end of each task. The reading practices at the end of each lesson include multiple-choice questions and short writing assignments. The sixteen readings that supplement the *Inferences Module* provide for additional application of the skills taught and for posttest checking of students' progress. A progress chart for the students' use is included on the inside front cover of the book.

Acknowledgments

I am indebted to several persons who work with me in the Communications Learning Center of the Metropolitan Campus of Cuyahoga Community College: John Arko, Harold Miller, Jane Miller, Margaret Payerle, Wendy Shapiro, and Ruth Williams. They have used the modules of *Concepts of Communication: Reading* and have provided me with valuable information about the effectiveness of the materials with students. I am especially grateful to my colleague Ray Ackley, whose insights helped me in the final development of the books. I am indebted most of all to John Kristofco, who has assisted me for several years with my students, with the monumental task of collecting and evaluating statistical data about students and instructional materials, and with many other chores. I am also indebted to Ray Fredman, Norman Prange, Ann Salak, and Colleen Wilson for providing me with data for the placement test in the *Instructor's Guide.*

I am more than appreciative of the contribution made by my reviewers. Their advice and counsel have been essential to the successful completion of the books. They are Suzette Elgin, California State University; William H. Engler, Mercer Community College; C. W. Hubbard, Lake-Sumter Community College; Judith Longo, Ocean County College; and Barbara Wainer, Prince George's Community College. I particularly want to thank John T. Becker of John Carroll University for his help not only in reviewing the manuscripts and readings but also in directing me to various studies and reports that proved relevant to the development of the books.

Last, but by no means least, I wish to thank my family: Charlie, Marc, Cassi, and John. They have also made a contribution to this project!

M. L. C.

To the Student

Suppose that your instructor asks you to read an article for a course you are taking. Do you know how to find the important ideas in the article? Do you know how to determine the meaning of those ideas? Can you remember the important ideas after you have read the article? Can you explain the ideas clearly to someone else? Are you able to form an opinion about what you read? Are you able to see how the ideas in different readings are alike? Can you see how the ideas are different?

If you answered no to any of the above questions, you will find that the lessons of the *Ideas* and *Inferences Modules* will help you. All the skills you were questioned about are related to reading. Some of the skills are not easy to acquire. However, there are techniques you can learn to make the job easier. These techniques are taught in the *Ideas* and *Inferences Modules.*

Ideas Module

Contents

Unit One Overview 1

Reading for Ideas 1
The Ideas Module Instruction 2
The Ideas Module Objectives 2

Unit Two Essays and Articles 5

Task 11 Controlling Ideas 9
Titles, Leads, and Headings 10
Key Words 12
Key Paragraphs 13
Key Sentences 14
Answer Key 16

Task 12 Major Points and Body Paragraphs 19
Topic Sentences 21
Transitional Paragraphs 28
Digressions 30
Single-Sentence Paragraphs 31
Transitional Statements 32
Answer Key 34

Task 13 Supporting Data and Body Paragraphs 37
Examples 37
Facts 39
Cause and Effect 41
Classification and Division 42
Comparison and Contrast 45
Analogy 47
Definitions 48
Answer Key 51

Task 14 Determining the Meaning of Ideas 57
Sentence Patterns 57
Problem Sentences 64
Answer Key 69

Task 15 Expressing the Meaning of Ideas 77
Paraphrasing 77
Summarizing 81
Answer Key 83

Overview **Unit One**

Reading for Ideas

An idea is a thought or opinion. The sentences and paragraphs of everything you read are made up of different ideas. In any one piece of writing, the ideas in the sentences of a paragraph explain the idea of the paragraph. The ideas of the paragraphs explain the idea of the whole composition. Thus, the different ideas are *related* to each other. The chart below shows you the way the ideas in writing are related.

Idea of the whole composition
- Paragraph idea
  - Sentence idea
  - Sentence idea
  - Sentence idea
- Paragraph idea
  - Sentence idea
  - Sentence idea
- Paragraph idea
  - Sentence idea
  - — — — — — —
- — — — — — — —

Most of the reading you do for your school courses will be of essays, articles, or textbooks. All of these composition forms are based on expository writing. **Expository writing** is simply writing in which a general or broad idea is explained through more specific information and ideas. The ideas are called the *content* of the writing.

Expository writing also has an *organization*—a pattern or structure. Perhaps you will find it helpful to think of expository writing as being something like a house. When you look at the outside of a house, you can see it has a structure. It has a foundation, walls, and a roof. Essays, articles, and chapters in a textbook have a similar outside structure. Sometimes, especially in the chapters of a textbook, you can *see* that structure. You simply look at the special headings, sizes and kinds of type, and spacings on the pages. Of course, you cannot always see the structure easily, any more than you can see the back of a house when you are standing in front of it. You know the structure is there, like the back of a house. But you have to look around a little to see it.

A house and expository writing have an inside organization or structure, too. A house may have any number of rooms, halls, and other spaces. Some are more important than others. Also, the rooms can be arranged according to many different plans.

In the same way, a composition, or piece of writing, may have any number of paragraphs and sentences. They can be arranged in many different ways. Some of the paragraphs and sentences (those that state the controlling idea, major points, and significant supporting ideas) are very important. Some (transitional paragraphs, statements, and markers) are useful—like the halls in a house—for getting you from one idea to another. Others (digressions) may sometimes be useful. But you might be able to get along without them. Still other paragraphs and sentences may be no more important than the useless spaces in a poorly planned house.

Reading is a little like examining a house you want to buy. You know something about the house from seeing it on the outside. But you need to know what is inside. Of course, reading is a more difficult task than examining a house. However, you can learn some skills to make reading less difficult than you may now find it.

The Ideas Module Instruction

The *Ideas Module* instruction will help you learn to read essays, articles, and textbooks. In Unit Two, "Essays and Articles," you will learn to find and work out the relationships of the controlling idea, major points, and supporting data in an essay or article. Then you will learn how to determine the meanings of the ideas and to express their meanings in your own words. In Unit Three, "Textbooks," you will learn about the reading and study aids included in a textbook. You will also use the skills you learned in Unit Two in reading for ideas in your textbooks. In Unit Four, "Readings," there are essays, articles, and textbook selections. Your instructor will want you to read some of these selections and show that you can use the skills you have learned. In Unit Five, you will find a list of the reading tasks you need to master to reach the objectives of the *Ideas Module.*

The Ideas Module Objectives

A. Objectives

To achieve the objectives, or learning goals, of the *Ideas Module,* you should show that you can do the following:

1. Find the ideas in an essay or article and in an excerpt (pages) from a textbook
2. Determine the relationships among the ideas
3. Find the meanings of the ideas
4. Express the ideas in your own words
5. Find and use the reading and study aids in a textbook

You should satisfy the objectives under the conditions and according to the criteria indicated below.

B. Conditions of performance

1. The reading selections should be assigned by your instructor.
2. You should read and demonstrate your understanding of the selections according to your instructor's directions.

C. Criteria for evaluation

1. You should show you can find ideas, work out their relationships, and determine their meaning by selecting the controlling idea(s), major points, and significant supporting data in the assigned readings.
2. You should show you are able to explain the ideas by stating the meaning of the controlling idea(s), major points, and important supporting data in your own words.
3. You should show you are able to find the reading and study aids in three different textbooks. You should show you can use the reading and study aids by finding specified information in a textbook chosen by your instructor.

Essays and Articles **Unit Two**

Essays and articles are prose, nonfiction compositions that are written to explain an idea. Usually, they are between 1,500 and 5,000 words long. You will find them printed in magazines, newspapers, and books.

An essay is often more formal in language than an article. However, they are alike in ways that are important to you as a reader. First, both compositions are based on an idea. The writer explains that idea through the different but related ideas within the sentences and paragraphs* of the composition. The writer thinks of these ideas as the **content** of an essay or article. But the writer must also think of the ideas in terms of their related importance. The idea on which a composition is based is called the **controlling idea** because that idea "controls" the other ideas that are included in the composition. The ideas that directly explain the controlling idea are called **major points.** Together, the controlling idea and major points explain the main ideas in the essay or article. These are the important ideas that you need to understand and remember if you are reading for a school course.

No essay or article is complete, however, without the ideas that are called the **supporting data.** These ideas are usually some kind of details—examples, facts, causes, and so on. These specific ideas are very important to you as a reader because they help you understand and believe the writer's major points and controlling idea.

The chart on the next page shows you the relations among ideas in essays and articles.

A second fact about essays and articles is also important to you as a reader. The ideas of a composition are arranged according to a pattern. This pattern is called the **organization** of the composition. There are usually three parts to the organization of an essay or article. These parts are called the **introduction,** the **body,** and the **conclusion.** Each part will usually contain at least one paragraph. The controlling idea, major points, and supporting data are expressed somewhere within the parts of the composition. A common practice is to state the controlling idea in the paragraphs that make up the introduction. Generally, the major points and supporting data are in the paragraphs of the body. The controlling idea

*There are various definitions for a **sentence**. What you see in print as a sentence is usually a group of words that begins with a capital letter and ends with a period, question mark, or exclamation point. A sentence should express an idea and, therefore, have a meaning that you find through reading. A **paragraph** usually consists of several sentences that are related to one another in explaining an idea of some importance in the composition. A paragraph is shown in print by indenting the first word or by some other spacing.

Relations among Ideas in an Essay or Article

- Controlling idea
  - Major point
    - Supporting data
    - Supporting data
  - Major point
    - Supporting data
    - Supporting data
    - Supporting data
  - Major point
    - Supporting data
    - Supporting data
  - Other major points and supporting data (as needed to explain the controlling idea)

and major points may also be stated or summed up in the paragraphs of the conclusion. The following chart shows you how the ideas (content) and the organization of an essay or article are usually combined.

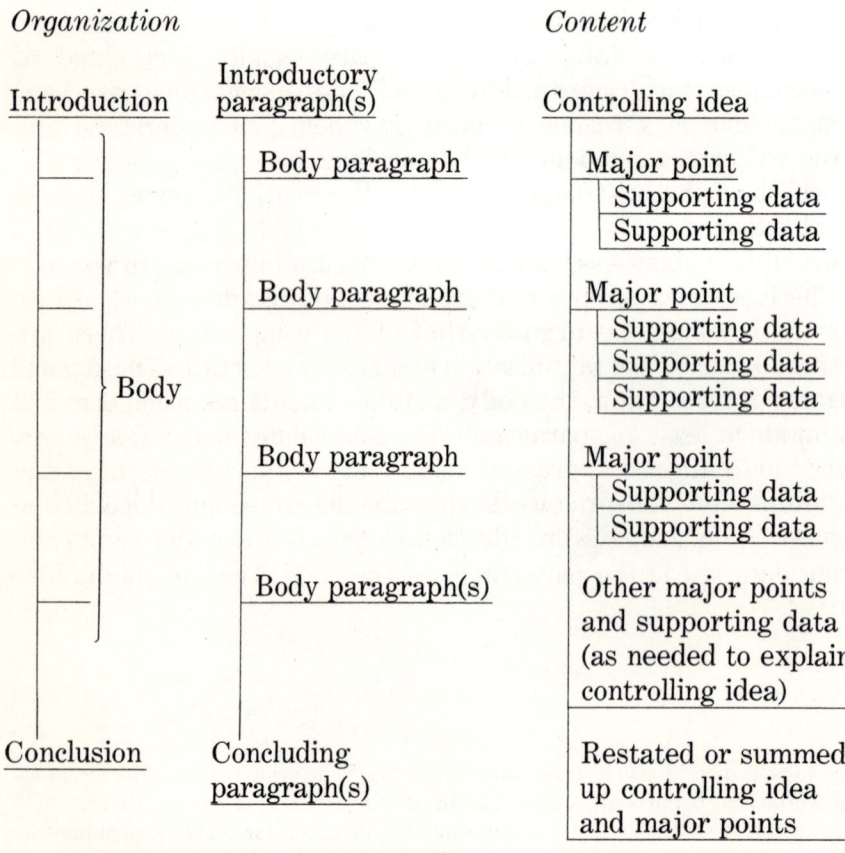

Organization		*Content*
Introduction	Introductory paragraph(s)	Controlling idea
Body	Body paragraph	Major point Supporting data Supporting data
Body	Body paragraph	Major point Supporting data Supporting data Supporting data
Body	Body paragraph	Major point Supporting data Supporting data
Body	Body paragraph(s)	Other major points and supporting data (as needed to explain controlling idea)
Conclusion	Concluding paragraph(s)	Restated or summed up controlling idea and major points

Understanding what you read involves finding ideas, working out their relations, and determining their meanings. In the following tasks, you will learn about these skills. You will learn to use the skills in reading for the stated ideas in essays and articles. You will find these same skills helpful when, in Unit Three, you work with textbooks.

Words and Terms to Know

sentence
paragraph
content of an essay or article
controlling idea
major points
supporting data
organization of an essay or article
introduction
body
conclusion

Concepts to Remember

1. Essays and articles are both prose compositions that are based on an idea of the writer.
2. In both compositions, the writer explains the idea of the whole composition through other related ideas.
3. The idea on which the composition is based is called the controlling idea. The ideas that explain the controlling idea are called the major points. The ideas that support the major points are called the supporting data. Examples, facts, causes, and definitions are some of the specific kinds of information used as supporting data.
4. A writer arranges the ideas in an essay or article according to a pattern. The pattern is called the organization of the composition.
5. The organization of an essay or article usually has three parts: introduction, body, and conclusion.
6. A writer usually expresses the controlling idea in the introduction and the major points, and supporting data in the body of an essay or article. In the conclusion, the writer generally restates or sums up the controlling idea and major points.
7. Understanding what you read involves finding ideas, working out their relationships, and determining their meanings.

Task 11
Controlling Ideas

Suppose one of your friends calls you and says, "How about going to a movie tonight?"

You might answer, "No, I can't go to a movie tonight." You have answered by stating an idea.

Next, you would probably explain that idea. You might say:

> I can't afford it. I just spent my last dollar putting gas in my car.
> Besides, I have to study. I'm having a test in English tomorrow.

You have now made your idea, "No, I can't go to a movie tonight," a **controlling idea.** You have explained that idea by stating different but related ideas. Your ideas are related in the following way:

Controlling idea	No, I can't go to a movie tonight.
Major point	I can't afford it.
Supporting data	I just spent my last dollar putting gas in my car.
Major point	Besides, I have to study.
Supporting data	I'm having a test in English tomorrow.

Writers explain an idea the same way you do. Of course, they must be more exact and orderly in their writing than people usually are in speaking. But they do follow the same general order you follow in speaking. Usually, writers express an idea and then state other ideas that explain or prove that idea, just as in the above example. Sometimes, they change that order—as you sometimes do. They may state the supporting ideas and then tell you the idea they determined from those ideas. For example, a writer might answer the question "How about going to a movie tonight?" by saying:

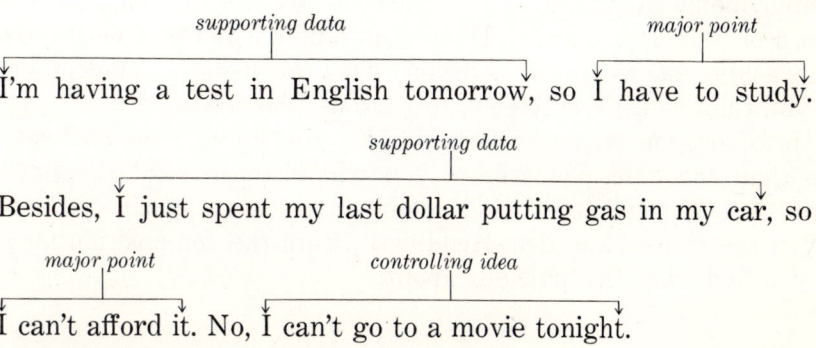

supporting data [I'm having a test in English tomorrow], so *major point* [I have to study].

Besides, *supporting data* [I just spent my last dollar putting gas in my car], so

major point [I can't afford it]. No, *controlling idea* [I can't go to a movie tonight].

Even if writers explain ideas as you do, you may still have trouble finding and understanding the writer's controlling idea. However, you can learn some reading skills that will help you. You should begin by prereading an essay or article. Prereading means looking for the (1) title, leads, and other headings; (2) key words; (3) key paragraphs; and (4) key sentences in the essay or article.

Titles, Leads, and Headings

Titles

The **title** of a composition often tells what the composition is about. Look at the following titles. Make a note by each title saying what you think each composition might be about.

How to Build a Fire ______________________

____

____

And Now . . . a Lawnmower That Doesn't Need Pushing ______________________

____

____

The first title indicates clearly that the article is about the way to build a fire. The second title tells you the article is about a lawnmower that does not have to be pushed. However, some titles do not indicate what a composition is about as clearly as the titles above. For example, you can probably list more than one idea for each of the following titles.

The Terrible 1930s ______________________

____

____

The Best Piece of Home Equipment You Can Own ______________________

____

____

For the title "The Terrible 1930s," you could list the Depression, unemployment, gangsters, or any "terrible" events that happened in the 1930s. For "The Best Piece of Home Equipment You Can Own," you could list a washing machine, clothes dryer, radio, television, or some other item that you think is especially good to have in a home.

However, you cannot be certain of the controlling idea until you read more than the title. Sometimes, you will have to read the first few sentences to learn what an article is about. In some magazines, a lead may tell you the controlling idea. Headings within the composition may also help you find what the article is about.

Leads

A **lead** is a short statement that follows the title of an article. The lead contains a brief statement or summary of the content of the article. Generally, the lead tells you the controlling idea. The lead sentences are usually printed in a different size and kind of type than is used for either the title or the article itself. For example:

title→ THE CORN THAT COULD CHANGE THE LIVES OF MILLIONS

lead→ *This remarkable new corn, richer in protein than milk, almost as rich as meat, holds promise of an end to the malnutrition that stunts minds and bodies across much of Asia, Africa and Latin America.* ["The Corn That Could Change the Lives of Millions," by Paul Friggens, *The Reader's Digest* (January 1975), p. 144. Copyright 1975 by The Reader's Digest Assn., Inc.]

title→ THE GHOSTLY MENACE OF FOG

lead→ *It can be deadly for travelers on land, in the air and at sea. But we are at last making progress in learning how to deal with it.* ["The Ghostly Menace of Fog," by Earl and Miriam Selby, *The Reader's Digest* (January 1975), p. 169. Copyright 1975 by The Reader's Digest Assn., Inc.]

Headings

Headings are words that are set off by a different type or spacing to identify sections or major points in the composition. Headings can help you find the controlling idea when the title is not specific. For instance, the title "Caring for Your Pet in Cold Weather" tells you a great deal about the content of the article. But if you found the headings "Dogs" and "Cats," within the article, you would know the particular kinds of pets the article is about.

Read the examples of titles, leads, and headings given below. Circle the letter of the answer that expresses the controlling idea of each article.

A. *title*→ NEW TAPE RECORDER GIVES SPEED LISTENING

lead→ *An ingenious circuit lets you play back tapes at twice the speed they were recorded, yet restores original pitch and close to original intelligibility.*

The controlling idea is

a. a new kind of circuit records tapes faster
b. a new kind of tape recorder plays back tapes at the same speed they were recorded and restores the original pitch
c. a new kind of tape recorder plays tapes twice as fast and almost as clearly as they were recorded
d. a special circuit lets you record tone and sound twice as fast as on an original tape

B. *title→* THE BEST PIECE OF HOME EQUIPMENT YOU CAN OWN

headings→ How You Can Use a Calculator to Save Money
How Your Kids Can Use a Calculator to Learn Math

The controlling idea is

a. kids can save money by learning to use a calculator to do their math problems
b. you can save money on your home equipment by learning to use a calculator to do math problems
c. if you have a calculator in your home you can learn how to use mathematics to save money
d. a calculator is the best piece of home equipment because it helps you save money and helps kids learn math

Look in the Answer Key for the answers.

Key Words

Key words are the words that are a key, or clue, to the writer's controlling idea. Key words are generally used in the first few sentences of a composition. The key words help define the controlling idea. For instance, the title in the example below tells you the article is about building a fire. However, the word *fireplace* in the first sentence defines the controlling idea more exactly. That key word tells you the article is about building a fire in a fireplace rather than in a furnace, barbecue, or camping area.

title→ HOW TO BUILD A FIRE
first sentence→ If you have a fireplace, it can be a source of both enjoyment and extra heat in a closed room.

Key words are especially helpful when the title of a composition does not tell you what the composition is about or when the composition does not have a lead or headings. For example, you can probably think of several ideas for an article titled "Measure for Measure." However, you would not know the article is about the metric system, a method of measuring. You would first have to read the key words *metric system* in the following sentences:

> Remember when travelers returning from Europe would refer to English money as illogical and quaint? The shoe is on the other footage now. Only five countries in the world are not on the metric system today: Brunei, Burma, Liberia, Yemen—and the United States.
>
> Metric system: it sounds un-American, vaguely threatening, authoritarian. Perhaps it is unconscious association with the "penal system," or the "Czerny system" of musical scales, that causes otherwise open-minded persons to declare flatly, "It'll never happen here," and refuse to discuss the matter.

But the metric system *is* happening in many areas of our lives. . . . [Carol Brener, "Measure for Measure," *New York* (August 25, 1975), p. 52.]

The key words are usually repeated within a composition. For example, in the first ninety-eight words of "Measure for Measure," the words *metric system* are used three times.

Read the titles and first sentences of the articles below. Underline the words that are keys or clues to what the article is about.

A. *title*→ A BEAN TO FEED THE WORLD?

first sentence→ We continue to sing of amber waves of grain, not dusty pods of beans; but soybeans, not wheat or corn, are the United States' number one cash crop, and by 1985, they are expected to occupy more acres than any other crop we grow. [Richard Rhodes, "A Bean to Feed the World?" *Atlantic Monthly* (January, 1975), p. 38.]

B. *title*→ DON'T TAKE IT LYING DOWN

first sentence→ For years, authorities have warned women that to resist rape is to court death. [Carole Wade Offir, "Don't Take It Lying Down," *Psychology Today* (January, 1975), p. 73.]

C. *title*→ THE SIMPLE STEPS TO CORRUPTION

first sentence→ Corruption is a fact of life in police departments, just as it is in politics, business and even the Boy Scouts. [Jack Horn, "The Simple Steps to Corruption," *Psychology Today* (January, 1975), p. 20. Reprinted by permission of *Psychology Today* Magazine. Copyright © 1974 Ziff-Davis Publishing Company.]

Look in the Answer Key for the answers.

Key Paragraphs

A paragraph generally contains several sentences that are related to one another in explaining one idea within a composition. You can *see* a paragraph when you look at a page. If you look at the page you are reading, you will see several "blocks" of print. The first word of each block may be indented. Each block is a paragraph.

As you learned earlier, the controlling idea is likely to be stated in the introduction and restated in the conclusion of a composition. Therefore, the **key paragraphs** for finding the controlling idea are the paragraphs at the beginning and at the end of the composition.

The paragraphs of the introduction and conclusion may be set off by headings or by extra spacing between the lines of print. If not, use some guesswork. First, count the number of paragraphs in the composition. Next, figure that two-thirds to three-fourths of the paragraphs in the middle of the composition are the body paragraphs. The rest of the paragraphs can be divided between the introduction and conclusion. Remember, you are only guessing. You won't know you have found the introduction and conclusion until you read the paragraphs more closely. But you can start by using such prereading methods and change your mind after you read the paragraphs.

Key Sentences

Key sentences are the sentences within the key paragraphs in which the controlling idea is likely to be stated. Of course, the controlling idea may be stated in any paragraph and in any sentence. But the controlling idea is often found in one or more of the following key sentences:

1. The last sentence or two of the first paragraph
2. The first sentence of the first paragraph
3. The first or last sentences of the last paragraph

Read the following key paragraphs. Underline the sentence(s) that are key sentences. Then, circle the letter of the answer that tells the controlling idea.

A. A TYPEWRITER IS HELPING CHILDREN LEARN NEW WORDS

There's a muffled rush of typewriter keys [and] an attentive look on children's faces. They're learning new words in a new way at Boyd Elementary School, a public school in Jackson, Mississippi. ["IBM Reports," *Harper's Magazine* (December, 1974).]

The controlling idea is

a. children pay attention to the sound of typewriters
b. Boyd Elementary School is in Jackson, Mississippi
c. children are using the typewriter to help them learn words
d. children who live in Mississippi pay attention when they use a typewriter

B. THE BANJO'S BACK IN TOWN

Banjos are back and booming. The instrument that once thrilled an entire nation in the 1800s and early 1920s is making a new sound in the air—a sound many have never heard before. [Paula O'Neil, "The Banjo's Back in Town," *House Beautiful* (November, 1974), p. 68.]

The controlling idea is

a. banjos are popular again, but they have a different sound than they used to have
b. in the 1800s and 1920s, banjos had a booming sound that made them a popular instrument

c. banjos make a booming sound that thrills everyone in the nation
d. the booming sound of a banjo thrills everyone in the nation and has been popular since the 1800s

C. ANGLO VS. CHICANO: WHY?

The cultural differences between Hispanic and Anglo-American people have been dwelt upon by so many writers that we should all be well informed about the values of both. But audiences are usually of the same persuasion as the speakers, and those who consult published works are for the most part specialists looking for affirmation of what they believe. So, let us consider the same subject, exploring briefly some of the basic cultural differences that cause conflict in the Southwest, where Hispanic and Anglo-American cultures meet. [*Western Review*, Vol. IX (Spring, 1972).]

The controlling idea is
a. specialists read published materials to find the ideas they believe in, and audiences believe the things speakers say
b. cultural differences cause conflicts between Hispanic and Anglo-American people who live in the Southwest
c. everyone should know about the differences between Chicanos and Anglo-Americans
d. the Southwest has a different culture than the culture of the rest of the United States

Look in the Answer Key for the answers.

Words and Terms to Know

title
lead
headings
key words
key paragraphs
key sentences

Concepts to Remember

1. The title, lead, and headings of a composition will often help you find out what the composition is about.
2. The key words of a composition name what the writer is writing about.
3. The key paragraphs are usually the beginning and ending paragraphs. The controlling idea is likely to be stated in the key paragraphs.
4. The key sentences are certain sentences within the key paragraphs. The controlling idea is likely to be stated in the key sentences.
5. The controlling idea may be stated anywhere in a composition, but it is likely to be stated in the first paragraph and restated in the last paragraph.

Assignment

Complete the worksheet at the end of this task according to your instructor's directions.

Answer Key Task 11

pages 11–12

A. The controlling idea is *c.*
B. The controlling idea is *d.*

page 13

A. The word *soybeans* is the key word.
B. The word *rape* is the key word.
C. The words *corruption* and *in police departments* are the key words.

pages 14–15

A. The key sentence is the last sentence in the paragraph. The controlling idea is *c.* In this example, the title tells you the controlling idea. The key word *typewriter* appears in both the title and the first sentence. You should associate *typewriter* with the "new way" of learning words.
B. Both sentences of the paragraph are key sentences. The first sentence tells you of the return of the banjo. The second is about the banjo's new sound. The controlling idea is *a.*
C. The key sentence is the last sentence in the paragraph. The controlling idea is *b.*

Task 11 **Worksheet**

NAME ______________________________ DATE ____________

Reading Practice

Read the paragraphs below. Circle the letter of the answer to the questions that follow the paragraphs.

A. THE CORN THAT COULD CHANGE THE LIVES OF MILLIONS

This remarkable new corn, richer in protein than milk, almost as rich as meat, holds promise of an end to the malnutrition that stunts minds and bodies across much of Asia, Africa and Latin America.

José Nuñez is typical of millions in today's developing countries. A wiry, barefoot little man, he grows corn in the volcanic mountains of Guatemala. Spading his postage-stamp-size plot, harvesting by machete, he barely ekes out a living. Worse, he and his family of eight, although they never really starve, are chronically malnourished. Deprived of protein even before birth, several of the Nuñez children were born forever stunted in mind and body. Their life expectancy is some 20 years less than that of people in better-fed countries.

Why are Nuñez and his children so undernourished? Because, like some 300 million other people in Asia, Africa and Latin America, they rarely taste meat or milk, and depend for their staple food on corn that is too poor in protein quality to sustain them.

But now comes a major nutritional breakthrough: an international team of scientists is developing a remarkable new type of corn called Opaque-2, which has nearly double the effective protein content of normal corn, nearly as much as that of meat, and surpasses that of milk. ["The Corn That Could Change the Lives of Millions," by Paul Friggens, *The Reader's Digest* (January, 1975), p. 144. Copyright 1975 by The Reader's Digest Assn., Inc.]

1. The controlling idea is
   a. people in Guatemala are undernourished because they have only corn to eat and milk to drink
   b. a man named José Nuñez has found a new kind of corn that he can grow on a small plot of ground in Asia
   c. scientists have developed a high-protein corn that may prevent malnutrition among people in many parts of the world

d. people who live in Asia, Africa, and Latin America do not eat enough meat or milk and are undernourished

B. WINDMILLS: GETTING THEIR SECOND WIND?

Is the answer to the energy crisis blowing in the wind. . . ?

While the United States imports crude oil energy, she still exports windmills, though sales of the latter are not exactly full-blown—about 5,000 annually as aid to emerging nations. As for helping with the balance of payments, they don't amount to a sneeze in a breeze. Only three companies still manufacture windmills: Heller-Aller of Napoleon, Ohio, Dempster Industries of Beatrice, Nebraska, and Braden Industries of Broken Arrow, Oklahoma. A hundred years ago, the American windmill became the most significant breakthrough for settling the Great Plains. Today, as with all but three of the factories that built them, the old mills are broken-down derelicts. Occasionally a beheaded tower, unable to snag the wind, has been reharnessed to capture a TV signal or, inadvertently, an ailing kite. . . .

Like the pioneers poised at the edge of the Great Plains over a century ago, Americans today are hoping with baited breath for an energy breakthrough. That it will come in the form of cheap, clean windpower is a hopeful, if distant, possibility. [La Vern J. Rippley, "Windmills: Getting Their Second Wind?" *Passages* (May, 1975), pp. 21, 23.]

2. The controlling idea is
   a. windmills made it possible to settle the Great Plains area
   b. windmills may provide us with energy in the future
   c. the United States imports crude oil to supply energy
   d. the windmills in the United States have all broken down

Task 12
Major Points and Body Paragraphs

The ideas that are directly related to explaining the controlling idea are called **major points.** The major points are explained, through the supporting data, in the paragraphs that make up the body of the composition. Consequently, when you read the body paragraphs you will find not only major points but also the ideas that support these points. Look again at the chart on page 6. The chart shows how the major points and supporting data are combined in the body of the composition.

Understanding the way body paragraphs are usually organized can help you in reading for ideas. First, remember that a paragraph is based on an idea. When a body paragraph has more than one sentence, that idea is usually stated in one of the sentences and explained in the other sentences. The sentence that expresses the idea is called a *topic sentence* because it states the idea (topic) of the paragraph.

Second, the topic of a paragraph may be a major point or an idea that supports a major point. The topic may even be an idea of very little importance in the composition as a whole. In this task, you will learn to preread a composition for its topic sentences. As you preread, you must begin to work out the relationships of the paragraph ideas.

In certain compositions, some or all of the body paragraphs are based on major points—ideas that are directly related to explaining the controlling idea. In such compositions, the paragraphs and their ideas are organized in the following way:

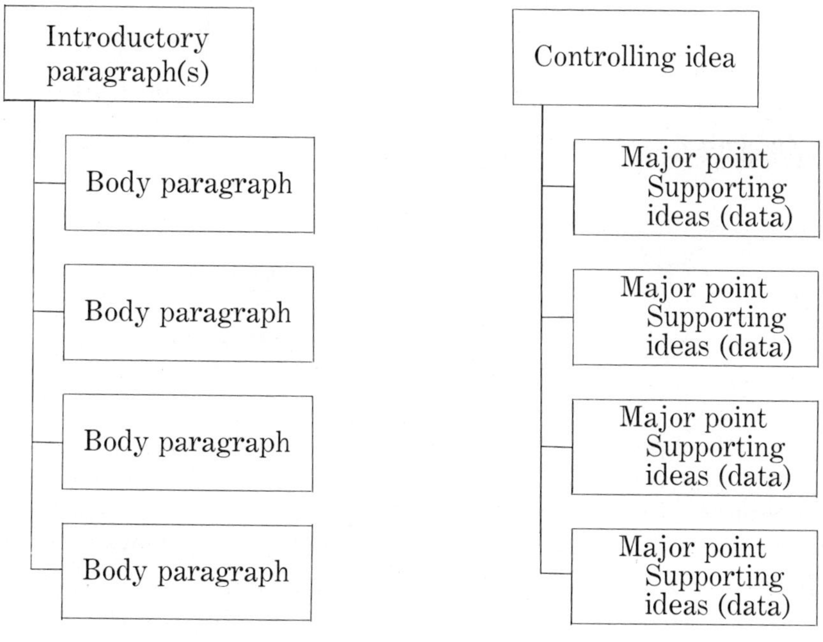

In other compositions, you will find that a *set,* or group, of paragraphs is based on a major point and the ideas that support that point. In that case, the paragraphs and their ideas are organized as the following chart shows:

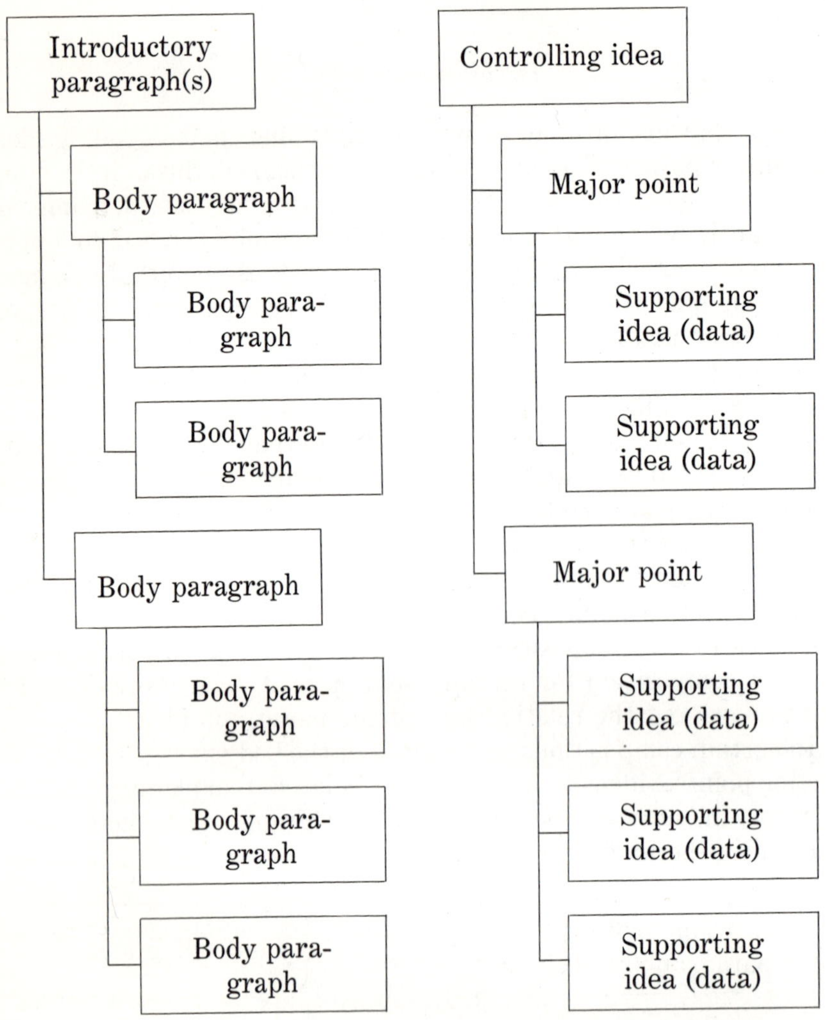

In the body of some articles, you may find three other types of paragraphs. One is called a *transitional paragraph* because it contains statements that help you make the change (transition) from one idea to another. The second is called a *digression* because it contains information that does not fit closely into the relation of the other ideas. The third is a *single sentence paragraph.* Such paragraphs can be a problem when you are trying to determine the related importance of the ideas in an article.

Transitional and digression paragraphs may appear between any of the paragraphs of a composition. The following chart shows you *some* of the places you might find such paragraphs:

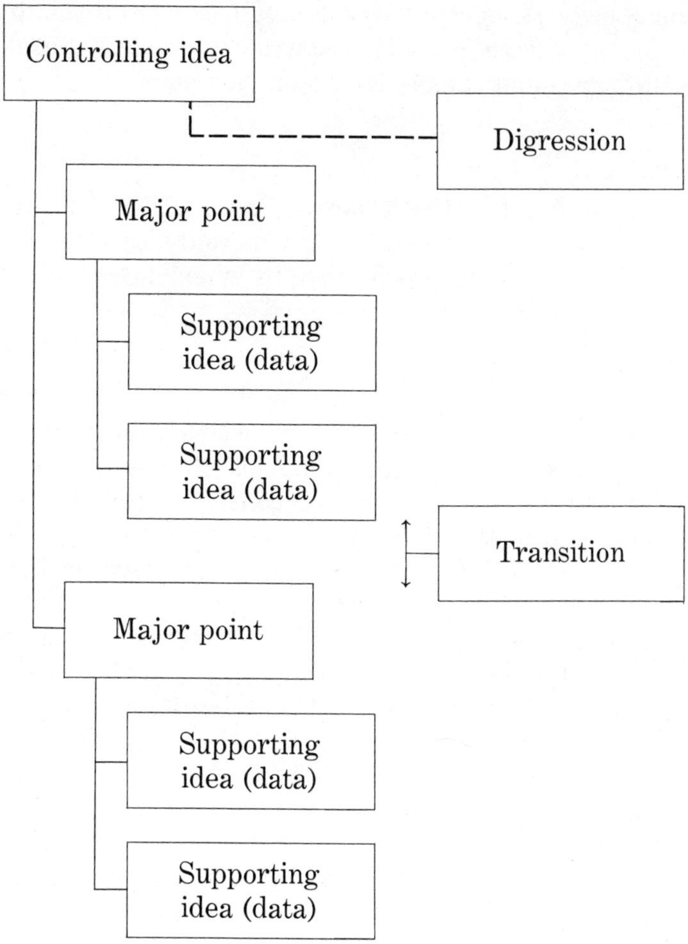

Single-sentence paragraphs may also appear anywhere in an article. Often in newspaper articles each sentence is printed as a paragraph. The sentence may be based on a major point, supporting idea, transitional statement, or other information.

You should begin your prereading of the body paragraphs of a composition by looking for topic sentences. This will help you find the relations among the ideas in the various paragraphs that make up the body of the composition. Prereading for topic sentences will also lead to finding transitional statements. *Transitional statements* are used to link ideas in the same way transitional paragraphs are.

Topic Sentences

If a composition is short, the writer may use each major point as the idea of a paragraph. The idea is sometimes given in a **topic sentence.** A topic sentence states the idea (topic) of the paragraph. Often, the first sentence of the paragraph is the topic sentence. Therefore, you can *sometimes* find the major points by prereading the first sentence of each body paragraph.

The following body paragraphs, for example, are from the article "The Simple Steps to Corruption." The controlling idea is stated for you. Underline the topic sentences that state major points.

controlling idea:
According to Psychologist Charles Bahn, police officers who become corrupt tend to follow a common route, called "socialization to corruption." The process begins when the recruit leaves the police academy for the streets.

body paragraphs:
(1) The recruit rapidly learns two secrets. First, much police work involves waiting around for something to happen, rather than saving lives or catching criminals. Danger is always a possibility, but boredom is a more constant problem. Second, police efficiency is low, individually and organizationally. Neither secret can be revealed to the outside world, because it would damage the police image and encourage crime.
(2) Socialization continues as the new officer learns to accept small gifts or favors from businesses on his beat: a haircut, a magazine, a pack of cigarettes. Small cash gifts are next, which the officer rationalizes are legitimate because he gives a little extra service for them—maybe he stops by the store an extra time or two to check that everything is OK. This is really part of his job anyway, so what's wrong with it?
(3) As the officer becomes accustomed to the small luxuries the extra cash makes possible, he comes to count on it. It's only natural to look for ways to make a bit more, usually by doing small favors for persons on his beat. Perhaps he tips off a storekeeper that the traffic squad is in his area, so he and his customers don't get ticketed for illegal parking. Or perhaps he sees a card game going on in the back room, and ignores it.
(4) At this point, Bahn says, the officer starts to distinguish between clean and dirty money. He gets clean money for ignoring victimless crimes such as illegal parking or gambling. The law isn't really being broken, just bent a little. And since no one is being hurt, it's all right to take the money.
(5) The next step is the pad, a list of businesses on the beat that can be counted on for regular gifts or money. This formal arrangement is always a two-way street; it depends on regular favors from the policeman to keep it going. Once the pad is institutionalized, it usually passes from officer to officer as beat assignments change. [Jack Horn, "The Simple Steps to Corruption," *Psychology Today* (January, 1975), pp. 20–21. Reprinted by permission of *Psychology Today* Magazine. Copyright © 1974 Ziff-Davis Publishing Company.]

You probably found that the first sentence in each paragraph is a topic sentence and a major point. In each of the sentences, a step in the corruption process is stated. However, the information in the second sentences of paragraphs 2 and 3 is also important. That information is part of the major point of each paragraph. For instance, the first sentence of paragraph 2 states that taking small gifts and favors from businesses is a step in the police officer's corruption. The second sentence adds that when the officer takes money and tells himself it is for his services, he continues the corruption process. This information is best treated as part of the major point of the paragraph, since the rest of the paragraph gives supporting data for the second sentence.

The ideas in paragraph 3 are organized in much the same way. The following chart shows you the organization and content of the two paragraphs.

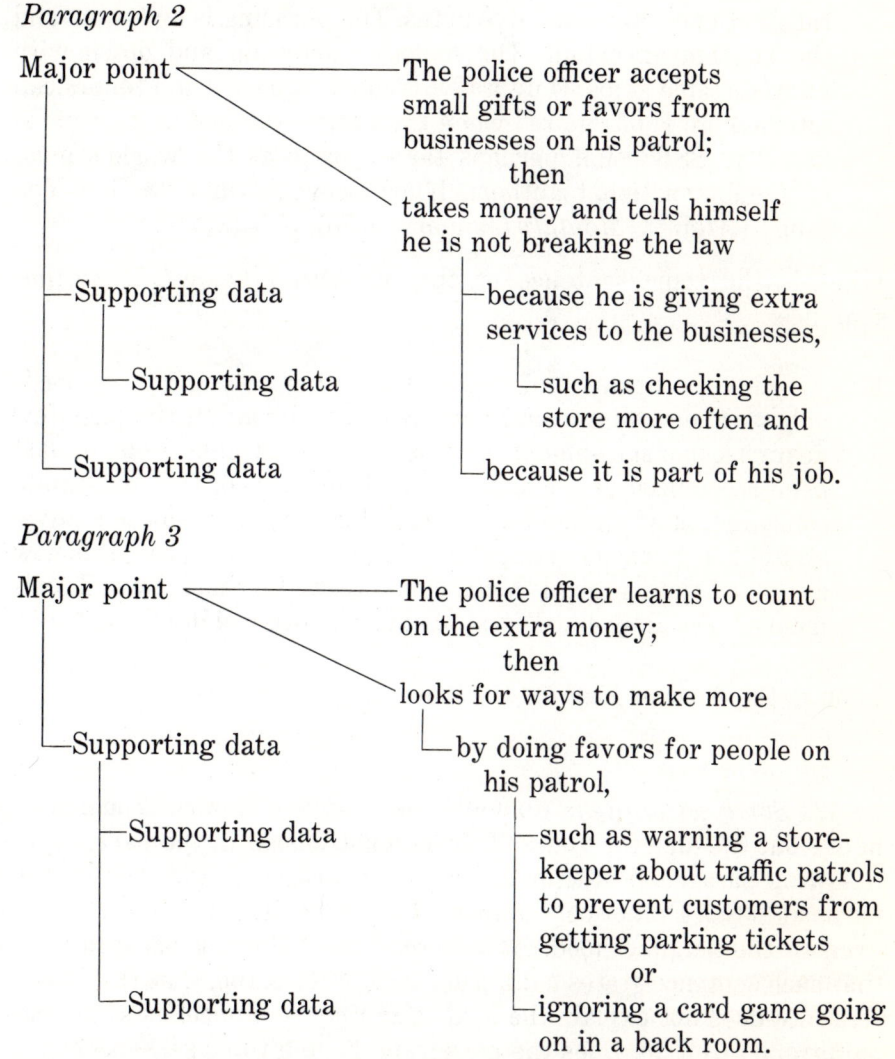

Paragraph 2

- Major point — The police officer accepts small gifts or favors from businesses on his patrol; then takes money and tells himself he is not breaking the law
  - Supporting data — because he is giving extra services to the businesses,
    - Supporting data — such as checking the store more often and
  - Supporting data — because it is part of his job.

Paragraph 3

- Major point — The police officer learns to count on the extra money; then looks for ways to make more
  - Supporting data — by doing favors for people on his patrol,
    - Supporting data — such as warning a store-keeper about traffic patrols to prevent customers from getting parking tickets
    - or
    - Supporting data — ignoring a card game going on in a back room.

As you can see, prereading generally involves more than looking at the first sentences of the paragraphs in a composition. While you are reading, remember that

1. A topic sentence can be placed anywhere in a paragraph
2. Some paragraphs do not have a topic sentence
3. A topic sentence may not fully state the idea of a paragraph
4. A topic sentence may state, instead of a major point, a supporting or lesser idea in the composition

These facts about topic sentences are explained in more detail in the following pages.

1. *A topic sentence can be placed anywhere in a paragraph.* For example, is the topic sentence the first or the last sentence of the paragraph below? In which sentence is the topic of the paragraph stated most clearly? Underline the topic sentence.

A. If the SSB [Star Spangled Banner] fills [Metropolitan Opera singer] George London with apprehension, think of what it must do to ordinary citizens whose musical talents may just get them through "Sweet Adeline" and "Abide with Me." If they remain silent, we should not be surprised. After all, the anthem has a range of one octave and five notes. The phrasing is awkward and the rhythm uncertain. The melody moves up and down with unpredictable skips. Only a few trained sopranos and tenors can hit the high F on "glare" when the song is pitched in its usual B flat. The SSB could perhaps take a prize as the world's most unsingable national anthem. [Carl Scovel, "Oh Say Can You Sing?" *Atlantic Monthly* (January, 1975), p. 54.]

What is the topic sentence of the paragraph below? Underline the sentence.

B. But the upsurge of problem drinking among the young is only part of a disturbing nationwide problem. In the past few years alcoholism—among youths and adults alike—has at last been recognized as a plague. From 1960 to 1970, U.S. per-capita consumption of alcohol has increased 26 percent—to the equivalent of 2.6 gallons of straight alcohol per adult per year. It is now at an all-time high. ["Alcoholism: New Victims, New Treatments," *The Reader's Digest* (August, 1974), p. 116.]

Look in the Answer Key for the answers.

2. *Some paragraphs do not have a topic sentence.* You must then figure out the idea for yourself, from what *is* said in the paragraph. The following paragraph is from an article about the Haight-Ashbury neighborhood in San Francisco, California. In the 1960s, hundreds of drug users lived in the neighborhood. As you read the following paragraph, notice that each sentence states a different idea. Notice, too, that the idea in one sentence does not explain the idea in another sentence, as sentences in a paragraph often do. Does the paragraph have a topic sentence?

To Middle America looking in, it was all a nightmarish zoo of drug abuse luring its runaway children. To the city of San Francisco, it was a major crime and health problem. And to the liberal, old Haight-Ashbury neighborhood, with its creaking, majestic Victorian houses near Golden Gate Park, it was too much to physically bear. [Tom Carter, "Hippie Haven, 10 Years After," *TWA Ambassador* (November, 1975), p. 23.]

The paragraph does not have a topic sentence. However, the different sentences are still related to one idea. Because the writer has not stated the idea, you must figure it out for yourself. The idea is that various groups felt that conditions in the Haight-Ashbury neighborhood were a serious problem.

Read the paragraph below. Then, read the question that follows the paragraph. Circle the letter of the answer that expresses the idea of the paragraph.

> Most of the brands of tequila popular in this country, José Cuervo, El Toro, Sauza and Gavilan, are available in both white and gold. Oddly enough, the white outsells the gold, five to one, because most Americans feel that the lighter a liquor is in color, the lighter and milder it will be in flavor, which, as any drinker of white corn moonshine will tell you, is not true at all. Joseph C. Haefelin, a vice president of the American Distilling Company, which imports El Toro, sees to it that his tequila is aged for three years before Jaimie Ruiz ships it from Mexico. Then it is strained through charcoal to remove its golden color before it is bottled as white El Toro for the U.S. market. ["Tequila," *Travel & Leisure* (November, 1974), p. 74.]

The idea of the paragraph is

a. tequila is a white and gold liquor that is aged for three years before it is shipped to Mexico
b. one distilling company ages its tequila for three years before shipping it from the United States to Mexico
c. to satisfy Americans, who think lighter liquor is better than darker, one company processes its tequila to make it white
d. white corn moonshine is a very strong kind of liquor

Look in the Answer Key for the answer.

3. *A topic sentence may not fully state the idea of a paragraph.* For example, look at the first sentence of the paragraph below. It is a topic sentence, but you must find the sentences that explain the "two secrets" to fully understand the idea of the paragraph. Underline the sentences that explain the two secrets.

> The recruit rapidly learns two secrets. First, much police work involves waiting around for something to happen, rather than saving lives or catching criminals. Danger is always a possibility, but boredom is a more constant problem. Second, police efficiency is low, individually and organizationally. Neither secret can be revealed to the outside world, because it would damage the police image and encourage crime. [Jack Horn, "The Simple Steps to Corruption," *Psychology Today* (January, 1975), p. 20. Reprinted by permission of *Psychology Today* Magazine. Copyright © 1974 Ziff-Davis Publishing Company.]

The sentences that explain the two secrets are *First, much police work involves waiting around for something to happen, rather than saving lives or catching criminals* and *Second, police efficiency is low, individually and organizationally.* The organization and content of the paragraph are shown in the following chart.

Topic sentence	The recruit rapidly learns two secrets.
—Supporting data	—First, much police work involves waiting around for something to happen, rather than saving lives or catching criminals.
—Supporting data	—Danger is always a possibility, but boredom is a more constant problem.
—Supporting data	—Second, police efficiency is low, individually and organizationally.
Concluding idea	Neither secret can be revealed to the outside world, because it would damage the police image and encourage crime.

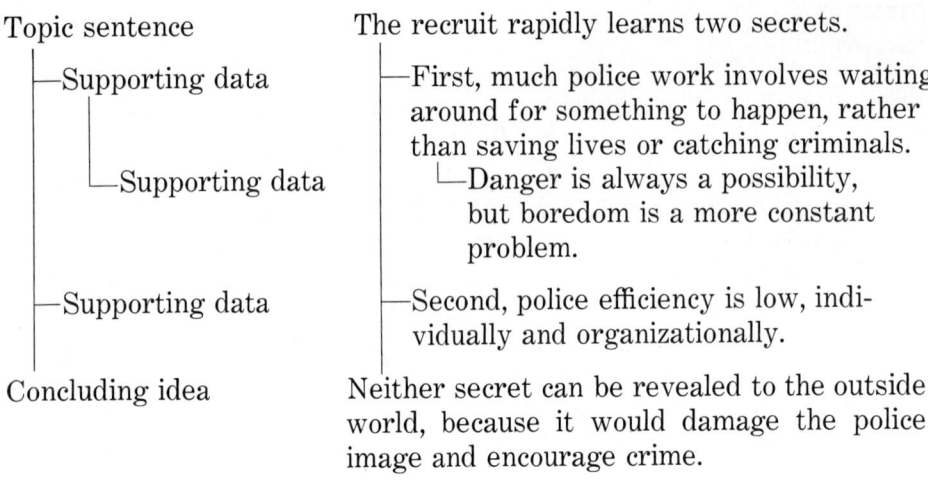

4. *A topic sentence may state, instead of a major point, an idea that supports a major point.* As you know, a major point is an idea that is directly related to explaining the controlling idea. However, most essays and articles are made up of sets, or groups, of paragraphs that explain a major point. Consequently, in prereading for major points, you must also begin working out the relationships between the major points and the ideas that explain them.

The set of paragraphs on the following page is from an article about containers and the problems we have getting rid of them. The first paragraph states a major point in the article. That idea is explained, in turn, by three other ideas. You can find these ideas by reading the following paragraphs and sentences:

First paragraph
First sentence of paragraph 2
First *two* sentences of paragraph 3
First sentence of paragraph 4
First sentence of paragraph 5

After you have read the paragraphs, complete the outline in the right-hand column. An *outline* is like a chart or diagram of the content of a composition. The ideas are numbered and lettered according to their relationships. In the following paragraphs, the major point is the most important idea. The supporting ideas that are numbered (1 and 2) are next in importance. The lettered ideas (*a, b,* and *c*) are less important. If the ideas from all the other sentences were added to the outline, those ideas would be the least important. Complete the outline by writing a sentence that states the major point from paragraph 1. Use your own words whenever possible in stating the point. Then, complete the rest of the outline either by copying the appropriate sentences or by stating the ideas of the sentences in your own words.

(1) Scientists all agree that packages are very necessary. They also agree that packages are a problem. But they do not agree on what to do about it.

(2) There is the make-it-attractive group. These designers concentrate on making the package so interesting that the buyer cannot bring himself to part with it—thus keeping it out of the trash. Corrugated boxes are made with psychedelic designs, in mod colors and all sizes. They can be used as temporary furniture. Jars are fashioned in eye-catching shapes to be used as vases, drinking glasses, candle holders. Children will not part with plastic cereal containers in the shape of teddy bears or jelly glasses with elephants on them.

(3) Next there is the no-package-package group. They have ideas like spraying a protein coating, derived from corn, on foods to protect them against loss of vitamins and spoilage. The coating is perfectly safe to eat and is used now on dried fruits, nuts, enriched rice, and frozen dehydrated foods. Someday soon it may also be sprayed on cheese in place of wax coating that must be removed before eating, or on fresh vegetables and fruits in place of miles of plastic wrap.

(4) In the no-package-package group is a new type of glass that may be the answer to the 26 billion bottles thrown away every year. The glass is coated on the inside as well as the outside by a water resistant film. When the bottle is smashed, the glass will dissolve in plain water, or hydralize. In three or four days, nothing remains but a little puddle.

(5) Another no-package is the plastic bag used to hold laundry bleach or bluing. Tossed into the laundry, it dissolves before the washing is finished. But the prize will go to the scientist who can come up with a container that is as successful as the ice cream cone! [From *How Do They Get Rid of It?* by Suzanne Hilton. Copyright © MCMLXX, Suzanne Hilton. Used by permission of The Westminster Press.]

Check your outline with the example on the following page.

Outline

Major Point ______________________

____

____

1. *Supporting Idea* ______________________

____

____

2. *Supporting Idea* ______________________

____

a. ______________________

____

____

b. ______________________

____

____

c. ______________________

____

____

Major Point Scientists do not agree on what should be done about packages.

1. *Supporting Idea* There is the make-it-attractive group.
2. *Supporting Idea* Next there is the no-package-package group.
   a. They have ideas like spraying a protein coating, derived from corn, on foods to protect them against loss of vitamins and spoilage.
   b. In the no-package-package group is a new type of glass that may be the answer to the billion bottles thrown away every year.
   c. Another no-package is the plastic bag used to hold laundry bleach or bluing.

Transitional Paragraphs

A paragraph may also consist of statements that link sections or major points in the composition. Such paragraphs are called **transitional paragraphs** because the statements help the reader make the change (transition) from one idea to another. A transitional paragraph does not have a topic sentence. Instead, the first sentence or two sums up or points back to ideas in preceding paragraphs. The last sentence or two directs the reader to the idea that will follow. Sometimes, the paragraph may refer to or restate the controlling idea.

Read the paragraphs below. The transitional paragraph has been marked for you. As you read, notice that the first sentence of the paragraph refers to the idea in the paragraph just before it. The last sentence refers to the information that follows it.

> Just to show how similar humans and apes are, Dr. Geoffrey Bourne, director of America's biggest primate research center—the Yerkes center at Emory University near Atlanta, Ga.—says there's no theoretical or even practical reason why people and apes cannot interbreed. . . .
>
> But Dr. Bourne, one of the world's top primate experts, isn't into far-out speculation. He's a fact man. And inside his center's fenced-in 20 acres, some myth-shattering research is going on. *transitional paragraph*
>
> A bouncing, five-year-old chimpanzee named Lana is shattering most of the myths. She's so smart it's scary—and there's no real evidence that she's any smarter than other chimps. It's just that she's been given a tool to communicate with. (Chimps don't have the physical equipment to vocalize like humans.)
>
> Her link with her still-expanding world is a colorful keyboard with about 90 symbols, each representing a word or concept. The keyboard is connected to a computer and a teletype machine, and what comes out on that machine is revolutionizing the way people view their primate cousins. [Dick Pothier, "What the Apes Are Teaching Us." Reprinted by permission by *The Philadelphia Inquirer*, issue of December 7, 1975.]

The following seven paragraphs are from an article titled "Who Will Do Tomorrow's Dirty Work?" The controlling idea of the article is that we are running out of people who are willing to do our necessary unskilled work. One of the paragraphs is a transitional paragraph that links two major points in the article. Mark the transitional paragraph. Then, answer the questions that follow the paragraphs.

(1) A number of other factors have been eroding the supply of people available for unskilled work. Economist Harold Wool, of the National Planning Association, points out that during the '60s society's efforts to keep young people in school reduced the number of dropouts entering the labor force. Moreover, minority groups, especially blacks, began pushing in earnest toward equality in employment.

(2) Today, a great many young black people refuse to take jobs they consider demeaning. A decade ago, 20 percent of the black young women who had graduated from high school worked as domestics; only three percent were settling for that kind of work in 1970. "Most service-type jobs," says Wool, "have become anathema to many blacks, even on a temporary basis." This explains why some service jobs are hard to fill even in cities where unemployment among young black people runs at dismayingly high rates.

(3) It seems clear, then, that in years ahead the traditional supply of low-status workers will not meet the demand. But a lot of unskilled work will *have* to be done, one way or another. Society will have to respond to the tightening of the labor supply by improving pay and working conditions.

(4) Right now, there are many places where the federal minimum wage of $2 an hour cannot buy work. Even members of the so-called "secondary labor force"—women and young people whose pay supplements a family's principal source of income—are usually not willing to work for $2. For those groups, around $2.50 is the real market "minimum" needed to balance supply and demand.

(5) It may be a portent of things to come that New York City now pays its unionized sanitation men $14,840 a year after three years (plus an extremely liberal pension). Hardly anybody ever quits, and thousands of men are on a waiting list for future job openings. At Chrysler Corp., unskilled "material handlers," whose job includes pushing carts around the plant floor by hand, get $5.56 an hour, which draws plenty of young married men. . . .

(6) Another way to improve the status of unskilled work is to raise the quality and complexity of the work itself. Some of the credit for a low turnover rate at Massachusetts General Hospital goes to a training program begun in 1968 for "building-service aides," who previously had gone by the titles of "maid" and "houseman." Today they go through a one-month program, which involves 80 hours in a classroom and a loose-leaf manual resembling one used by more highly skilled workers at the hospital.

(7) A pleasanter work climate can also help make low-status work less lowly. . . . Jan Lovell, former president of the Dallas Restaurant Association, believes his industry is improving the work atmosphere but will have to do more in order to survive. "A few years ago," says Lovell, "it wasn't unusual for a restaurant to buy a $12,000 dishwashing machine and then hire two drunks off

the street at $75 a week who might forget to turn the water on. Today, you pay one guy $150 a week who does the work of two. But maybe we also need to put in a radio and a rug on the floor." [Edmund Faltermayer, "Who Will Do Tomorrow's Dirty Work?" *Fortune* (January, 1974). As condensed in the January, 1975 *The Reader's Digest*, pp. 164 and 166. Courtesy of *Fortune* Magazine, Edmund Faltermayer.]

1. The first sentence of the transitional paragraph refers back to the statement that
   a. unemployment among young black people runs at dismayingly high rates
   b. many young black people refuse to take jobs they consider demeaning
   c. some service jobs are hard to fill
   d. a decade ago, 20 percent of the black young women who had graduated from high school worked as domestics

2. The third (last) sentence of the transitional paragraph points to ideas about
   a. training workers to be skilled operators
   b. improving pay and working conditions for unskilled jobs
   c. changing the titles of unskilled jobs
   d. hiring alcoholics to run dishwashing machines

Look in the Answer Key for the answers.

Digressions

A **digression** is a statement or idea that is not closely related to the other ideas being explained. A digression may be a single sentence or a paragraph or more in length.

The paragraphs below explain the difference between reproducing pianos and player pianos. However, the article is mainly about the restoration of player pianos. Is the information about reproducing pianos important to the article as a whole? Read the paragraphs and mark the sentences and paragraphs that are digressions.

(1) Thousands of tunes ago the old time player piano practically disappeared. Banished into barns, basements and tinderboxes, it was largely displaced by its lower cost, more versatile modern counterparts—the radio and the record player. Approximately 2,500,000 player pianos were built between 1900 and the Depression years, and most of these, like the black-iron wood stoves of the period, were never expected to be seen again.

(2) But just as necessity has rekindled flames in the once-banished wood stove, so nostalgia has served to pump air into those big wooden music boxes of yesteryear. Stocked with as little as $75 worth of service manuals (usually reprinted from the original), instruction books and a few basic tools and materials, enthusiasts can transform what they call the "player action" (as opposed to simple piano innards) from a weather-weary, mouse-molested reject to an orchestration of expanding and collapsing

bellows—the pumps that breathe life into these vacuum-operated machines.

(3) Enthusiasts collect all manner of roll-actuated instruments, but the player piano and its more elaborate relative, the reproducing piano, are the most popular. The reproducer does not have the pedal-and-pump mechanism that activates the player—it operates electrically, moving a complex series of special bellows that reproduce the phrasing and modulation of whoever created the piano roll. That is why such composers as Debussy, Stravinsky and Grieg made rolls for these instruments, which were also produced as concert grand pianos.

(4) In the words of Theodore DeWitt, a meticulous professional restorer in Chesapeake, Va., who began as a hobbyist, "Comparing a reproducing piano to a player is like comparing a stereo set to a transistor radio."

(5) However, reproducers are so much more intricate that most novices choose to work on the simpler player pianos first. Restoration always requires a complete rebuilding of what is commonly called the "player action" (the mechanical series of bellows and valves that operate the piano rolls), as well as a complete refinishing of the outer cabinet in most cases. [Jourdan and Alan Houston, "Those Old Player Pianos Roll Again," *New York Times* (February 9, 1975), D-35. © 1975 by The New York Times Company. Reprinted by permission.]

Paragraphs 3 and 4 and the first sentence of paragraph 5 should be marked as the digression. Try reading paragraphs 1 and 2; then skip to the second sentence of paragraph 5. As you read, notice that these paragraphs are all related to restoring player pianos, which is the subject of the article. The information about reproducing pianos is not closely related to that subject.

Single-Sentence Paragraphs

In some articles, you will find **single-sentence paragraphs.** In newspaper articles, for instance, the first paragraph usually contains all the essential information. The additional paragraphs include less important information. These paragraphs may have a single sentence. All the sentences, and all the ideas, thus seem to be of equal importance. But they are not. In fact, when you read articles with single-sentence paragraphs, you may find it difficult to determine the relationships and importance of the ideas. Such articles are difficult because they do not have paragraph organization or topic sentences to help you.

The following article has some single-sentence paragraphs. Label the controlling idea. What are the major points of the article? You may have to combine the information in some of the paragraphs to decide the major points.

title→ HELPING HAND

lead→ *If a handicapped person cannot travel alone, he now can take along a companion free, thanks to a new bus service instituted by the world's largest bus line.*

(1) Thousands of physically handicapped Americans now will be able to travel to faraway places to visit friends and relatives and admire America's scenic wonders at close range . . . thanks to the "Helping Hand" extended by the world's largest bus line.

(2) Under the new service, a companion travels free to assist the handicapped person who needs help in boarding, leaving and traveling on a Greyhound Lines' bus. Both travel on a single ticket and must complete the trip together.

(3) All that's needed by a handicapped person to be eligible for the special two-for-the-price-of-one fare is a written statement from a doctor that the assistance of a companion is essential to travel, the bus company said.

(4) The Helping Hand fare applies to all of the company's regular rates as well as to special fares, such as the Ameripass which offers unlimited travel over Greyhound's 100,000 route miles of service in the U.S. and Canada.

(5) An Ameripass good for 15 days of travel for the handicapped traveler and companion will cost $125; a one-month pass is $175 and a two-month pass is $250. Special discounts on meals, lodgings and sightseeing at stopover points are available to Ameripass holders. [Murray J. Brown, "Helping Hand," *Miami Herald* (December 21, 1975), 4-J. Copyright United Press International.]

The controlling idea of the paragraphs above is stated in paragraph 1. Paragraphs 2 and 3 are about conditions of the travel service, the first major point. Paragraphs 4 and 5 are about the rates for travel, the second major point.

Transitional Statements

As you preread a composition, you may find transitional paragraphs. You may also find transitional statements at the end or the beginning of a paragraph. The statements may be whole sentences or part of a topic sentence. **Transitional statements** refer to ideas that have already been explained, to ideas that follow, or to both. The statements link the ideas together. Thus, they help you make the change (transition) from one idea to the next. They can even help you find ideas when the paragraphs are not clearly organized.

The following five paragraphs are from an article titled "Rape." The major point of the paragraphs has been marked for you. Notice that the major point has two parts. Read the paragraphs and underline the transitional statements.

(1) Still other assailants look for environments that are easily entered and relatively safe. They make certain that the victim is alone, and that they will not be interrupted. They often commit their crimes in the run-down section of town, where residences are rickety, and where many women live alone. More than three fourths of the Denver victims were single women. *major point*

(2) Older homes, converted into apartments, are the easiest residences for a rapist to get into; basement or first-floor

apartments are especially tempting. Two thirds of Denver's sex offenses that took place in buildings during a two-year period occurred in the basement or on the ground floor. Large apartments with doormen or security guards are the most difficult residences for a rapist to enter.

(3) Rapists often select their victims long before they actually approach them, and they may be very consistent in how they do it. One rapist in Denver always identified single women living alone in a second-story apartment with an accessible window. He used a ladder to reach his victims and to flee the scene.

(4) Rapists may have a sixth sense for identifying women who live alone, or be particularly good at finding streets, empty laundromats or theater restrooms that are isolated, but draw unsuspecting victims.

(5) . . . While housing that is easy to enter and the isolation of the victim are two obvious factors that make women particularly vulnerable to rape, women who are characteristically friendly and who like to help others also are courting danger. One fourth of the women in Denver who were attacked by strangers from 1970 to 1972 were responding to the offender's request for help. Teachers, nurses and other women who have learned to serve others, be charitable, and give of themselves are especially vulnerable to sexual exploitation. [James Selkin, "Rape," *Psychology Today* (January, 1975), p. 72. Reprinted by permission of *Psychology Today* Magazine. Copyright © 1974 Ziff-Davis Publishing Company.]

The first part of the first sentence in paragraph 5 is a transitional statement. The statement refers to both parts of the major point. The second part of the sentence states the topic of the paragraph.

Words and Terms to Know

major point
topic sentence
transitional paragraph
digression
single-sentence paragraph
transitional statement

Concepts to Remember

1. A paragraph is based on an idea. The idea is usually stated in one of the sentences of the paragraph and explained in the other sentences.
2. The sentence that expresses the most important idea (topic) of the paragraph is called a topic sentence. The idea may be a major point or a supporting idea in the whole composition.
3. The topic sentence is often the first sentence in a paragraph. However, a topic sentence can be placed in any position in a paragraph.
4. In some paragraphs, the idea or topic is not directly stated in a sentence. Because such paragraphs do not have a topic sentence, you must determine the idea of the paragraph from what *is* said.

5. A topic sentence may not fully state the idea of the paragraph.
6. A major point may be explained in a single paragraph or in a set of paragraphs.
7. A transitional paragraph contains sentences that sum up or point back to ideas that have been explained and/or to ideas that follow.
8. A digression is a statement or idea that is not closely related to the other ideas being explained.
9. A single-sentence paragraph may be based on a major point, supporting idea, or an idea of less importance in the composition. Combining single-sentence paragraphs in the composition can help you determine the major points.
10. A transitional statement refers to ideas that have been explained and/or to ideas that follow.

Assignment

Complete the worksheet at the end of this task according to your instructor's directions.

Answer Key Task 12

page 24

A. The topic sentence is the last sentence.
B. The topic sentence is the second sentence.

page 25

You need to combine information from sentences 2, 3, and 4 of the paragraph to determine the idea. The answer to the question is *c.*

pages 29–30

The third paragraph is the transitional paragraph. The first sentence of the paragraph refers to *b*: "many young black people refuse to take jobs they consider demeaning" (paragraph 2). The relationship between the ideas is that young black people, who have been the "traditional supply of low-status workers," are refusing jobs they feel are undignified (demeaning) and that their refusal will result in not having enough people, in the future, to fill unskilled jobs. The same meaning relationship occurs between the first sentence and the quotation in paragraph 2: "Most service-type jobs . . . have become anathema to many blacks. . . ." However, the quotation was not among the answers. The last sentence of the paragraph points to ideas about improving pay and working conditions for unskilled jobs (statement *b*). Notice that paragraphs 4 and 5 discuss information related to improving pay. Paragraphs 6 and 7 discuss ways to improve working conditions.

Task 12 **Worksheet**

NAME ____ DATE ____________

Reading Practice

The paragraphs below are from the article "Zebras Offer Clues to the Way Wild Horses Once Lived." The paragraphs contain two major points. Each major point is concerned with one type of zebra behavior. Each type of behavior results in specific zebra actions. Those actions are explained in the paragraphs. As you read the paragraphs, underline and label the

a. Topic sentences that state major points
b. Sentences that state ideas which support the major points
c. Transitional statements
d. Paragraphs that are digressions

After you have read and marked the paragraphs, complete the outline in the right-hand column.

(1) Although generally quiet, zebras can be very noisy when disturbed or on the move in large bands. The loudest and most frequently heard cry sounds like something between a bark and a bray; the Hottentot name, *quagga* (pronounced *kwacha* in Afrikaans), represents this sound. It maintains or re-establishes contact between herd members.
(2) A quiet call often heard in a concentration of grazing animals is blowing with loose lips, exactly like a horse. It is a sound of contentment or well-being. The opposite is the short squeal emitted when a zebra is bitten or kicked, or simply afraid. There are two alarm calls: a snort, the nearly universal alarm call of hoofed animals, and a hoarse, open-mouthed breathing in and out, a quiet cry. Foals have their own distress call, a drawn-out squeal which alarms the herd and instantly brings the stallion and mother to its defense.
(3) A good deal of time is spent in grooming. Zebras like to rub themselves on large rocks and tree trunks, embankments, termite mounds or other objects of the right height, which are apt to be scarce on the

A. ______________________________
____
1. ______________________________
____
2. ______________________________
____
3. ______________________________
____
4. ______________________________
a. ______________________________
b. ______________________________
5. ______________________________

B. ______________________________
1. ______________________________
____

plains. They will wait in line, if necessary, for a chance to rub their necks, sides, rumps and bellies. Aside from warthogs and elephants, few other savanna animals appear to have the rubbing habit.

(4) Polished rubbing rocks with tracks around them are still to be seen on the South African High Veld, where herds of *quagga*—a zebralike animal that was either a subspecies of the plains zebra or a species in its own right—lived until they were exterminated in the 19th century. Today even most local residents have no idea of what kind of animal left these memorials.

(5) Confirmed dust bathers, zebras are indebted to wildebeests for their stamping grounds of bare earth. Wildebeests, too, like to roll, but cannot roll completely over as a zebra (or a horse) can. The secret may lie in having a rounded back—plains zebras always seem to look round and fat.

(6) Even more important in zebra behavior than rolling and rubbing is social grooming, a mutual activity which seems to cement relationships between members of a stallion's herd. Two zebras stand face to face and nibble (not lick) one another's neck and back with their incisors, removing dead skin and loose hair. When they have finished one side, each animal, as if on signal, takes one step backwards, swings its head to the partner's opposite side and resumes currying. All the members of a herd groom one another, but mares groom most often with their offspring, especially the latest one, while adult females are paired least often. The stallion prefers to groom some mares more than others, without regard to social rank, and apparently with no sexual overtones. Zebras do not groom with strangers; when a new mare is introduced to a herd, at first only the stallion, her sponsor, will groom her. [Richard D. Estes, "Zebras Offer Clues to the Way Wild Horses Once Lived." Copyright 1974 Smithsonian Institution, from *Smithsonian* magazine, November 1974, pp. 102–103.]

2. ______________________________

____

3. ______________________________

____

Task 13
Supporting Data and Body Paragraphs

We all use the same kinds of information to explain our ideas. We may use an example or fact. We may describe the steps in a process. We may point out causes and effects of an event or condition. We may explain the parts of an object or problem, or the similarities and differences between things or ideas. We may use a definition.

Writers use these same kinds of information as **supporting data** or details to explain an idea. They explain or prove a major point, for instance, through examples, facts, or other specific information.

Being able to identify the information used to explain an idea can help you in several ways. First, understanding what you read depends, in part, on recognizing that certain information is an example, fact, or other detail that explains an idea. Second, recognizing that the supporting data has not explained or cannot prove an idea is a necessary part of deciding whether you can accept the idea as reasonable or true. Third, remembering the examples, facts, or other details in an article is often important in your school courses.

The kind of supporting data that is used is sometimes indicated by words such as *for example, in fact,* or *because.* Such words are called **transitional markers.** Through their meaning, transitional markers help you determine the relation of the supporting data to another idea. Also, if the writer does not use such markers, you can use them to "test" the relation of ideas.

Examples

An **example** is a specific illustration of a more general idea. In the paragraph below, *rice, sugar,* and *flour* are examples. They explain the idea in the first sentence of the paragraph.

topic sentence It is one of the oddities of "progress" that many of our foods are so refined that most of the valuable food nutrients have been removed. *example* White rice is not nearly so good for you as the brown rice it is made from. Brown sugar is better, honey better yet, than *examples* any refined sugar. Bleached white flour has had the best part of the wheat, the vitamin E, removed. Unbleached white flour, available every place, is better than bleached flour. Whole wheat or other whole grain flour is better still. [Bernice Kohn, *The Organic Living Book* (New York: Viking Press, 1972), p. 16.]

The transitional marker *for example* is often used to indicate that the information you are reading is an example of another idea. Some other phrases that are used to indicate examples are *for instance, such as,* or *as an example.*

If there are no transitional markers used, you can test for the relationship of information to another idea with the words *for example.* The information in the above paragraph about refined foods could be tested in the following way:

Paragraph		*Meaning*
It is one of the oddities of "progress" that many of our foods are so refined that most of the valuable food nutrients have been removed.	→ *topic sentence* →	The nutritional value of many of our foods is greatly reduced when they are refined or processed.
White rice is not nearly so good for you as the brown rice it is made from.	→ *for example* →	White (refined) rice is not as good for you as brown (unrefined) rice.
Brown sugar is better, honey better yet, than any refined sugar.	→ *for example* →	Refined sugar is not as good for you as brown (unrefined) sugar or honey.
Bleached white flour has had the best part of the wheat, the vitamin E, removed. Unbleached white flour, available every place, is better than bleached flour. Whole wheat or other whole grain flour is better still.	→ *for example* →	Bleached (refined) flour has had its vitamin E removed and is not as good for you as unbleached (unrefined), whole wheat or other whole grain flour.

Read the following paragraphs. As you read, label the examples you find and draw a line from each example to the idea it explains. Next, circle the transitional markers that identify examples. Then, label the examples you identified by using the "for example" test.

A. *(1)* It is not the best of times, and it is not the worst of times, just somewhere discouragingly in between. New York no longer has the look of a city in construction, which means that at least fewer good old buildings are being torn down for bad new ones. The developers are crying all the way to the Caribbean. And the city's planners, theoretically, have time to sit and think.

(2) They have plenty to think about. Planning is in a quiet crisis in New York. The Times Square area, for example, faces a fateful 12 months in which it will either be lost or revitalized. This will depend on whether currently projected major construction will be able to go ahead. [The condition of Times Square, the symbolic heart of the city, somehow seems to represent the condition of the whole city.] [Ada Louise Huxtable, "More Bad News About Times Square," *New York Times* (February 9, 1975), 32-D. © 1975 by The New York Times Company. Reprinted by permission.]

B. Americans have been dosing themselves with patent medicines since colonial times, when they sought relief in such nostrums as Turlington's Balsam of Life, Daffy's Elixir Salutis and Monsieur Torres' Chinese Stones. Unlike Monsieur Torres, today's manufacturers of nonprescription drugs don't tout their products as cures for cancer and the bites of mad dogs and rattlesnakes. But they do claim that their products will cure or at least relieve the symptoms of a variety of temporary minor ills, from tension headaches down to athlete's foot. [Caroline Donnelley, "Dose-It-Yourself Drugs," *Money* (December, 1974), p. 92.]

Look in the Answer Key for the answers.

Facts

A **fact** is information that can be checked for its accuracy. Figures or statistics that refer, accurately, to prices, percentages, or other numbers are facts. Dates—whether of days, months, or years—are facts. So, too, are specific details about a place, object, or event, providing the details can be checked and are accurate. Facts may be used as supporting data alone or in combination with an example or other kind of information.

The paragraphs below show you some of the different kinds of information that are facts. Notice that there are some statements that may be facts. But you cannot completely accept the statements as true because the statements cannot be checked.

A. When a motorist, driving at 65 mph, sights a sudden hazard, his foot moves sharply to the brake pedal. But, incredibly, the car has traversed another 70 feet between the sighting and contact with the brake. Another 250 feet will be covered before the car is brought to a halt. For the total procedure: a distance longer than a football field. So brakes are important and they deserve a checkup at least twice a year. ["The Ping of the Road," *Saturday Evening Post* (January/February, 1975), p. 102.]

possible fact, but all motorists may not react this way

facts, used within an example that explains why brake checkups are important

B. *(1)* If you use either the Sinclair Executive ($79.95) or the Cambridge ($29.95), you will have not only the right answer, but also one of the best-designed calculators available. In fact, the Executive has been selected for the Permanent Design collection at the Museum of Modern Art. It is small—shirt-pocket-size—thin, and lightweight. The buttons are tiny, very light and springy to the touch, and make no sound when pressed. The Executive also has a "memory" unit, which enables you to do a set of calculations, store the result, do another set, then multiply, divide, add, or subtract the second result with the one already in the "memory."

facts (prices)

facts, explaining "best-designed calculators"

(2) The Cambridge is even smaller, though slightly thicker and about the same weight. The buttons are larger and make a dignified, quiet click. Both models operate on batteries only. The

facts, comparing and contrasting the calculators

Executive's batteries last for twelve hours, the Cambridge's for twenty-four. Neither can be recharged. These calculators are available where other calculators are sold, or from us (add $2 for postage and handling). ["Calculating Look," Wraparound, *Harper's* Magazine (April, 1975), p. 114.]

facts, information about buying calculators

Some of the transitional markers that are used to indicate facts are *the fact is, the facts are, the point is, the truth is.* However, such markers are sometimes followed by an opinion rather than a fact. Look at the following sentence:

> An automatic washing machine is a good investment: In fact, it's the best appliance you can buy.

The statement *In fact, it's the best appliance you can buy* is an opinion, not a fact. Furthermore, the statement cannot really be checked. In contrast, the statement *In fact, stoves come in twenty- to forty-inch widths* can be checked. You can go to an appliance dealer, for instance, and find out if the information is accurate.

To test supporting data, you can say *the fact is* or *the facts are* to see if the information has a factual relation to another idea. In addition, you must think about whether the information can be checked to see if it is true. Dates, figures, and other numbers can usually be checked in encyclopedias, reports, or other documents kept in libraries. But you should not accept as facts any statements that are actually opinions or that cannot be checked or proved.

Read the paragraphs below. As you read, label the facts and circle the transitional markers that identify the facts. Then label any statements that are opinions or that cannot be checked or proved. Use the paragraphs on pages 39–40 as examples in marking the paragraphs.

A. During the past three months [May–June, 1975] Alaska, Maine, Colorado, and California have joined Oregon in enacting laws that make the possession of at least one ounce of marijuana for personal use a civil offense punishable by a small fine, rather than a crime. Alaska's Supreme Court went even further, ruling that the constitutionally guaranteed right to privacy entails the right to possess marijuana for consumption in the citizen's own home. In the language of the court: "It appears that the use of marijuana, as it is presently used in the United States today, does not constitute a public health problem of any significant dimensions." ["What Will Happen When Middle-Class America Gets the Straight Dope?" *New York* (August 25, 1975), p. 28.]

B. Ninety per cent of the Haight-Ashbury was built before 1923, most of it before the 1906 fire and earthquake. Seldom has the resident population exceeded 20,000. Many buildings are two- and three-story flats with turrets and domes, pillars and detailed façades and beautiful stained-glass windows. The hippie invasion—with its attendant, illegal doubling-up and the rising incidence of absentee-ownership—caused more deterioration than the heavy population influxes during the Depression and World War II. [Tom Carter, "Hippie Haven, 10 Years After," *TWA Ambassador* (November, 1975), p. 24.]

Look in the Answer Key for the answers.

Cause and Effect

A **cause** explains "why." An **effect** explains what happened or the result of certain causes.

We depend on cause and effect explanations in making decisions, solving problems, creating laws, and explaining diseases. For example, you have seat belts in your car as a result of cause and effect investigations of deaths and injuries in auto accidents. You may want a gun-control law because you think the law will have the effect of reducing crime. You may not want a gun-control law because you think such a law takes away your rights or because you think the law will not have the effect of reducing crime. As you can see, cause and effect relationships are very important. Consequently, you will find many cause and effect explanations in your reading.

Causes are often indicated by the transitional marker *because.* If the information is not identified as a cause, you can use the word *because* to "test" the relationship of the information to another idea.

Sometimes cause and effect explanations are simple and easy to understand. In the following paragraphs, for example, a single cause (amplified rock-'n'-roll music) is related to a single effect (deafness).

> *effect*
> *cause*
>
> *(1)* Otologists* report that youngsters are going deaf as a result of blasting their eardrums with electronically amplified rock 'n' roll. . . .
>
> *cause (repeated)*
>
> *(2)* In discotheques and rock-'n'-roll joints, the trouble is not so much in the instruments themselves, or even the sustained fortissimi or the close quarters. The blame goes to the electronic amplifiers. An old-fashioned oompah military band, playing a Sousa march in Central or Golden Gate Park, generated as much sound. But the sound was not amplified, and was dissipated in the open air. A trombonist sitting in front of a tuba player might be a bit deaf for an hour or so after a concert; then his hearing returned to normal. A microphone hooked up to a public-address system did not much increase the hearing hazard. What did was multiple mikes and speakers, and the installation of internal mikes in such instruments as guitars and bouzoukia. ["Going Deaf from Rock 'n' Roll," *Time* (August 9, 1968), p. 47.]

In a cause and effect explanation, there may be several causes that are related to a single effect. Or, there may be one cause for several effects. In the paragraphs below, the writer states two reasons or causes for Mrs. Rosa Parks's refusing to give up her seat on a bus to a white man. The writer tells you these two causes were disproved (although you should notice that you are not told how or by whom they were disproved).

*An *otologist* is an ear specialist.

Then, you are told the reason the writer says is the "truth." As you read, underline and label (in paragraph 3) the causes that explain why Mrs. Parks would not give up her seat. Then, answer the questions following the paragraphs. If necessary, use the "because" test.

> *(1)* "Lord, Child," a Mississippi woman once said to me, "we colored people ain't nothing but a bundle of resentments and sufferings going somewhere to explode."
>
> *(2)* The explosion—and no one would have then taken it for that—came on December 1, 1955, the day Mrs. Rosa Parks boarded the Cleveland Avenue bus in Montgomery, Alabama. And the Negro revolt is properly dated from the moment Mrs. Parks said, "No" to the bus driver's demand that she get up and let a white man have her seat.
>
> *(3)* There have been scores of attempts to discover why Mrs. Parks refused to move. The local white power structure insisted that the NAACP had put her up to it, but this charge was quickly disproved. The extremists spread the word that Mrs. Parks was a Communist agent, that the whole thing had been hatched in the Kremlin; that rumor collapsed under the weight of its own preposterousness. The truth is that Mrs. Parks was a part of the deepening mood of despair and disillusionment that gripped the American Negro after World War II. She had been an official in the Montgomery NAACP; Mrs. Parks was an alert woman, a dedicated Negro and fully aware of the continuing injustices Negroes all over the nation were enduring. The only way to account for Mrs. Parks is to say she was a part of the times; that, at long last, her cup ran over. [From p. 81 in *The Negro Revolt* by Louis E. Lomax. Copyright © 1962 by Louis E. Lomax. Reprinted by permission of Harper & Row, Publishers, Inc.]

1. The paragraphs say that the black civil rights movement began because
   a. white people got the best seats on buses
   b. white people insisted on having all the power
   c. a black woman was blown up on a bus
   d. a black woman refused to give up her bus seat to a white man

2. The paragraphs say that Mrs. Parks did not give up her bus seat because
   a. she lived in Montgomery, Alabama, in December, 1955
   b. She felt black people were treated unjustly
   c. The NAACP (National Association for the Advancement of Colored People) wanted her to start trouble
   d. a Russian agent had worked out a plan for her to start a revolution

Look in the Answer Key to check your marking of the paragraphs and your answers to the questions.

Classification and Division

A **classification** system is a way to group people, places, objects, or even information. We decide who or what belongs to a particular group on the basis of certain features, qualities, or characteristics that are alike. For example, the yellow pages of the telephone book are called the *classified* pages. In those pages, business places and agencies are grouped according to the product sold, produced, or serviced. Newspapers also have a section called the *classified* advertisements. In that section, ads are grouped according to the kind of information they have in common. For example, the ads list "jobs available," "jobs wanted," "apartments for rent," "houses for sale," and so on.

Thus, a classification is based on characteristics that make a group alike. Then, a group is divided according to characteristics that make its parts different. These differences are the **divisions** of the classification. For instance, in the yellow or classified pages of the phone book, you may find a classification for "clocks." You may also find divisions of that classification, such as "clocks—parts," "clocks—dealers," or "clocks—repairing." In newspaper ads, you may find "jobs available" ads divided into "factory jobs," "sales jobs," "secretarial jobs," and so on. "Apartments for rent" and "houses for sale" ads may be divided according to different neighborhoods.

A writer often treats an idea as a classification and then explains the idea through divisions. For example, in the paragraph below, a *policeman's job* is the classification. The three ways of handling the job are the divisions.

> *classification* — *division 1* — *division 2* — *division 3*
>
> The presidential crime commission offered a partial solution to overworked police forces: Split up the policeman's job three different ways. Under this plan, a "community service officer," often a youth from the ghetto, would perform minor investigative chores, rescue cats, and keep in touch with combustible young people. A police officer, one step higher, would control traffic, hold back crowds at parades, and investigate more serious crimes. A police agent, the best-trained, best-educated man on the ladder, would patrol high-crime areas, respond to delicate racial situations, and take care of tense confrontations. ["The Police Need Help," *Time* (October 4, 1968), p. 27.]

The divisions are sometimes indicated by such transitional markers as *for one thing, also,* or *in addition.* In the paragraphs below, the divisions are shown by the words *first, second,* and *third.*

> *classification*
>
> [A safe city street must have three main qualities.]
>
> *division 1*
>
> First, there must be a clear demarcation between what is public space and what is private space. Public and private spaces cannot ooze into each other as they do typically in suburban settings or in projects.
>
> *division 2*
>
> Second, there must be eyes upon the street, eyes belonging to those we might call the natural proprietors of the street. The buildings on a street equipped to handle strangers and to insure the safety of both residents and strangers, must be oriented to the street. They cannot turn their backs or blank sides on it and leave it blind.
>
> *division 3*
>
> And third, the sidewalk must have users on it fairly continuously, both to add to the number of effective eyes on the street and to induce the people in buildings along the street to watch the sidewalks in sufficient numbers. Nobody enjoys sitting on a stoop or looking out a window at an empty street. Almost nobody does such a thing. Large numbers of people entertain themselves, off

and on, by watching street activity. . . . [Jane Jacobs, *Death and Life of Great American Cities* (New York: Random House, 1961).]

Read the paragraphs below. As you read, underline and label the classification and divisions in each paragraph. Then, answer the questions that follow each paragraph. Use the paragraphs on page 43 as examples in marking the paragraphs below.

A. In the nineties and the early 1900s, gold teeth were as much a part of the fashion scene as peg-top trousers, choker collars, and chatelaine watches. There were, of course, certain practical reasons for this popularity. From the viewpoint of the average dentist, gold-shell crowns provided a simple method of securely anchoring artificial teeth; at the same time they covered ugly, broken-down, and discolored natural teeth, as well as much inferior dental work. And to the patient, gold seemed to represent the most in value received. [Charles I. Stoloff, *Natural History* (February, 1972).]

1. The paragraph is about reasons for the popularity of
   a. peg-top trousers
   b. gold teeth
   c. choker collars
   d. chatelaine watches

2. The paragraph says that gold teeth were used by dentists for the following reasons:
   a. to anchor artificial teeth
   b. to cover natural teeth
   c. to hide poor dental work
   d. all of the above (*a, b,* and *c*)

B. The metric system seems dreamlike in its consistency. First of all, it is a decimal system—the units it employs are almost always related by powers of ten. For example, the meter, the basic unit of length in the metric system, is equal to 10 decimeters, or 100 centimeters, or 1,000 millimeters. Therefore, converting 38.61 meters to centimeters requires only shifting the decimal point two places to the right. Also, the metric system utilizes a consistent system of prefixes to designate multiples and submultiples of its basic units. Greek-derived prefixes are assigned to the multiples (*deca* equals multiplication by 10, *hecto* equals multiplication by 100, *kilo* equals multiplication by 1,000). Latin prefixes are assigned to the submultiples (*deci* equals division by 10, *centi* equals division by 100, and so on). Easy to memorize, not much to forget. [Frank Kendig, "The Coming Changeover," *Saturday Review* (November 25, 1972).]

3. The paragraph is about
   a. decimal units
   b. the metric system
   c. number prefixes
   d. Greek and Latin numbers

4. The paragraph says the basic unit of length in the metric system is
   a. a decimal
   b. a prefix
   c. the meter
   d. a unit of ten

5. The paragraph says that the meter is equal to
   a. 10 decimeters
   b. 100 centimeters
   c. 1,000 millimeters
   d. all of the above (*a, b,* and *c*)

6. The paragraph says that the prefixes used in the metric system are
   a. consistent
   b. basic
   c. multiples
   d. submultiples

7. The divisions are indicated by the words
   a. therefore
   b. for example
   c. also
   d. first of all and also

Look in the Answer Key for the answers.

Comparison and Contrast

A **comparison** explains the ways in which people, objects, or ideas are alike. A **contrast** explains the ways in which they are different.

In the paragraph below, the writer explains that dogs and cats are alike in being carnivores (flesh- or meat-eating animals) and in serving man as hunters. Thus, these two characteristics compare the two animals. The dog and cat are different, or in contrast, because the dog has changed its way of life but the cat has not. The writer also explains that the cat is still wild and independent (in contrast to the dog, who is dependent on man). The cat, unlike the dog, is mysterious and remote.

comparison characteristics
1. carnivores
2. hunters

contrast characteristic
1. dog-changed
2. cat-not changed

Only two animals have entered the human household otherwise than as prisoners and become domesticated by other means than those of enforced servitude: the dog and the cat. Two things they have in common, namely, that both belong to the order of carnivores and both serve man in their capacity of hunters. In all other characteristics, above all in the manner of their association with man, they are as different as the night from the day. There is no domestic animal that has so radically altered its whole way of living, indeed its whole sphere of interests, that has become domestic in so true a sense as the dog; and there is no animal that, in the course of its centuries-old association with man, has altered so little as the cat. There is some truth in the assertion that the cat, with the exception of a few luxury breeds, such as Angoras, Persians and Siamese, is no domestic animal but a completely wild being. Maintaining its full independence it has taken up its abode in the houses and outhouses of man, for the simple reason that there are more mice there than elsewhere. The whole charm of the dog lies in the depth of the friendship and the strength of the spiritual ties with which he has bound himself to man, but the appeal of the cat lies in the very fact that she has formed no close bond with him, that she has the uncompromising independence of a tiger or a leopard while she is hunting in his stables and barns, that she still remains mysterious and remote when she is rubbing herself gently against the legs of her mistress or purring contentedly in front of the fire. [*Man Meets Dog* by Konrad Lorenz. Copyright © Konrad Lorenz 1953. Reprinted by permission of Houghton Mifflin Company and Methuen & Co., Ltd.]

The paragraph below is also based on two like characteristics and one contrast characteristic. Read the paragraph. As you read, underline and label (1) the two comparison characteristics and (2) the one contrast characteristic. Use the paragraph about dogs and cats as an example in marking the paragraph below. Then, answer the questions that follow the paragraph.

America's cities were already jammed with cars and its landscape defaced with billboards in 1939, but in other ways things looked a good deal different from the way they look now. New urban building, which had gone through a fantastic boom during the twenties, had been at a virtual standstill for a decade, so the nation's cities had a certain look of faded splendor. Now, though, a small crop of new buildings were beginning to appear, many of them pioneering low-cost housing projects; with their unadorned rectilinear planes they anticipated the joyless boxes that were to be a feature of the postwar period. Some new buildings, such as a high-rise apartment house under construction on New York City's Riverside Drive, represented the last gasp of the elegant past, with such elaborations as decorative towers, filigree in stone, perhaps even a gargoyle or two; but the tide had turned. In New York three more end-of-the-century merchant palaces on Fifth Avenue were about to go under the wrecker's hammer, and the brand-new Museum of Modern Art, designed by Philip L. Goodwin and Edward D. Stone, foretold the future in its simple lines and generous use of glass. [From p. 18 in *The Great Leap* by John Brooks. Copyright © 1966 by John Brooks. Reprinted by permission of Harper & Row, Publishers, Inc.]

1. The paragraph compares and contrasts American
   a. cars
   b. landscapes
   c. cities
   d. billboards

2. The paragraph says that after a "standstill" in building, new buildings began to be put up
   a. after World War II
   b. in 1939
   c. in 1920
   d. in 1899

3. The paragraph gives three examples of "new urban building." Circle the letter of the answer that is *not* an example of new urban building.
   a. low-cost housing projects
   b. high-rise apartment houses
   c. merchant palaces on Fifth Avenue
   d. the Museum of Modern Art

Look in the Answer Key for the answers.

Analogy

An **analogy** is a comparison between items that belong to different groups or classes. For example, a comparison of a man to a bird is an analogy. Writers use analogies to explain or describe things and ideas. The paragraph below, for example, compares a forest to a cathedral (church).

> The cliché often used for the forest is "cathedral-like." The comparison is inevitable: the cool, dim light, the utter stillness, the massive grandeur of the trunks of forest giants, often supported by great buttresses and interspersed with the straight, clean columns of palms and smaller trees; the gothic detail of the thick, richly carved, woody lianas plastered against the trunks or looping down from the canopy above. [Marston Bates, "The Rain Forest," *The Forest and the Sea* (New York: Random House, 1960).]

Read the paragraphs below. Then, answer the questions that follow the paragraphs.

> *(1)* Broiling either mud pies or water seems impractical. But the experiment has important implications for the weather. Suppose the mud pie were the continent of the United States, the dishpan of water the oceans around it, and the gas flame the sun. When the sun rises, what happens?
>
> *(2)* The surface of the earth, like the upper crust of the mud pie, warms rapidly. All the heat it receives from the sun is absorbed within the first foot or so of topsoil. But the dishpan of water—the ocean—warms little. The sun's rays are distributed through a large volume of water. All this water must be heated before the temperature at the top changes perceptibly. By midafternoon, the surface temperature of the land may have risen 10 degrees. That of the ocean may be less than 1 degree higher.
>
> *(3)* After sunset, the process is reversed. The earth cools quickly. Much of its heat stays close to the surface and escapes. The ocean, on the other hand, keeps at about the same temperature. The heat it gives off during the night represents an infinitesimal part of what it has stored up in its depths. Over a twenty-four hour period, the surface temperature range may equal 20 degrees for land but only 1 degree for water. [From pp. 28–29 in *How About the Weather?*, Revised Ed., by Robert Moore Fisher. Copyright 1951, 1958 by Robert Moore Fisher. Reprinted by permission of Harper & Row, Publishers, Inc.]

1. The paragraphs compare
   a. mud pies to the sun's rays
   b. a dishpan of water to a mud pie
   c. a mud pie to a gas flame
   d. mud pies to the continent of the United States

2. The paragraphs also compare
   a. a dishpan of water to a gas flame
   b. a mud pie to the sun's rays
   c. a dishpan of water to the oceans
   d. the gas flame of a broiler to mud pies

3. The paragraphs compare, in addition,
   a. a dishpan of water to the sun's rays
   b. the gas flame of a broiler to the sun
   c. the gas flame of a broiler to mud pies
   d. a dishpan of water to the crust of the earth

Look in the Answer Key for the answers.

Definitions

A **definition** is an explanation of the meaning of a word. Writers often need to define a word. A word, like a major point or other idea, may be defined by using various kinds of information. The word may be explained in a formal definition, which is based on the classification and division method of explaining. Examples, facts, cause and effect, or comparison and contrast may also be used to define.*

The set of paragraphs below has been marked to show the ways of explaining that are used to define the word *map.*

formal definition { *(1)* A map is a <u>conventional picture</u> of an <u>area of land, sea, or sky</u>. Perhaps the maps most widely used are the <u>road maps</u> given away by the oil companies. They show the cultural features such as states, towns, parks, and roads, especially paved roads. They show also natural features, such as rivers and lakes, and sometimes mountains. As <u>simple maps</u>, most automobile drivers have on various occasions used sketches drawn by service station men, or by friends, to show the best automobile route from one town to another.

classification: conventional picture
division: area of land, sea, or sky
example: road maps

example: simple maps

(2) The distinction usually made between "maps" and "charts" is that a chart is a representation of an area consisting chiefly of water; a map represents an area that is predominantly

contrast:
chart - represents water
map - represents land

*For a detailed explanation of the methods of defining, see Unit Two, "Word Clues," in the *Vocabulary Module* of *Concepts of Communication: Reading* (Boston: Houghton Mifflin, 1978).

land. It is easy to see how this distinction arose in the days when there was no navigation over land, but a truer distinction is that charts are specially designed for use in navigation, whether at sea or in the air.

(3) Maps have been used since the earliest civilizations, and explorers find that they are used in rather simple civilizations at the present time by people who are accustomed to traveling. For example, Arctic explorers have obtained considerable help from maps of the coast lines showing settlements, drawn by Eskimo people. Occasionally maps show not only the roads, but pictures of other features. One of the earliest such maps dates from about 1400 B.C. It shows not only roads, but also lakes with fish, and a canal with crocodiles and a bridge over the canal. This is somewhat similar to the modern maps of a state which show for each large town some feature of interest or the chief products of that town. [From pp. 198–199 in *Astronomy, Maps, and Weather* by C. C. Wylie. Copyright 1942 by Harper & Row, Publishers, Inc. Reprinted by permission of Harper & Row, Publishers, Inc.]

example: use of maps

example: features of some maps

comparison: features of early maps to modern maps

As you read the paragraphs below, underline and label the kinds of supporting data used to define the term *liberal democracy.* Use the paragraphs that define *map* as an example in marking the paragraphs below. Then, answer the questions that follow the paragraphs.

(1) Liberal democracy is the form of self-government that stresses individual liberties. (A democracy is liberal to the degree that it permits minority views to flourish.) It's the type of government that most North Americans and Western Europeans are used to.

(2) Governments in liberal democracies are granted their power by the people they govern. Not by God, grandparents, and guns. [Not by] divine right, ancestry, and force—the way most authoritarian governments get their power. ["Is There a Better Way? *Senior Scholastic* (October 10, 1974), p. 11.]

1. The paragraphs say that liberal democracy stresses
   a. divine right, ancestry, and force
   b. the right to own guns
   c. individual liberties
   d. the power of God

2. The paragraphs also say that liberal democracies get their power from
   a. the people they govern

b. God, grandparents, and guns
c. divine right, ancestry, and force
d. North Americans and Western Europeans

Look in the Answer Key for the answers.

Words and Terms to Know

supporting data
transitional marker
example
fact
cause
effect
classification
division
comparison
contrast
analogy
definition

Concepts to Remember

1. The major points in a composition may be explained through examples, facts, or other kinds of information. Such information is called supporting data or details.
2. The kind of supporting data is sometimes indicated by words called transitional markers. If such markers are not used, the markers can sometimes be used to test the relationship of information to other ideas.
3. An example is a specific illustration of a more general idea. An example is often used to explain an idea.
4. The words *for example* can be used to test information to see if it is an example of another idea.
5. A fact is information that can be checked and is accurate.
6. The transitional markers *the fact is* or *the facts are* can be used to test information for its factual relationship to another idea.
7. A cause tells "why." An effect is the result of the cause or causes.
8. The word *because* can be used to test information to see if it is a cause.
9. A classification system groups people, objects, and so on according to the characteristics that make them alike. The parts of a classification system are called the divisions.
10. A comparison explains the ways in which people or things are alike. A contrast explains the ways in which they are different.

Assignment

Complete the worksheet at the end of this task according to your instructor's directions.

Answer Key Task 13

pages 38–39

A. The example is in paragraph 2: "The Times Square area, for example, faces a fateful 12 months. . . ." and "The condition of Times Square . . . somehow seems to represent the condition of the whole city." The example explains "Planning is in a quiet crisis in New York," which is the topic sentence of paragraph 2. You should have circled "for example" in paragraph 2. You should not have needed to use the "for example" test.

B. The examples are "Turlington's Balsam of Life, Daffy's Elixir Salutis and Monsieur Torres' Chinese Stones." The examples explain "when they sought relief in such nostrums as . . ." You should have circled "such nostrums." You should not have needed to use the "for example" test.

pages 40–41

A. The following are facts:

 the date, "May-June, 1975"
 the names of the states and their enactment of marijuana laws
 Alaska's Supreme Court decision
 the quotation from the court decision

B. The first sentence states facts. The size of the population is a fact, but is qualified by "seldom." The description of the buildings is fact, but is qualified by "many." The deterioration of Haight-Ashbury being caused by the hippie invasion is perhaps a fact, but the statement may be opinion.

page 42

The following statements are causes: "NAACP had put her up to it"; "Mrs. Parks was a Communist agent, that the whole thing had been hatched in the Kremlin"; "she was a part of the times"; "that, at long last, her cup ran over." You might also have underlined and labeled "Mrs. Parks was a part of the deepening mood of despair and disillusionment that gripped the American Negro after World War II," which says she "was a part of the times," as in the last sentence. The answers to the questions are 1-*d* and 2-*b*.

pages 44–45

A. The classification is "reasons for this popularity [of gold teeth]." The divisions could be labeled from the viewpoint of the dentist and the viewpoint of the patient. The divisions could also be labeled according to (1) simple method of anchoring artificial teeth, (2) covered ugly, broken-down, and discolored natural teeth, (3) [covered] inferior dental work, and (4) represented value received. The answers to the questions are 1-*b* and 2-*d*.

B. The classification is "metric system . . . consistency." The divisions are (1) decimal system and (2) prefixes to designate multiples and submultiples of its basic units. The answers to the questions are 3-*b*, 4-*c*, 5-*d*, 6-*a*, 7-*d*.

pages 46–47

The two comparison characteristics are "jammed with cars" and "landscape defaced with billboards." The contrast characteristic is "new urban building" (in contrast to building being at "a virtual standstill for a decade"). The answers to the questions are 1-*c*, 2-*b*, 3-*c*.

pages 47–48

The answers to the questions are 1-*d*, 2-*c*, 3-*b*.

pages 49–50

The paragraphs should be underlined and labeled as shown below. The answers to the questions are 1-*c*, 2-*a*.

> *(1)* Liberal democracy is the form of self-government that stresses individual liberties. (A democracy is liberal to the degree that it permits minority views to flourish.) It's the type of government that most North Americans and Western Europeans are used to. — *classification* / *division*
>
> *(2)* Governments in liberal democracies are granted their power by the people they govern. Not by God, grandparents, and guns. [Not by] divine right, ancestry, and force—the way most authoritarian governments get their power. — *division* / *contrast* / *contrast*

Task 13 **Worksheet**

NAME ______________________________ DATE ____________

Reading Practice

Read the paragraphs below. Answer the questions that follow the paragraphs.

A. In recent years, a number of social scientists have come up with a model called "social traps" to describe situations in which people are caught in a conflict between their own immediate interests and their long-run interests as members of society. Take the decay of passenger railroads, for example, as people began using their own cars. As rail service deteriorated, more people switched to private vehicles, which in turn caused a further decline in the railroads. This self-accelerating process has ended up with no one riding the trains, while traffic clogs the highways. [Berkeley Rice, "Fighting Inflation with Buttons and Slogans," *Psychology Today* (January, 1975), p. 49.]

1. The paragraph explains what is meant by
   a. social scientists
   b. social traps
   c. immediate interests
   d. passenger railroads

2. The paragraph explains by using
   a. facts
   b. classification
   c. example
   d. divisions

3. A transitional marker that is used in the paragraph is
   a. a model called
   b. for example
   c. more people
   d. further decline

B. Why does a battery, which roars into life during summer, become a recalcitrant child in winter? The answer is that the battery grows weaker as the thermometer drops. Full power at 80 degrees has dropped to 65 percent at freezing and 40 percent at zero. A checkup is the only way to assure reliable winter starts. A worn battery should be replaced before the cold weather begins. ["Ping of the Road," *Saturday Evening Post* (January/February, 1975), p. 102.]

4. The paragraph explains
   a. what a checkup is
   b. why the temperature drops 65 percent at freezing
   c. why a battery is weaker in winter than in summer
   d. why a battery drops full power at 80 and 40 percent at zero
5. The paragraph explains by using (*more than one answer may be correct*)
   a. facts
   b. cause
   c. classification
   d. analogy
6. The words that could be used to test the information are
   a. *example* and *the fact is*
   b. *full* and *checkup*
   c. *because* and *the fact is*
   d. *checkup* and *for example*

C. *(1)* All international [labor] unions are power centers through which workers try to win improvements in their jobs they could not hope to win alone. Moreover, all rely on the same methods. One is collective bargaining with employers over wages, hours, and working conditions. The other is political action to obtain through laws what cannot be won through bargaining. Most also are deeply involved in recruiting new members and organizing new locals to increase their strength and bargaining power.
(2) One quickly learns, however, that unions differ markedly. There are, for example, giant unions like the Teamsters, the Auto Workers, and the Steelworkers with over a million members, hundreds of local unions, and staffs of over a thousand. But there also are unions like the Watch Workers, the Window Cutters, and the Cigar Makers, which have only a few thousand members.
(3) There are craft unions, like the Carpenters and the Plumbers, which restrict their membership to workers with a particular skill. There also are industrial unions, like the Rubber Workers, which recruit everyone from factory hands to office clerks. There are unions which have fully organized the occupations or industries with which they deal. Thus, every airline pilot carries a union card and so do almost every actor and almost every barber. But other unions like the Textile Workers and the Farm Workers devote most of their efforts and resources to organizing the unorganized, often in the face of severe opposition from employers. [Alvin Schwartz, *The Unions* (New York: The Viking Press, Inc., 1972), pp. 26, 28. © 1972 by Alvin Schwartz.]

7. In paragraph 1, unions are classified according to
   a. being international power centers
   b. methods of winning job improvements
   c. number of members and kinds of workers
   d. methods of organizing their members
8. In paragraph 2, unions are classified according to
   a. the number of members

b. the kind of workers
c. Teamsters and Steelworkers
d. Watch Workers and Cigar Makers

9. In paragraph 3, the divisions are (*more than one answer may be correct*)
a. craft unions
b. industrial unions
c. unions organized by occupations or industries
d. unions that organize the unorganized workers

D. *(1)* There is a big difference between politicians and statesmen. Politics means the art of compromise. Most politicians are all-too-well schooled in this art. They compromise to get nominated; they compromise to get elected; and they compromise time and time again, after they are elected, to stay in office. In times of crisis, the politician flexes his muscle. During these next few months, you will see other Presidential candidates flexing their muscles, twisting arms politically to get delegate votes at the party conventions or offering the dividends of political appointment for delivering the vote in November.

(2) The statesman, on the other hand, flexes his mind in times of crisis. Like myself he is a dreamer, with a vision of the very best life has to offer and a determination to see all men have their rightful share of this offering; not as a reward, but because justice will tolerate nothing less. The statesman's devotion is to humanity, to the alleviation of suffering, to the creation of a decent and peaceful human environment throughout the world. The statesman cannot compromise with what he knows to be right, nor can he make any political deals which will allow a form of evil or injustice to be even temporarily victorious. These are indeed times of crisis in America. Lest there be the slightest doubt in the mind of any voter, I am serving notice *now* that I will be a statesman and not a politician. [From *Write Me In!* by Dick Gregory; copyright © 1968 by Dick Gregory. Reprinted by permission of Bantam Books, Inc.]

10. The paragraphs contrast
a. elections and compromise
b. humanity and suffering
c. delegates and presidents
d. politicians and statesmen

11. A characteristic used to contrast is
a. nominations
b. compromise
c. time
d. elections

12. Another characteristic used to contrast is
a. ways of reacting in a crisis
b. ways of daydreaming
c. ways of getting votes in an election
d. ways of getting nominated

E. American recipes look like doctors' prescriptions. Perfect cooking seems to depend on perfect dosage. Some [cookbooks] give you a table of calories and vitamins—as if that had anything to do with eating well! [Raoul de Roussy de Sales, "Love and Cookery," *Atlantic Monthly* (May, 1938). Copyright Atlantic Monthly, 1938, 1966.]

13. The paragraph explains by using
    a. classification
    b. division
    c. facts
    d. analogy

14. The paragraph says cooking recipes are like
    a. tables of calories
    b. vitamin charts
    c. doctors' prescriptions
    d. perfect dosage

F. Poverty is associated with low income, but it cannot be identified with it. To be in a state of poverty is to be entrapped: that is, to be in a situation without choices, an environment without options. Hence, adherents of the New Left who plunge themselves into the ghetto, or graduate students in the major universities whose material conditions are not significantly different from those of the poor, are not actually impoverished; for them there is always another place: the middle-class environment to which they can return, the future toward which they can strive. Poverty produces the sense of being shaped by forces beyond one's understanding and control, which renders the self insecure in all its aspects—physical well-being, personal relationships, moral and intellectual beliefs. Finally, and as a result of these conditions, poverty is a feeling of personal unimportance. The conviction that the *self* is worthless is what distinguishes modern poverty from the "honest poor" of old or the ascetics of religious tradition. [Wilson C. McWilliams, "Poverty: Public Enemy Number One," *Saturday Review* (December 10, 1966).]

15. The paragraph defines
    a. tradition
    b. the New Left
    c. poverty
    d. religion

16. The paragraph defines by using (*more than one answer may be correct*)
    a. example
    b. cause and effect
    c. comparison and contrast
    d. facts

Task 14
Determining the Meaning of Ideas

You have learned how to find the controlling idea, major points, and supporting data in an essay or article. Next, you must read the composition carefully to determine the meaning of the ideas. Of course, you could not have recognized the ideas or their relations without having some understanding of their meaning. However, through close reading of any difficult sentences, you should make sure you understand the ideas.

"Close" reading does not mean you need to read word by word. Of course, you may sometimes have to find the meaning of a certain word, in order to understand an idea.* Close reading means reading in which you work out the meaning of the ideas in the sentences.

Many teachers who have studied the way people read think that readers sometimes need to read sentences or parts of sentences over again. When readers do this, they often use sentence patterns to find meaning. Sentences, like a whole composition, have patterns of organization that writers use to convey meaning. Readers may use the patterns to find meaning. Certain types of sentences, however, may be hard to read and understand. Some of these sentences are discussed later in this task, under "Problem Sentences."

Sentence Patterns

Basic patterns

In the English language, a sentence is made up of a word or word group called the **subject** and a word or word group called the **predicate.** The predicate is made up of a verb and the words that complete the meaning or receive the action of the verb. The subject tells you who or perhaps what is being talked about. The **verb** tells you the action or state of the subject.

A subject and verb form the basic sentence pattern. By adding words to basic sentences, we can make an endless number of sentences and express an endless number of ideas. We can also put basic sentences together in many ways. Of course, we must use words according to their meaning. We must also put the words in a certain order. In fact, we usually put the subject before the verb. However, some sentences, such as questions, have a different order.

The order in which the subject, verb, and certain other words occur in

*See the *Vocabulary Module* for explanations of the different ways to determine the meaning of words.

a sentence is called the **sentence pattern.** The following sentences, for example, have subject-verb patterns:

subject verb
↓ ↓
The man cried.

subject verb
↓ ↓
Birds fly.

Many sentences contain a word or word group that completes the meaning or receives the action expressed in the verb. Depending on the verb that is used, the word(s) following the verb are called a **complement** or an **object.** Such sentences have subject-verb-complement and subject-verb-object patterns. For example:

subject verb complement
↓ ↓ ↓
She is a doctor.

subject verb object
↓ ↓ ↓
He wrecked the car.

A third pattern is often used to make sentences. The pattern is like that of the sentences above, except that it has an additional object word called an indirect object. The object is then called a direct object. The **direct object** receives the action of the verb directly. The **indirect object** receives the action *indirectly.* The following sentence is an example of this pattern:

subject verb indirect object direct object
↓ ↓ ↓ ↓
The parents asked the teachers some questions.

Another pattern is used in questions and in sentences that begin with words such as *there.* In questions and *there* sentences, the verb is placed *before* the subject. If the verb is made up of two words, those words are usually placed on either side of the subject. For example:

verb subject verb object
↓ ↓ ↓ ↓
Did the parents ask questions?

verb subject verb object
↓ ↓ ↓ ↓
There are parents asking questions.

Most sentences contain other words and phrases that modify either the subject, verb, objects, or complement. A **phrase** is two or more words that do not have a subject and predicate but that are related in meaning. To *modify* means to "change or limit the meaning of." Thus, **modifiers**—words and phrases that modify or complement the subject, verb, or objects—will change or limit the meaning of the word they modify.

In English sentences, modifying words and phrases are usually placed next to the word they modify. In the following sentence, the modifying words are underlined. The arrows point to the words that each underlined word or phrase is modifying.

subject ↓ *verb* ↓ *indirect object* ↓

The children's parents asked the elementary school teachers

direct object ↓

some very specific questions about the textbooks.

You can sometimes learn the meaning of a sentence through its pattern. Suppose that you found, first, the subject, verb, and object words in the following sentence:

subject ↓ *verb* ↓

The young woman in the yellow car recently completed an electri-

object ↓

cal engineering degree.

The subject tells you that the sentence is about a *woman.* The verb tells you the woman *completed* something. The object tells you that the woman completed a *degree.*

However, this is only part of the information in the sentence. You have to "chunk," group, the information added by the modifiers with the subject, verb, and object words. These chunks of words form units of meaning. The curved lines over the sentence below show you the units of meaning.

subject ↓ *verb* ↓

The young woman in the yellow car recently completed

object ↓

an electrical engineering degree.

Even though the above sentence is fairly short, it contains all the following information:

The woman completed a degree.
The woman is young.
The woman is in a yellow car.
The woman completed a degree recently.
The degree the woman recently completed is in electrical engineering.

The meaning of the whole sentence depends on *all* the information. However, once you know the units of meaning within the sentence, you will usually understand the whole sentence.

Each of the sentences on the next page has a pattern like one of the patterns explained above. These patterns are

Subject-verb
Subject-verb-object/complement

Subject-verb-indirect object-direct object
Verb-subject-verb

Label the pattern of each sentence by writing *subject, verb, object/ complement, indirect object*, or *direct object* above the correct words. Next, "chunk" any modifying words and phrases with the words they modify. Draw a curved line over the words to show they are a unit of meaning. Use the sentence about the woman as an example in marking the sentences below. Then, answer the questions that follow each sentence.

A. The security system sometimes prevented the communication of signals.

1. What kind of system is being talked about?

____

2. What did the system do?

____

3. What is it that the system prevented?

____

4. How often did the system prevent communication?

____

5. What kind of communication did the system prevent?

____

B. The labor negotiations over the workers' wages ended in a strike.

1. What kind of negotiations are being talked about?

____

2. What were the negotiations for or about?

____

3. Whose wages were being negotiated?

____

4. What happened to the negotiations?

____

C. Does the police department know any reason for the high crime rate?

1. What kind of department is being talked about?

____

2. The sentence is asking whether the police department knows (*circle the correct answer*)
   a. the high crime rate
   b. the reason

3. What kind of reason is being talked about?

D. The angry residents showed their representative the run-down houses on their street.

1. What kind of residents are being talked about?

---

2. What did the residents do?

---

3. What did the residents show?

---

4. What kind of houses did the residents show?

---

5. Where were the houses located?

---

6. To whom did the residents show the houses?

Look in the Answer Key for the answers.

Combined patterns

A basic sentence pattern can contain a lot of information, as you have seen. However, many sentences are made up of combinations of the patterns. Each subject-verb group of words in the combination is then called a **clause.** Because each clause has a subject and its verb, the clause expresses an idea. When a sentence contains more than one clause, the sentence has more than one idea. For example:

subject *verb* *subject* *verb*
↓ ↓ ↓ ↓
Paul works in a law office, and his wife goes to medical school.

The words used to join clauses are called **function words.** Their function, or purpose, is to join words, phrases, or clauses. For now, we are concerned only with their use to join and show the relations of clauses in a sentence. The word *and,* in the sentence above, is an example of a function word. By looking for function words, you will sometimes know whether a sentence has more than one idea.

The word used to join the clauses also has a meaning. The meaning helps you decide the relation between the ideas. For example, the word *and* means "in addition" or "also." Thus, when clauses are joined by *and,* you know the idea in one clause is "in addition to" the idea in the other clause.

The relations shown by some of the function words are listed on the next page.

Addition or "also" Relations

and
moreover
furthermore
not only . . . but also

Contrast, Condition, Exception, or "in spite of" Relations

but	although
however	even though
otherwise	if
yet	unless
nevertheless	

Result or Effect Relations

thus
so
therefore
consequently
accordingly

Choice, "instead of," or "one or the other" Relations

or
nor
either . . . or
neither . . . nor

Time Relations

then	until
after	when
as	while
since	

Reason or "because" Relations

for
because

Each of the sentences below has at least two clauses. Label the pattern of each clause by writing *subject, verb, object/complement, indirect object,* or *direct object* above the correct words in the clauses. Next, circle the function words that join the clauses. Use the list of words above to find the function words. Then, answer the questions that follow each sentence.

A. Child abuse occurs among all classes of people, but incidents in upper-income families are often not reported to the police.

1. What kind of abuse is being talked about?

____

2. Where does child abuse occur?

3. What kind of incidents are being talked about?

4. What happens when child abuse occurs in upper-income families?

5. What does the word *but* mean in the sentence?

B. The students prepared for their field trips by discussing the products manufactured by different industries; consequently, they asked worthwhile questions during their visits to those industries.

1. What did the students do? (*first clause*)

2. What kind of trips did the students prepare for?

3. How did the students prepare for the field trips?

4. What did the students ask?

5. What does the word *consequently* mean in the sentence?

C. Some writers classify the people of the United States on the basis of income, even though the United States supposedly has a classless society.

1. Who is being talked about?

2. What do some writers do?

3. Who is classified by some writers?

4. What people do some writers classify?

5. How do some writers classify people?

____

6. What kind of society is talked about?

____

7. What do the words *even though* mean in the sentence?

____

D. The coal-mining companies destroyed some land when they strip-mined and did not replace the vegetation.

1. What companies are being talked about?

____

2. What did the companies do?

____

3. How much land did the companies destroy?

____

4. How did the companies destroy the land?

______________________ and ______________________

5. What does the word *when* mean in the sentence?

____

Look in the Answer Key for the answers.

Problem Sentences

A sentence may have a subject-verb pattern that you can easily identify. However, the sentence may still be hard to understand. The four kinds of sentences discussed below are sometimes difficult.

1. *A sentence may be hard to understand if its subject is not doing the action.* In the example sentences on pages 60–61, the subject is doing the action that is expressed in the verb. In the sentence below, the subject is *not* doing the action.

The burglars were searched by the police.

The *burglars* (subject) were not doing the searching (the action expressed in the verb). The *police* were doing the searching.

Such sentences can sometimes be changed and still have the same meaning. For example, *The burglars were searched by the police* can be changed to *The police searched the burglars.* The two sentences have the same meaning.

Read the sentence below. Then, answer the questions that follow the sentence.

The natural beauty of the canyonlands of southern Utah was

destroyed when the utility companies built power plants in the area.

1. What was destroyed?
   a. canyonlands
   b. beauty
   c. companies
   d. power plants

2. Who or what did the destroying?
   a. Utah
   b. companies
   c. power plants
   d. natural beauty

3. Which sentence has the same meaning as the sentence above?
   a. The natural beauty of the power plants destroyed the canyonlands of southern Utah.
   b. The utility companies destroyed the power plants in the natural beauty of the southern Utah canyonlands.
   c. The power plants built by utility companies destroyed the natural beauty of the canyonlands of southern Utah.
   d. The utility companies destroyed the canyonlands and the natural beauty of the power plants in southern Utah.

Look in the Answer Key for the answers.

2. *A sentence may be hard to understand if some of the information you need is missing from the sentence.* For example, a sentence may not have a subject word. Often, the missing subject word is *you.* If so, you can easily read a sentence like *Tell him about the good news* as [*You*] *tell him about the good news.*

Other sentences that have omitted information will usually become clear in meaning when you read them *with* other sentences in the article. For example, the sentence below does not tell you where *she* wanted *to go.*

She said she wanted to go.

But now read the sentence with another sentence.

The director asked her if she planned to attend the conference.
She said she wanted to go.

When you link the information in the sentences, you know that *the conference* is where *she wanted to go.*

Read the sentences below. Then, answer the questions that follow each sentence.

A. Try to describe the car and the accident.

1. What is the subject of the sentence?

____

2. What is the subject told *to describe?*

____

B. It was dark by the time they were ready to leave. That's why they had trouble finding their way out of the park.

1. What is the place they were ready to leave?

____

2. Why did they have trouble finding their way?

____

Look in the Answer Key for the answers.

3. *A sentence may be hard to understand if it is very long.* A long sentence may contain several clauses. A sentence, or a clause, may also be difficult if it has many modifying words or phrases.

Some long sentences may have a clause within another clause. For example, the underlined words in the following sentence are a clause:

subject ↓ (who) *verb* ↓ (asked)

The person who asked so many questions at the meeting is the governor of New Mexico.

The underlined clause tells you about the *person.* The other clause of the sentence is *The person is the governor of New Mexico.* But you must read across the clause *who asked so many questions at the meeting* to find the verb (*is*) that goes with *person.*

In other sentences, several modifying words may be placed before the subject of the sentence. In the sentence below, you must read across several words before you find the subject of the sentence (*person*) and know "who" or "what" is being talked about.

A goal-oriented, highly-motivated person tends to work very hard at his or her chosen occupation.

In still other sentences, there may be a long series of phrases. Phrases in a series may modify the subject, verb, or object in the sentence. However, a phrase can modify a word in another phrase. The sentence below is an example. The phrases are underlined, and the arrows from the phrases point to the word that each phrase modifies.

object ↓ (reasons) *phrase* ↓ (for the collapse)

The president gave several reasons for the collapse of the

phrase ↓ (provisional government) *phrase* ↓ (of the colonies) *phrase* ↓ (in the west)

provisional government of the colonies in the west.

If a sentence is long and hard to understand, start by finding the clauses. Next, find the modifiers of the subject, verb, and object words. Then, work out the units of meaning in the clauses. If you find a series of phrases, decide whether they modify a word in another phrase or the subject, verb, or object words.

Read the sentences on the next page. Then, answer the questions that follow each sentence.

A. Children who have normal vision for the first two or three years of life and then become blind may eventually lose all their visual learning.

1. How many clauses are there in the sentence?

____

2. Underline the clause that is placed within another clause.
3. What is the subject of the clause that is within another clause?

____

4. What is the subject in the other clause of the sentence?

____

5. What is the verb in the other clause of the sentence?

____

B. Unified, determined, well-directed protest movements have been effective in gaining civil rights for many minority groups.

1. What is the subject of the sentence?

____

2. What are the words that modify the subject?

_______________, _______________, _______________, and _______________

3. What is the verb in the sentence?

____

4. What word does the phrase *for many minority groups* modify?

____

5. What word does the phrase *in gaining civil rights* modify?

____

Look in the Answer Key for the answers.

4. *A sentence may be hard to understand if it contains a word that refers to a word or idea in another sentence.* For example, the word *it* in the sentences below refers to Pearl Harbor. However, you might have trouble deciding whether *it* (second sentence) refers to *Pearl Harbor* or to *catastrophe* (first sentence). In the last sentence of the paragraph, the reference of *it* is even harder to decide because *it* is so widely separated from the words *Pearl Harbor.*

> Pearl Harbor is not an isolated catastrophe. It can be matched by many examples of effective surprise attack. The German attack on Russia in the summer of 1941 was preceded by a flood of signals, the massing of troops, and even direct warnings to Russia by the governments of the United States and the United Kingdom, both of whom had been correctly informed about the imminence of the onslaught. Yet it achieved total

surprise. [Roberta Wohlstetter, "Surprise," *Pearl Harbor: Warning and Decision* (Stanford, Cal.: Stanford University Press, 1962).]

Read the paragraphs below. Then, answer the questions that follow each paragraph.

A. The ordeal and spectacular death of King Kong, the giant ape, have been witnessed by millions of American movie-goers. Yet, year after year, ticket-buyers by thousands still pursue King Kong's luckless fight against the forces of technology, tabloid journalism, and the DAR. They see him chloroformed to sleep and machine-gunned by model airplanes. [Adapted from X. J. Kennedy, "Who Killed King Kong?" *Dissent* (Spring, 1960).]

1. What are the words that *They* (last sentence) refers to?

_______________ and _______________

2. The word *him* (last sentence) refers to which words?

____

B. While our progress can be measured by the fact that the machine is clearly recognized as the servant of man and not his better, the fear is now widespread that it could become our master. Since this is so, we must understand how it could become our master in reality as it already is in our delusions. [Adapted from Bruno Bettelheim, "Imaginary Impasse," *The Informed Heart* (New York: The Free Press, 1960) © The Free Press, a Corporation, 1960.]

1. What is the word that *it* (first sentence) refers to?

____

2. What is the idea that the word *this* (second sentence) refers to?

____

____

____

3. What is the word that *it* (second sentence) refers to?

____

Look in the Answer Key for the answers.

Words and Terms to Know

subject
predicate
verb
sentence pattern
object/complement
indirect object

direct object
phrase
modifier
clause
function word

Concepts to Remember

1. A sentence is made up of a subject and predicate. The predicate is made up of a verb and the words that complete the meaning or receive the action of the verb.
2. Some of the basic English sentence patterns are subject-verb, subject-verb-object/complement, subject-verb-indirect object-direct object, and verb-subject-verb.
3. Modifying words and phrases can be added to the subject, verb, and object/complement words in a sentence.
4. Modifying words and phrases are usually placed next to the word they modify.
5. A unit of meaning in a sentence is made up of any modifying words and the word they modify.
6. When subject-verb patterns are combined, each subject-verb group of words is called a clause. Each clause in a sentence expresses an idea.
7. Function words (*and, but, for, because*, and so on) are used to join clauses. The meaning of the function word indicates the relation between the clause ideas.
8. A sentence may be hard to read for various reasons. Some of the sentences that may be hard are those in which (1) the subject is not doing the action expressed in the verb, (2) some information is missing, (3) many clauses or modifying words are used and the sentence is very long, and (4) words are used that refer to a word or idea in another sentence.

Assignment

Complete the worksheet at the end of this task according to your instructor's directions.

Answer Key Task 14

pages 60–61

subject ↓ *verb* ↓ *object* ↓

A. The security system sometimes prevented the communication of signals.

1. security
2. prevented/prevented communication
3. communication/communication of signals
4. sometimes
5. signals

subject ↓ … verb ↓

B. The labor negotiations over the workers' wages ended in a strike.

1. labor
2. wages/workers' wages
3. the workers'
4. ended/ended in a strike

verb ↓ … subject ↓ … verb ↓ … object ↓

C. Does the police department know any reason for the high crime rate?

1. police
2. b (any reason)
3. for high crime rate

subject ↓ … verb ↓ … indirect object ↓

D. The angry residents showed their representative the run-down

direct object ↓

houses on their street.

1. angry
2. showed/showed houses
3. houses/run-down houses
4. run-down/on their street
5. on their street
6. representative

pages 62–64

subject ↓ … verb ↓ … subject ↓

A. Child abuse occurs among all classes of people, (but) incidents in upper-

verb

income families are often not reported to the police.

1. child
2. among all classes of people
3. child abuse/in upper-income families
4. often not reported to the police
5. except

subject ↓ … verb ↓

B. The students prepared for their field trips by discussing the products

subject ↓ … verb ↓

manufactured by different industries; (consequently,) they asked

object ↓

worthwhile questions during their visits to those industries.

1. prepared/prepared for their field trips
2. field
3. by discussing the products manufactured by different industries
4. worthwhile questions
5. as a result

subject ↓ *verb* ↓ *object* ↓

C. Some writers classify the people of the United States on the basis of

subject ↓ *verb* ↓

income, (even though) the United States supposedly has a classless

object ↓

society.

1. some writers
2. classify/classify people
3. people/people in the United States
4. in the United States
5. by income/on the basis of income
6. classless
7. in spite of the fact

subject ↓ *verb* ↓ *object* ↓ *subject* ↓ *verb* ↓

D. The coal-mining companies destroyed some land (when) they strip-

verb ↙ ↘ *object* ↓

mined and did not replace the vegetation.

1. coal-mining
2. destroyed/destroyed some land/strip-mined/did not replace vegetation
3. some
4. strip-mined/did not replace vegetation
5. at the time that

page 65

1. *b*
2. *c*
3. *c*

pages 65–66

A. 1. you
   2. car/accident

B. 1. the park
   2. it was dark

page 67

A. 1. two

2. The clause that is placed within another clause is *who have normal vision for the first two or three years of life and then become blind.*
3. who
4. children
5. may . . . lose

B. 1. movements
2. unified, determined, well-directed, protest
3. have been
4. rights
5. effective

page 68

A. 1. ticket-buyers/movie-goers
2. King Kong

B. 1. machine
2. the fear is now widespread that it [the machine] could become our master
3. machine

Task 14 **Worksheet**

NAME ______________________________ DATE ____________

Reading Practice

For sentences **A** through **F** below, label the pattern of the sentences by writing *subject, verb, object/complement* above the correct words. Circle the function words that join clauses. Next, draw a curved line over the units of meaning in each sentence. A unit of meaning is made up of any modifying words and the word they modify. Then, answer the questions that follow the sentences.

A. An accountant keeps financial records.

1. Who is being talked about?

____

2. What does an accountant do?

____

3. What kind of records does an accountant keep?

____

B. The president appointed several women to his cabinet.

4. Who is being talked about?

____

5. What did the president do?

____

6. What kind of cabinet is being talked about?

____

7. What word does *his* refer to?

____

C. The natural resources of the world are not distributed evenly among all countries; therefore, countries sometimes trade their resources.

8. What kind of resources are being talked about?

____

9. What is the problem related to natural resources?

____

10. What do countries do with their resources?

____

11. What does the word *therefore* mean in the sentence?

____

12. What word does *their* refer to?

____

D. An older person may feel anxious about going back to school; however, an older student usually gets good grades in school.

13. What kind of student is being talked about?

____

14. How does an older person feel about going back to school?

____

15. What does an older student usually do in school?

____

16. What does the word *however* mean in the sentence?

____

E. Martin will get the job if he can pass the physical exam.

17. Who is being talked about?

____

18. What does Martin have to do to get the job?

____

19. What does the word *if* mean in the sentence?

____

F. Biologists found a rare animal while they were examining a wildlife region in Africa.

20. What did the biologists do?

____

21. What kind of animal was found?

____

22. When was the animal found?

____

23. Where was the animal found?

---

24. What does the word *while* mean in the sentence?

---

25. What word does *they* refer to?

G. Many people were laid off during the cold weather by industries that were short of natural gas.

26. Circle the letter of the sentence that has the same meaning as the above sentence.
    a. During the cold weather, industries were short of natural gas.
    b. Industries that were short of natural gas laid people off during the cold weather.
    c. The natural gas shortage made it necessary for people to close down industries.
    d. The cold weather caused a shortage of natural gas.

27. The industries that laid people off were
    a. employing only a few people
    b. operating in cold weather
    c. natural gas companies
    d. short of natural gas

H. If you lend your car to a friend, are you legally liable if he or she has an accident? A man who loaned a car with a dirty windshield was held not responsible for a later collision. The court said he had a right to assume that the borrower would have enough sense to clean the windshield on his own.

28. Underline (in the second sentence) the clause that is within another clause.

29. What word does the word *he* (third sentence) refer to?

---

30. What word does the word *his* (third sentence) refer to?

Task 15
Expressing the Meaning of Ideas

Suppose that someone called you on the telephone and asked you to give a message to another person. Even if you repeated the message right after the call, you might not use exactly the same words that the caller used. But you would probably deliver the meaning of the message accurately.

Usually, your instructor will want to know that you understood the meaning of what you read. If you repeated the important ideas exactly as you read them, your instructor might think you did not really understand what you read. Therefore, you should use your own words to express the meaning of the ideas you find in reading. Using your own words to express the same ideas that you heard or read is called **paraphrasing.**

Often, your instructor will want you to write a paragraph or short paper to explain the meaning of something you read. You will need to write sentences in which you paraphrase (restate in your own words) the controlling idea, major points, and important supporting data. Consequently, you need to know how to use synonyms, modifiers, and clauses in your own sentences to explain the ideas you read.

Paraphrasing

Synonyms

Synonyms are words that have the same meaning. **Synonymous expressions** are groups of words that have the same meaning.

Using synonyms or synonymous expressions is part of expressing a writer's ideas in your own words. For example, you might use synonyms for the underlined words in the following sentence:

> In Peter's paper on freeway fatalities, the controlling idea is that the 55 miles per hour speed limit does reduce the number of people killed on the nation's roads each year.

The sentence might then read:

highway deaths ↓ *thesis/main idea* ↓

In Peter's paper on freeway fatalities, the controlling idea is

lessen ↓

that the 55 miles per hour speed limit does reduce the number

yearly/annually ↓

of people killed on the nation's roads each year.

Write a synonym or synonymous expression above each of the underlined words in the sentences below.

A. Our firm interviewed home gardeners to discover why they favored some varieties of flower seeds and ignored others.

B. The designer studied hundreds of paper samples to select a paper compatible with the corporation's new image.

Look in the Answer Key for suggested synonyms.

Modifiers

Modifiers are words, phrases, or clauses that modify another word. To *modify* means to "change or limit the meaning of." Modifiers change or limit the meaning of the word they modify.

Changing the form of the modifiers in a sentence is another way of paraphrasing. Sometimes you can change a phrase to a single word without changing the meaning of the phrase. For example, the underlined phrase in the sentence below tells you that the *car* is owned by or is the possession of the *uncle.*

The car belonging to her uncle was stolen.

You could express the same meaning by using the possessive form of the word *uncle* (*uncle's*) to replace the phrase. For example:

Her uncle's car was stolen.

In the sentence below, the information in the phrase can be stated in an easier-to-read way.

The church was destroyed by the bomb.

The sentence could say *The bomb destroyed the church* and have the same meaning.

Sometimes clauses can be changed to single words without changing the meaning of the original sentence. A clause is underlined in the following sentence:

The water that you drink may not be free of pollution.

The clause could be changed to *drinking,* and *the* could be changed to *your.* The sentence would have the same meaning as the sentence above.

Your drinking water may not be free of pollution.

You could also use a synonym for the words *free of pollution.* You could say, for example, "Your drinking water may not be *pure.*"

Rewrite the following sentences by changing the underlined phrases and clauses. Be sure your new sentence has the same meaning as the original sentence.

A. The farmers stored the seed grain that they harvested in boxes and bags.

B. The training of a modern nurse-midwife bears little resemblance to the training of the early midwife.

C. A considerable number of the drugs that are artificially synthesized are based on natural compounds.

D. If you are in debt, you may be able to get advice from a person who is a consumer-credit counselor. (Hint: Replace the word *person* with the information given in the underlined clause.)

E. The grass in the park was mowed by a crew of ten men.

Look in the Answer Key for the answers.

Clauses

Another way of paraphrasing is to combine sentences. For example, the following two sentences could be combined:

> Science has helped create problems—serious ones.
>
> And we must labor to solve them.

The sentence would then have two clauses and would say:

> Science has helped create problems—serious ones, and we must labor to solve them.

You would also want to paraphrase the wording of the clauses. You could write the sentence in the following ways and still keep the meaning of the original two sentences:

> Science has helped create serious problems, and we must work to solve them.

We must work to solve the serious problems that science has helped create.

Science has helped create serious problems that we must work to solve.

Sometimes you may want to express the ideas in the clauses of a long sentence by using several sentences. For example, you might use two or more sentences to express the ideas in the following long sentence:

One of the outstanding and best-known nurse-midwife programs in this country, and a prototype for others that followed, is the Frontier Nursing Service in the Appalachia area of eastern Kentucky, established 45 years ago to meet the needs of a community with very few doctors. [Elizabeth B. Connell, "The Modern Nurse-Midwife," *Redbook Magazine* (July, 1974), p. 64.]

Your sentences might say:

The Frontier Nursing Service is an outstanding, well-known nurse-midwife program. The service was founded forty-five years ago in the eastern Kentucky Appalachia region. Its purpose was to provide medical services in an area with few doctors. The service has been a model for other nurse-midwife programs.

Rewrite the sets of sentences below as one sentence. Reword the original sentences by using synonyms and/or changing modifiers. Be sure your sentence has the same meaning as the original sentences.

A. Some people get into financial trouble by buying too many things on credit. They only take on a bigger debt by borrowing at high interest rates to pay off their debts.

____

____

____

B. The Indian people are gone now from the plateau where they once lived. The plateau is still almost as beautiful as it was when the Indians left.

____

____

____

C. A group of Japanese people attended the meeting. They told about people getting sick more than ten years after they had stopped eating fish that were polluted with mercury.

____

____

____

Rewrite the following long sentence as two or more sentences. Be sure your new sentences have the same meaning as the original sentence.

D. It has been through the investigations of the scientist, who is supposedly cold and unconcerned about people, that we have been provided with steam, electricity, and radio beams, which do our work for us and make our lives comfortable.

____

____

____

____

____

____

Look in the Answer Key for suggested answers.

Summarizing

If you were to paraphrase all the ideas in an article, your paper might be as long as the original article. Besides paraphrasing the controlling idea and major points, you need to condense the number of ideas you express. To *condense* means to "reduce in volume." Because the ideas in the supporting data are often the least important, you should condense those ideas.

When you paraphrase and condense ideas, you are **summarizing** what you have read. For example, you might summarize the ideas in the paragraph below by rewriting the paragraph as shown in the right-hand column.

Development of new foods is a long, tedious process. Last year scientists at Purdue University bred a high-lysine variety of sorghum—but only after working on it for seven years and analyzing 10,000 varieties of the grain. It could be another ten years before that high-protein type will be ready for planting on commercial scale. After the new foods are developed, they sometimes do not satisfy local tastes. For example, residents of India were not satisfied with the soft-kernel, protein-rich, high-lysine corn, preferring their traditional flinty, hard corn. ["What to Do: Costly Choices," *Time* (November 11, 1974), p. 78.]

The process of developing new foods is long and tiresome. Scientists may spend many years breeding and preparing a grain for commercial planting and then find people do not like the product.

Summarize the following paragraph:

Science and technology are getting a bad press these days. Increasingly scornful of the materialism of our culture, young people speak about returning to a simpler, pre-industrial, pre-scientific day. They fail to realize that the "good old days" were really

____

____

____

____

the horribly bad old days of ignorance, disease, slavery and death. They fancy themselves in Athens, talking to Socrates, listening to the latest play by Sophocles—never as a slave brutalized in the Athenian silver mines. They imagine themselves as medieval knights on armored chargers—never as starving peasants. [From Isaac Asimov's "There's No Way to Go But Ahead." © 1975 courtesy of Field Newspaper Syndicate.]

Look in the Answer Key for a suggested summary of the paragraph.

Words and Terms to Know

paraphrasing
synonym
synonymous expression
modifier
summarizing

Concepts to Remember

1. Paraphrasing is using your own words to express the meaning of an idea you have heard or read.
2. A synonym is a word that has the same meaning as another word. A synonymous expression is a group of words that has the same meaning as another word or expression.
3. Using synonyms or synonymous expressions is part of paraphrasing.
4. Changing modifiers, such as phrases and clauses, to single-word modifiers is another method of paraphrasing.
5. Combining sentences into a single sentence is another method of paraphrasing.
6. Separating the clauses of a long sentence and rewriting the clauses as sentences is another method of paraphrasing.
7. Summarizing means to condense and paraphrase the ideas in what you have read.

Assignment

Complete the worksheet at the end of this task according to your instructor's directions.

Answer Key Task 15

page 78

company *talked to* *find out* *preferred*
↓ ↓ ↓ ↓
A. Our firm interviewed home gardeners to discover why they favored

kinds *didn't use/didn't choose*
↓ ↓
some varieties of flower seed and ignored others.

examined *find/locate/choose*
↓ ↓
B. The designer studied hundreds of paper samples to select a paper

suitable to/to fit
↓
compatible with the corporation's new image.

pages 78–79

A. The farmers stored the harvested seed grain in boxes and bags.
B. The modern nurse-midwife's training bears little resemblance to the early midwife's training.
C. A considerable number of the artifically synthesized drugs are based on natural compounds.
D. If you are in debt, you may be able to get advice from a consumer-credit counselor.
E. A crew of ten men mowed the grass in the park. Or: A ten-man crew mowed the grass in the park.

pages 80–81

A. Buying too many items on credit gets some people into financial trouble, and borrowing at high interest rates to pay off debts only gets them more deeply in debt.
B. The Indians have left the plateau, but it is almost as beautiful as it was when they went away.
C. Several Japanese people came to the meeting and told about people who became ill more than ten years after they had stopped eating mercury-polluted fish.
D. The scientist is thought to be cold and unconcerned about people. Yet, because of the investigations of scientists, we have steam, electricity, and radio beams to do our work and make us comfortable.

pages 81–82

These days, science and technology get bad publicity. However, young people who talk about returning to the prescientific "good old days" don't know that conditions were very bad for people then.

Task 15 **Worksheet**

NAME ______________________________ DATE ____________

Reading Practice

Read the paragraphs below. Write a summary of them. Be sure you paraphrase and condense the ideas.

> *(1)* Why would people who aren't in love want to get married? For one thing, during the courtship people tend to lose their sense of judgment. Nature makes men and women so attractive to each other, they don't stop to consider whether they have any other qualifications for making a life together, until it's too late. *(2)* Another reason people get married is that society expects it of them. Although social attitudes are beginning to change, there are still a lot of people who think that a woman who has passed the usual age without getting married simply hasn't been able to find herself a man. And there are many who suspect that a middle-aged man who remains a bachelor must be a homosexual. [William J. Lederer and Don D. Jackson, "Do People Really Marry for Love?" *Family Circle* (August, 1973), p. 20.]

____

____

____

____

____

____

____

____

____

____

____

____

____

Textbooks **Unit Three**

Early in your school years, you began to read textbooks in your history, mathematics, and other courses. A textbook is simply a book that contains information about a certain subject or area of study.

Some of your textbooks may be hard to read and understand. First, some words used in the book may have a meaning that differs from the meaning you already know. Other words, which you must know to understand the subject, may be new to you. Second, the book will usually contain a great amount of information. You may not see how the information is organized. It may be hard to find certain information when you need it. Third, the ideas in the book may be complex and hard to understand.

You can often learn the meanings of words by using the definitions you find within the book. Some books also have lists that define the special words used in the book. The skills needed to determine word meanings are explained in detail in the *Vocabulary Module.* Definitions are also explained in Task 13. Word lists (glossaries) are discussed in Task 16, "Reading and Study Aids."

A textbook usually contains a lot of information. You will understand how that information is organized and how to find specific information if you "survey" a book before you begin reading it. In Task 16, you will learn to survey or examine a book for the reading and study aids that can help you use and understand the contents of the book.

Even though the ideas in a textbook are often complex, they will be explained as they are in essays and articles. Thus, in reading a textbook, you can use the general reading skills you learned in Tasks 11 through 15. In Task 17, you will use those skills in reading a chapter in a textbook.

The particular subject matter will influence the way that information is organized and explained. You will learn about some of the methods of organizing and explaining ideas that are commonly used in the textbooks for specific subjects. Task 18 deals with books about mathematics and the natural sciences. Task 19 is about books in the humanities and the behavioral sciences. Task 20 is about books on business and other careers.

Task 16
Reading and Study Aids

Most textbooks contain special kinds of information that you will find helpful when you study the book. Before you begin your first assignment in any textbook, you should survey the book. To **survey** a textbook, you look through it to find any special information that the book contains. By surveying, you should learn whether the book contains the following information and where to find the information:

Contents/Table of contents
Introduction
Glossary
Index
Appendix
Footnotes
Bibliography
Charts and graphs

Contents

The **contents** or **table of contents** is a list of the information included in a book. The contents pages are placed within the first few pages of the book.

If the pages are numbered, they are numbered with small roman numerals (i, ii, and so on). The contents lists the chapters and special information in the book. It also gives the page number on which the chapters and, perhaps, their sections begin. The contents helps you find the chapters or sections that you want to read.

Look at the contents in Figure 16.1. Then, answer the following questions:

1. Suppose that you were using this textbook and your instructor asked you to read about electric meters. What chapter number and section within that chapter would you read?

   Chapter Number ______________________ Section Number ________

2. What page number would you look for to begin reading about electric meters?

   Page Number ____

3. Suppose that your instructor asked you to read about "changing inches to feet and inches." What chapter number and section within that chapter would you read?

   Chapter Number ______________________ Section Number ________

Contents

Part I Computation in Industry

Chapter 1 Industrial Measurements (1) *first page of chapter*

Reading meters

sections within the chapter { 1-1 Electric meters (1); 1-2 Gas meters (3); 1-3 Whole numbers (4); 1-4 Tachometer (7) *first pages of sections*

Reading graphs
1-5 Bar graphs 9; 1-6 Broken-line graphs 12; 1-7 Curved-line graphs 14

Career Profile 18

Reading rules
1-8 Rules and lengths 20; 1-9 Equivalent fractions 23; 1-10 Comparing lengths 26; 1-11 Metric scales 28

Reading technical drawings
1-12 Lines 32; 1-13 Dimensions 34; 1-14 Curves and angles 36

Taking Inventory 39; *Measuring Your Skills* 40

Chapter 2 Using Fractions 43

Adding and subtracting fractions
2-1 Fractions with the same denominator 43; 2-2 Fractions with different denominators 45; 2-3 The least common denominator 48

Adding and subtracting mixed numbers
2-4 Whole numbers and mixed numbers 52; 2-5 Adding mixed numbers 54; 2-6 Subtracting mixed numbers 58

Dimensions in feet and inches
2-7 Changing inches to feet and inches 61; 2-8 Conserving materials 64

Research With A Computer 68; *Taking Inventory* 70; *Measuring Your Skills* 70

Chapter 3 More on Fractions 73

Multiplying fractions
3-1 Multiplying a fraction and a whole number 73; 3-2 Multiplying a mixed number and a whole number 75; 3-3 Multiplying two fractions 78; 3-4 Cancellation 80

Dividing fractions
3-5 Reciprocals 82; 3-6 Dividing a fraction by a whole number 82; 3-7 Dividing by a fraction 85

v

Figure 16.1. Sample Contents Page

From Merwin Lyng, L. J. Meconi, and Earl J. Zwigk, *Career Mathematics: Industry and the Trade* (Boston: Houghton Mifflin Company, 1974), p. v. Copyright © 1974 by Houghton Mifflin Company. Used by permission.

4. What page number would you look for to begin reading about changing inches to feet and inches?

   Page Number ____________________

Look in the Answer Key for the answers.

Introduction

A textbook may contain several sections that are part of the **introduction** to the book. The sections may be called *preface, foreword, overview,* or *introduction.* They are found in the first few pages of the book. In some books, these sections are placed before the contents. In other books, these sections follow the contents. Sometimes, as in this book, the overview or introduction is the first chapter or unit of the book.

Although the various sections have somewhat different purposes, together they introduce you to the book. They may tell you about the objectives or learning goals that you should achieve by studying the book. They may define some of the technical terms used in the book. Sometimes they describe the organization of the chapters or units within the book.

In the *Ideas Module*, the objectives are explained in Unit One, "Overview." You are now studying a task that is related to the reading and study aids found in a textbook. Read the objectives and find the objective you should gain through the task you are now studying. Write the number of the objective on the following line: ______. Look in the Answer Key for the answer.

In some textbooks, the important technical terms used in the book are defined in the introductory sections. The page of definitions in Figure 16.2 is from an engineering mechanics textbook. The terms are called *concepts,* which means "general ideas." These concepts are important ideas in engineering mechanics. List the terms or concepts that are defined.

____

____

____

____

Look in the Answer Key for the answers.

In the sample preface in Figure 16.3, the organization of the book is explained. Read the preface. Then, answer the following questions:

1. What is the first thing you would expect to see or read in each unit of this textbook?

____

2. What kind of information would you find in the second section of each unit?

____

Look in the Answer Key for the answers.

1.3 Fundamental Concepts

The concepts fundamental to a study of mechanics are those of space, time, inertia, and force.

Space By space we mean a geometric region in which physical events occur. It can have one, two, or three dimensions. Or, more than three dimensions can be conceptualized. Here we shall be concerned with, at most, three-dimensional space. Position in space is ascertained relative to some reference system. The basic reference system necessary for Newtonian mechanics is one that is considered fixed in space. Measurements relative to this system are considered as absolute.

Time Essentially a measure of the orderly succession of events occurring in space, time is considered as an absolute quantity. The unit of time is a *second,* which was originally related directly to the earth's rate of spin. Today, the standard of time is established by the frequency of oscillation of a cesium atom.

Inertia The ability of a body to resist a change in motion is called inertia.

. . .

Force A force is the action of one body on another. This action may exist due to contact between the bodies, which is called the push-pull effect; or this action may exist with the bodies apart, which is called the field-of-force effect.

Figure 16.2. Sample Page of Definitions

From D. K. Anand and P. F. Cunniff, *Engineering Mechanics: Statics* (Boston: Houghton Mifflin Company, 1973), p. 3. Copyright © 1973 by Houghton Mifflin Company. Used by permission.

xviii Publisher's Preface

A INTRODUCTORY GRAPHICS

Each unit begins with a visual summary of what it is about—a picture-and-caption X ray of the central problems and processes of the topic. The sequence in each case consists of three panels: *input*—the initiating elements; *process*—the dynamic operations involved; and *output*—the end result, or the behavior, in which we are most interested. These graphics thus pinpoint the unit topic in ordinary experience before it becomes the subject of more technical discussion and help you anticipate some of the variables that integrate the unit.

B DEFINITION AND BACKGROUND

1. DEFINITION

This section begins with a brief discussion of the general topic. A DEFINITION is given to specify how psychologists see the topic as a problem to investigate. When the same problem is approached from a variety of viewpoints, the definition encompasses all the viewpoints discussed in the unit.

. . .

2. BACKGROUND

Psychology as a scientific discipline separate from philosophy, physics, and physiology has less than a century of history. Yet there are many figures in that short history who have initiated research on the topics considered in this text. For many units it was difficult to choose a single background figure. In choosing, we were guided by our desire to present a good sample of those people who are responsible for psychology as we know it. In each unit we have described the events surrounding early investigation of the topic and the role the background figure played in those events.

Figure 16.3. Sample Preface Page

From *Psychology '73–74,* pp. xviii-xix, edited by Joseph Rubinstein. Copyright © 1973 by The Dushkin Publishing Group, Inc. Guilford, Ct. 06437.

GLOSSARY

CONE (p. 353): A solid whose base is a circular region and which has a curved surface which comes to a point, called the *vertex*.

CONGRUENT (p. 11): Having the same size and shape.

CONGRUENT ANGLES (p. 214): Two or more angles that have equal degree measures.

CONSECUTIVE ANGLES ABOUT A POINT (p. 218): A set of angles which, with their interiors, completely fill the region about a given point. The angle-sum of any set of consecutive angles about a point is 360°.

COORDINATE (p. 7): The number that is paired with a point on the number line.

CORRESPONDING ANGLES OF SIMILAR TRIANGLES (p. 331): The pairs of congruent angles of two similar triangles.

CORRESPONDING SIDES OF SIMILAR TRIANGLES (p. 333): Pairs of sides opposite corresponding angles; corresponding sides of similar triangles are proportional.

COSINE OF AN ANGLE (p. 344): For one of the acute angles of a right triangle, the ratio of the length of the side adjacent to the angle to the length of the hypotenuse.

CROSS PRODUCT (p. 145): In comparing two fractions $\frac{a}{b}$ and $\frac{c}{d}$, the cross products are $a \times d$ and $b \times c$.

CYLINDER (p. 352): A solid whose bases are congruent circles and which has a curved surface.

DATA (p. 396): Statistical facts.

DECIMAL (p. 238): A symbol that represents a decimal fraction.

DECIMAL FRACTIONS (p. 238): Common fractions whose denominators are place values (10, 100, 1000, and so on) in the Hindu-Arabic system of numeration.

DECIMAL POINT (p. 238): The dot separating the whole-number part from the fractional part of a decimal numeral.

DEGREE (p. 210): The basic unit for measuring angles; $\frac{1}{360}$ of a complete revolution.

DENOMINATOR (p. 134): The second term of a fraction; the term below the fraction bar.

DESCENDING ORDER (p. 152): Order from greatest to least.

DIAMETER (p. 320): A chord that passes through the center of a circle.

DIFFERENCE (p. 72): The amount by which one number exceeds another, found by subtraction.

DIGIT (p. 38): Any of the numerals 0, 1, 2, 3, 4, 5, 6, 7, 8, 9.

DIRECTED NUMBERS (p. 364): The set consisting of the positive numbers, the negative numbers, and zero.

DIRECTION NUMBER (p. 206): The number paired with a ray.

DISCOUNT (p. 301): A reduction in the list price of an article.

DIVIDEND (p. 83): The number to be divided in the division process.

DIVISOR (p. 83): The number by which the dividend is divided.

EDGE OF A SOLID (p. 352): A segment formed by the intersection of two faces of the solid.

ENDOWMENT INSURANCE (p. 411): A term insurance policy for which the policyholder receives cash value at the end of the term.

ENLARGEMENT (p. 279): A scale drawing that is larger than the object it pictures.

EQUATION (p. 111): A statement that two expressions are equal.

Figure 16.4. Sample Glossary Page

From Lawrence Hyman, Irwin N. Sokol, Richard L. Spreckelmeyer, *Modern Basic Mathematics* (Boston: Houghton Mifflin Company, 1975). p. 423.

Glossary

The **glossary** of a textbook is a list of the special terms used in the book and their definitions. The terms are listed in alphabetical order.

When you are studying a subject, you need to learn the special terms used in that subject. A glossary can help you learn and review the meanings of the terms.*

Generally, the glossary is placed in the back of the book. In some books, there may be a glossary at the end of each chapter. You should know whether each of your textbooks has a glossary and where it is in the book.

Look at the sample glossary in Figure 16.4. Then, answer the following questions:

1. What is the meaning of the word *data*?

____

____

2. What is the meaning of the term *discount?*

____

____

3. What is the meaning of the term *equation?*

____

____

Check your answers by looking at the glossary again.

Index

An **index** is an alphabetical list of the ideas, processes, terms, and other important information in a book. The index lists the page numbers on which each word or term is discussed. Thus, the index helps you find all the information in the book about a certain topic.†

In most indexes, you will find subtopics listed under some of the words. The subtopics are also listed in alphabetical order, followed by the page numbers on which the topics are discussed.

Besides using an index to find reading assignments, you should remember to use the index if you have an open-book examination. You may find the answer to a question if you look up the topic of the question in the index and then read quickly through the pages on which the topic is discussed. Look at the index page in Figure 16.5 and answer the following questions:

1. On what page are *potato chips* discussed? _______________

2. On what pages is *pressure cooking* discussed? _______________

*For a more detailed explanation of how to use a glossary, see Task 9 in the *Vocabulary Module.*

†For a more detailed explanation about how to use an index, see Task 9 in the *Vocabulary Module.*

3. On what pages are *pies, fillings for* and *pies, shell for* discussed?

______________________________ and ______________________________

Look in the Answer Key for the answers.

Perfringens, 565
Pesticide residue in food, 27
Pesticides Chemical Act of 1954, 27
Phosphorus, 7
PHS (Public Health Service), 29–30; Grade A Pasteurized Milk Ordinance, 30, 32–33, 148_n
Piccalilli, 625
Pickles and pickling, 624–631: causes of difficulties, 630–631; choice of methods, 626–630; defined, 624; effect of ingredients in, 625–626; making cross-cut pickle slices, 628–629; types of, 624–625
Pies, 334–344: convenience forms of, 344–348; fillings for, 342–344; freezing of, 347; shell for, 338, 339; varieties of, 334
Pigments of foods, 113–115
Pineapples: cost of, 48; nutritive value of, 54; selection of, 46
Pizza, 317
Plan of work, 476–477, 482–485
Planning of meals. *See* Meal planning
Plastic, 459
Plate table service, 523
Plums, 46, 54
Poaching, 183
Poisoning, food, 563–565: botulism, 565, 593; defined, 563; perfringens, 565; staphylococcal, 563–565
Polysaccharides, 4
Polyunsaturated fatty acids, 289
Popovers, 304–305, 309
Poppy, 381
Porcelain enamelware, 456–457
Pork: cuts of, 202; grades of, 213, 216; methods of cooking, 219; and trichinosis, 206. *See also* Meat
Potassium iodide, 370
Potato chips, 118
Potato starch, 265
Potatoes: characteristics and cooking of, 125; grades of, 108; nutritive value of, 118; selection of, 108–109; vitamin content of, 122
Poultry, 232–244: amount per serving, 236–238; classes of, 234–236; color changes of, 244; composition of cooked, 240; cost per serving, 236–238; frozen, 244; grading of, 233–234; home freezing of, 600; inspection of, 233; as a meat substitute, 232; nutritive value of, 239; preparation of, 239–244; selection of, 233–239; storage of, 238–239; terms used to identify, 235
Poultry Products Inspection Act of 1957, 24–25
Powdered sugar, 351
Preparation of food. *See* Cooking; Meal preparation
Prepared foods, 425–426
Preservation of food, 568–580: by additives, 577–580; canning, 573–575, 581–594; by drying, 571–573; by freezing, 569–571; by radiation, 575–577; by storage and chilling, 568–569
Preservatives, chemical, 578
Preserves, 617–623: causes of difficulties in making, 622; defined, 617; making of, 620–622
Pressure cooking, 124–127
Prices of food: factors affecting, 423–427; trends in, 435. *See also* Cost of food
Protection of food supply, 22–34: by Department of Agriculture (USDA), 22–25; egg inspection, 31–32, 175–179; by federal agencies, 23–30; by Food and Drug Administration (FDA), 25–30; grading of food, 426–429; GRAS list, 26; interrelationship among agencies, 30; meat inspection, 23–24, 209–213; misbranding, 27–28; poultry inspection, 24–25; by Public Health Service (PHS), standards of identity, 28–29; by state and local agencies, 30–33
Proteins, 5–6: in cereals, 71–72; complete or adequate, 6; composition of, 5; cost of recommended dietary allowance for a day, 440; in flour, 281; foods high in, 5–6, 13; functions of, 13; incomplete and inadequate, 6; in meat, 215–217; in milk, 163, in poultry, 239, 240; sources of, 13
ProTen, 228
Prothrombin, 9
Protopectin, 609
Provitamins, 8
Public Health Service (PHS), 29–30, 32
Puddings, 270–272
Pumpkin pie, 344
Pumpkins, 125
Purchasing of food, 417–443: convenience foods as price factor, 425–426; determining factors in, 418–423; determining food to be purchased, 431–443; grades and brands as aids to, 426–431; guide for, 441–442; packaging as price factor, 422; quality as price factor, 421–422; source and season as price factor, 421; suggestions for, 441; supply and demand as price factor, 423–424; supply for a week, 439–440; weights and measures in, 419–420
Pyroceran, 457, 497

Quality of food: grading of, 210–212; as price factor, 421–422
Quick breads, 298–310: biscuits, 305–318; causes for deviations in making, 308–310; griddle cakes, 301–303; muffins, 298–301; popovers, 304–305; proportions in, 298; waffles, 303

Radiation, 575–577
Radishes, 109–110
Rancidity of fats, 292
Range: cleaning of, 469–470; electronic, 451–452; selection of, 450–452
Raw-pack canning, 585–586
Receptions, 531–534
Refrigerator selection, 452–453
Relish, 625
Rennin, 155
Reverse osmosis, 573
Rhubarb, 110
Riboflavin (Vitamin B_2): functions of, 10, 14; in milk, 163; sources of, 14, 18–19; in vegetables, 118
Rice: characteristics of, 67–68; nutrients in, 72; preparation of, 78–79; varieties of, 68
Rice starch, 264
Rigor mortis, effect on meat, 203
R.O. (reverse osmosis) process, 573
Roasting: of meat, 221–225; of poultry, 241–243
Roller milling, 258
Rolls, 316–317, 318
Rosemary, 378

Figure 16.5. Sample Index Page

From Gladys E. Vail, Jean A. Phillips, Lucile Osborn Rust, Ruth M. Griswold, Margaret M. Justin, *Foods,* 6th edition (Boston: Houghton Mifflin Company, 1973), p. 642. Copyright © 1973 by Houghton Mifflin Company. Used by permission.

Appendix

An **appendix** is a section at the end of a book. An appendix contains materials that supplement the information within the textbook.

The information included in an appendix will depend upon the subject matter of the book. For example, you might find tables of numbers, such as a table of square roots, in the appendix of a mathematics book. You might find a copy of the Constitution, Declaration of Independence, or other important documents in the appendix of an American history book. In any case, if a textbook has an appendix, it will contain materials that you will probably need to use.

The materials included in an appendix differ widely by subject matter and even among the books about a particular subject. Therefore, an example is not included here. At the end of this task, however, you will be asked to survey three textbooks and list the items in the appendix of each book.

Footnotes and Notes

A **footnote** or a **note** has two parts. The first part consists of a number, symbol, or other reference. This part is usually placed within the sentences or paragraphs of the book. The second part consists of the particular information that the writer wants you to know. The second part (the note) is sometimes placed at the bottom (foot) of the page on which the number or other symbol is found. In some books, however, the notes are placed at the end of each chapter. In other books, the notes may all be found at the end of the book.

Footnotes or notes have, in general, two purposes. The first purpose is to tell you the book, article, or other document in which you can find the specific information the writer has used in the text. This is called a *citation footnote.* The second purpose is to give you information that supplements what the writer has said in the text. This is called an *information footnote.* Sometimes one footnote may include both a citation and information.

All of your textbooks may not follow the same note system. In English, history, and other humanities textbooks, the note generally consists of a number placed just above the line within the printed page. The citation or information (the second part of the note) is numbered the same as the number in the printed page. The note may be at the bottom of the page, the end of a chapter, or the end of the book. Figure 16.6 is an example of this system of footnoting. Notice that the citations tell you the author's name, the title of the document, the place of publication, the name of the publisher, the date of publication, and the page(s) on which the cited information can be found.

In science, education, psychology, and other textbooks, a different system of noting is generally used. Under this system, certain information is given within parentheses in the printed page. The information includes the last name of the author of the document being cited, the year of publication of the document, and sometimes the page number of the specific information. For example, you might find the following kinds of references within your psychology textbook:

(Brown 1974, p. 114)
(Haywood 1977)

The information given in parentheses refers you to a *list of references* or *bibliography.* The list of references is generally in the back of the book, but it might be located at the end of each chapter. The reference list contains, alphabetically arranged according to the author's last name, the titles of the documents cited.

UTOPIA: THE LURE OF THE IDEAL

The ideal of utopia, the perfect society, has long exerted a powerful influence upon the thinking, feeling, and action of human beings. Some of the most influential movements in history—Judaism, Christianity, Confucianism, Islam, communism, democratic socialism—have developed from a utopian vision and been sustained by a commitment of masses of people to the achievement of a utopian goal.[1] Utopian thinkers have claimed that the major advances in civilization would not have taken place without utopian aspirations and aims. H. G. Wells said that "the human mind has always accomplished progress by its construction of Utopias."[2] This is of course debatable.[3] But whether utopia has been conceived of as a paradisial garden from which man has been expelled; or as a promised land of milk and honey into which, after trial and testing, a chosen people would someday enter; or as a kingdom of God which promised salvation from sin and suffering to the elect; or as a classless society in which the state had withered away and the governance of persons had been replaced by the administration of things; or as a land of freedom and equality in which each person would be seeking his own greatest happiness; or as a unified and peaceful world controlled by an international government—no matter how it has been conceived, the ideal of utopia has retained a central place in the hopes, desires, fantasies, and spiritual aspirations of humanity. To dismiss utopia as a foolish and discredited notion without relevance to the world today would be to dismiss an ideal which has an irresistible attraction for large numbers of people and which helps to explain behavior that otherwise would seem incomprehensible.[4]

[1] The Western utopian tradition, with its roots in Greek, Judaic, and Christian cultures, is surveyed in Joyce O. Hertzler, *The History of Utopian Thought* (New York: Macmillan, 1923). For a recent survey of the less well known Eastern utopian tradition, see Jean Chesneaux, "Egalitarian and Utopian Traditions in the East," *Diogenes* 62 (Summer 1968): 76–102.

[2] Quoted by Mulford Q. Sibley, "Apology for Utopia: II Utopia and Politics," *The Journal of Politics* 2 (May 1940): 165.

information and citation footnotes

[3] See Georg G. Iggers, "The Idea of Progress: A Critical Reassessment," *The American Historical Review* 71 (October 1965): 1–17.

[4] For example, several of the problems confronting the United States today—the hostility of a monolithic communist power in China, the presence of a Marxist experiment at her doorstep in Cuba, the conflicting demands made by the Israelis and Arabs—cannot be understood fully without taking into account the powerful emotional, moral, and intellectual appeals of a utopian ideal.

information footnote

Figure 16.6. Sample Textbook Page with Footnotes

From Peyton E. Richter, *Utopias, Social Ideals and Communal Experiments* (Boston: Holbrook Press, Inc., 1971), pp. 1–2. Used by permission.

The following is an example of the information you would find within the printed page, under this system of footnoting:

> Thus, subjects who were anxious or became angry with themselves appeared to respond as if they were in an emergency; the others did not react in an emergency manner (Funkenstein *et al.*,* 1957).

In the back of the book, under the reference list section, you would find the following information:

> Funkenstein, D. H.; King, S. H.; and Droletter, M. E. (1957) *Mastery of Stress.* Cambridge, Mass.: Harvard University Press.

You should read the notes in your textbooks because they often contain information you need to know. Generally, the citation footnotes will be most useful when you want to study a certain topic in more detail than your textbook provides. The citation footnotes will then be useful in helping you choose other books and articles to read.

Bibliography

A **bibliography** is a list, alphabetically arranged according to the authors' last names, of the documents the writer used in preparing the book. Besides the author's name, each entry gives the title of the document, place of publication, name of the publisher, and year of publication. The purpose of a bibliography is to provide you with the titles of documents you might want to read if you study a subject in detail. Another purpose of a bibliography is to give credit to the persons who wrote the books or articles that the writer has used.

Generally, the bibliography is placed toward the back of the book. The bibliography may be organized in a single, alphabetical list. Sometimes it is arranged according to the chapters or even the topics in the book. In some books, there is a bibliography at the end of each chapter. The sample bibliography in Figure 16.7 is from a book about cities. Look at the bibliography. Then, answer the following questions.

1. If you wanted to read about bridges, which book would you choose?

___

___

2. If you wanted to read about real estate taxes, which book would you choose?

___

___

Look in the Answer Key for the answers.

*The words *et al.* mean "and others." They are used when there are several authors.

Bibliography

Gerberding, William and Smith, Duane (eds.). *The Radical Left: The Abuse of Discontent.* Boston: Houghton Mifflin, 1970.

Ginger, Ray (ed.). *Modern American Cities.* New York: Quadrangle Books, 1969.

Heilbrun, J. *Real Estate Taxes and Urban Housing.* New York: Columbia University Press, 1966.

Holland, Laurence B. (ed.). *Who Designs America?* Garden City: Doubleday, 1966.

Jacobs, Jane. *The Economy of Cities.* New York: Random House, 1970.

Kammerer, Gladys M.; Farris, Charles D.; De Grove, John M.; and Clubok, Alfred B. *The Urban Political Community: Profiles in Town Politics.* Boston: Houghton Mifflin, 1963.

Krislov, Samuel and Musolf, Lloyd D. (eds.). *The Politics of Regulation: A Reader.* Boston: Houghton Mifflin, 1964.

McHarg, Ian. *Design With Nature.* Garden City: Doubleday, 1969.

Morlan, Robert L. (ed.). *Capitol, Courthouse, and City Hall: Readings in American State and Local Government.* Boston: Houghton Mifflin, 1966.

Overman, Michael. *Roads, Bridges and Tunnels.* Garden City: Doubleday, 1968.

Overman, Michael. *Water: Solutions to a Problem of Supply and Demand.* Garden City: Doubleday, 1969.

Page, Alfred N. and Seyfried, Warren R. (eds.). *Urban Analysis: Readings in Housing and Urban Development.* Glenview, Ill.: Scott, Foresman, 1970.

Perloff, Harvey S. and Wingo, Lowdon, Jr. (eds.). *Issues in Urban Economics.* Baltimore: The Johns Hopkins Press, 1968.

Rodwin, Lloyd. *Nations and Cities: A Comparison of Strategies for Urban Growth.* Boston: Houghton Mifflin, 1970.

Rudofsky, Bernard. *Architecture Without Architects.* Garden City: Doubleday, 1964.

Figure 16.7. Sample Bibliography Page

From James E. McKeown and Frederick I. Tietze, eds., *The Changing Metropolis*, 2nd ed. (Boston: Houghton Mifflin Company, 1971), pp. 186, 195. Copyright © 1971, 1964 by James E. McKeown and Frederick I. Tietze. Used by permission.

Charts and Graphs

Many of your textbooks will contain charts and graphs. **Charts** and **graphs** use drawings, words, and various symbols to present information.

Perhaps you find charts and graphs hard to read. However, they give you important information in a compact, picture form. Consequently, you will find it useful to learn to read charts and graphs easily and quickly.

Charts and graphs usually have a title and a legend. The *title* tells you, of course, the kind of information the drawing represents. For instance, the chart in Figure 16.8 tells you about the location of different kinds of jobs. The legend is usually found in one of the corners or at the bottom of the drawing. The *legend* shows you the symbols used in the drawing and tells you what each symbol stands for. The legend is in the upper left corner of the chart on jobs. The symbol ▪ indicates the kinds of jobs with the greatest number of openings expected in the next five years. The symbol × indicates jobs for which there is now a shortage of workers. The symbol * indicates jobs that have openings now and that will have openings in the next five years.

Charts and graphs are generally organized according to a "two-way" system. This means that information is represented both across (horizontally) and up and down (vertically) in the drawing. In Figure 16.8, the kinds of jobs are listed across (horizontally). The states in which the jobs are found are listed up and down (vertically). If you want to know the states with openings in a certain kind of job, you read *across* the chart to find the kind of job and *down* the chart to find the states. Thus, you actually read *two* lines. One line is read horizontally, and the other is read vertically. Where the two lines meet, you will find a symbol. The symbol tells you about the openings in the kind of job in a particular state. For example, suppose you are trained in television and home-appliance repair work and you are looking for a job. If you read across the chart, you will find a column headed "TV & home appliance repairers." If you read down that column, you will find that the states of Iowa, Massachusetts (Mass.), Michigan (Mich.), New York (N.Y.), and Texas (Tex.) have a shortage of TV and home-appliance repairers.

Read the chart in Figure 16.8 and answer the following questions.

1. Suppose that you are a computer specialist and you want to find a job now. In which states would you be most likely to find a job?

   ____________, ____________, and ____________

2. Suppose you want to move to Florida in the next year or two. In what kind of work are you most apt to find job openings? (Hint: Read *down* the column of states to find Florida [Fla.], *across* the Florida line to the symbol for job openings in the next five years, then *up* each column to find the kind of job.)

   ____________, ____________, ____________,

   and ____________________________

3. Suppose that you are about to enter college and you want to learn the occupation that will have the most job openings in the next five years. What occupation would you choose? (Hint: Find the column with the greatest number of ▪ symbols in it. Then, read the kind of job listed at the top of the column. There are three columns with an almost equal number of ▪ symbols. You will have to count the number of symbols to find the *one* occupation with the greatest number of job openings expected in the next five years.)

   ____

Look in the Answer Key for the answers.

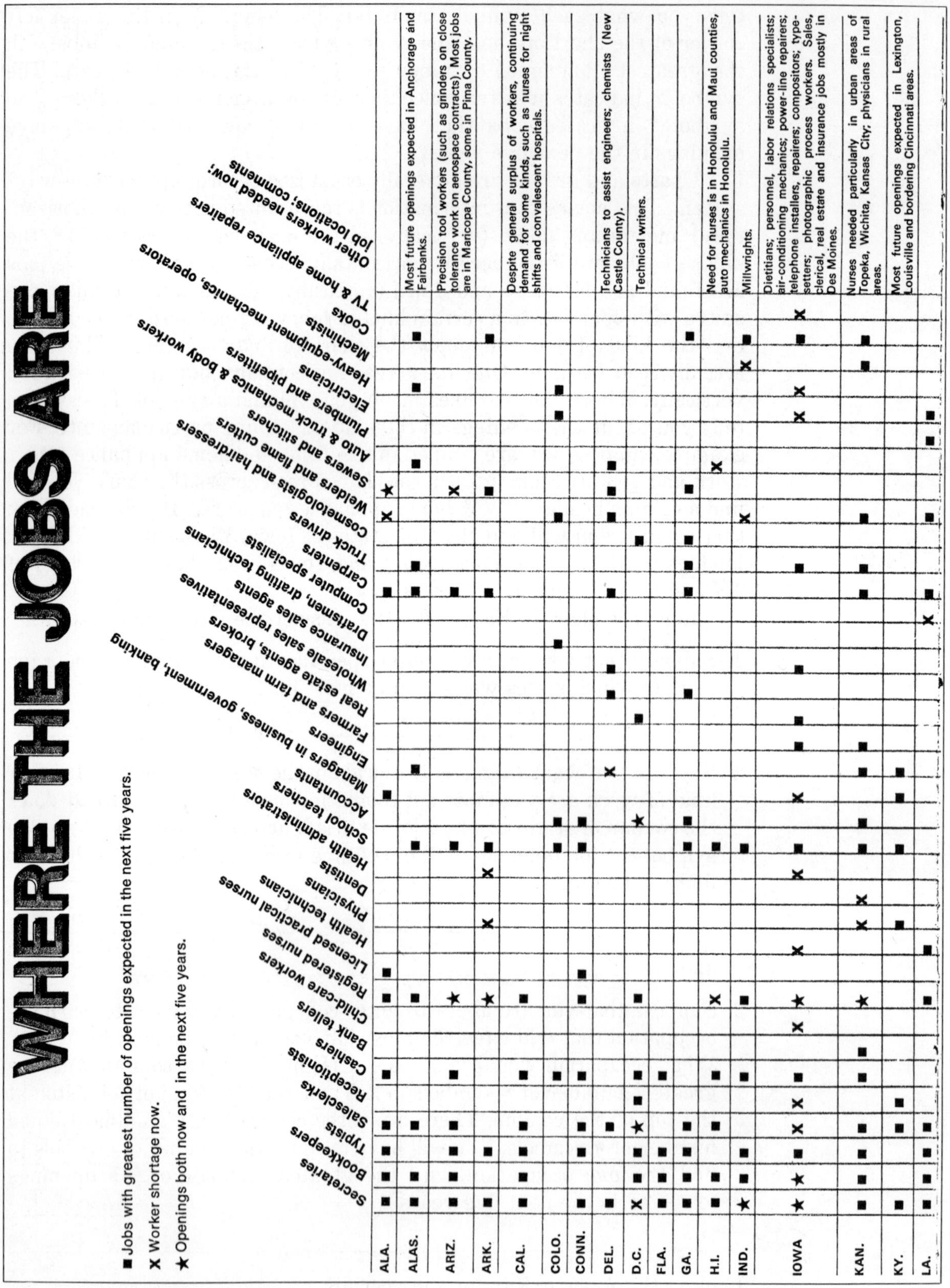

Figure 16.8. Sample Chart

Reprinted with permission from *Changing Times* Magazine, © 1976 Kiplinger Washington Editors, Inc., May 1976.

ME.	■	■	■						★	X					■							X			■									X			Wood harvesters.
MD.																																					Possible shortage of nurses (both LPN and RN) on Maryland's eastern shore.
MASS.	■	■	■						★	■		X	X		■	■		■											X							X	Data processing machine repairers.
MICH.	■	■	■	■		■			■																						X	X				X	Legal secretaries; machine & electric motor repairers; automatic screw, special gear, jig boring, centerless grinder, bridgeport, heavy forge press operators; offset pressmen; millwrights; diesel mechanics; air-conditioning & heating designers.
MINN.	■	■	■	■		■			■						■																						
MO.	■	■	■	■		■			★	X		X	X		■	■													■						■		Optometrists.
MONT.	■	■	■					■	■						■				■					X			■								■		
NEB.	★			■					■	■				■			■													■							Auto mechanic jobs will be in southeast Nebraska.
NEV.	■	■		■					★			X				■	■			■					■	■	■					■			■		Physician and nurse shortage is in rural areas. Other jobs mainly in Las Vegas and Reno areas.
N.H.	■	■	■			■			■						■			★							■	■			■	■			■	X	■		Skilled machinists in certain specialties; medical technicians in some areas. Generally, jobs are in southern part of state.
N.J.	■	■	■	■		■			■								■																				
N.M.	■	■	■	■		■			★	■					■	■			■						■		■		■	X					■		Legal and medical secretaries; uranium miners; diesel mechanics. Nurse shortage in small towns and rural areas.
N.Y.	■	■	■	■					■						■			X														X				X	Physical and occupational therapists; job and die setter and other kinds of experienced machinists; electrical, nuclear and biomedical engineers.
N.C.	■	■		■																									■								
N.D.	■	■	■					■	■						■		■																				
OHIO	■	■	■	■	■	■			■	■					■	■			■		■					■	■	■					■		■		
OKLA.	■	■	■			■	■		★	■	★	X	X	■		■	■	■					■		■	■		■	■	■	■	■		■	■		Shortage of health professionals is in rural areas.
ORE.	★	■	X						X	X											X				X												Carpenters and LPN's needed in Portland.
PA.	■	■	■	■		■			■	■					■	■									■	■	■		■						■		
S.C.	★	■		★	★	★	■	■	★		■														■	■			■		■		■	■			Textile jobs will be in the six northwest counties.
S.D.	■		■	■		■			★	■	X	X			■										■	■	■	■							■		Need for physicians, nurses and other health workers is in rural areas.
TENN.		■	■	■					■						■										■				■								
TEX.	★	■	■	★	■	■		■	★	★					■	★		X			■	X			■	■	■	X	★	X		X		X	★	X	Diesel mechanics; keypunch operators. Types of engineers needed are civil, mechanical. Jobs will be mostly in Dallas-Fort Worth and Houston areas.
UTAH	■	■	■	■		■			■							■											■		■						■		
VT.	■	■	■			■			■						■			■							■		■							■	■		
VA.	X	■	■	■		■			★						■	■		■						X	★				X	X					★		Commission sales workers.
WASH.	■	■	■	■		■																															
W. VA.	■	■	■						■						■																						
WIS.	■	■	■	■												■							■					■		■							
WYO.																																					Jobs open now and in years ahead in crude petroleum, natural gas and coal mining; petroleum refining; construction of related facilities, including power generating plants.

Note: Idaho, Illinois, Mississippi and Rhode Island did not respond.

BEHIND THOSE SKYROCKETING HEALTH-CARE COSTS—

A Tripling in National Health Bills

■ Americans on average spent $547 per person for health in 1975 — or $2,188 for a family of four — compared with $198 a year per person in 1965.

■ Medical costs take a growing share out of the nation's economy — accounting for 8.3 per cent of total output of goods and services in 1975, compared with 5.9 per cent in 1965 and 4.6 per cent in 1955.

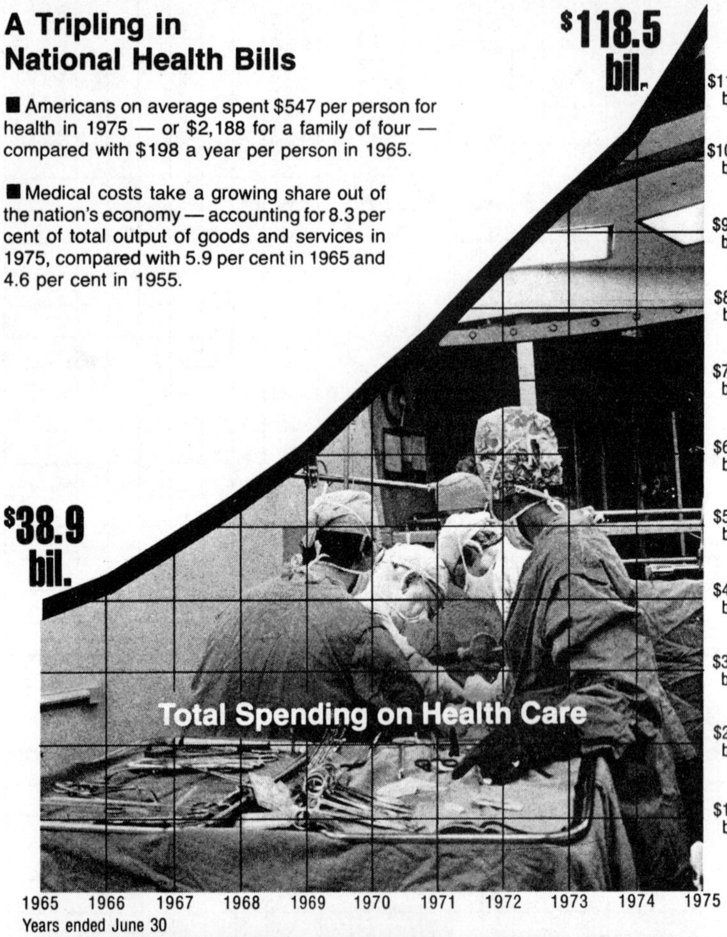

[redacted]

Of the 118.5 billion dollars spent on health in 1975 —

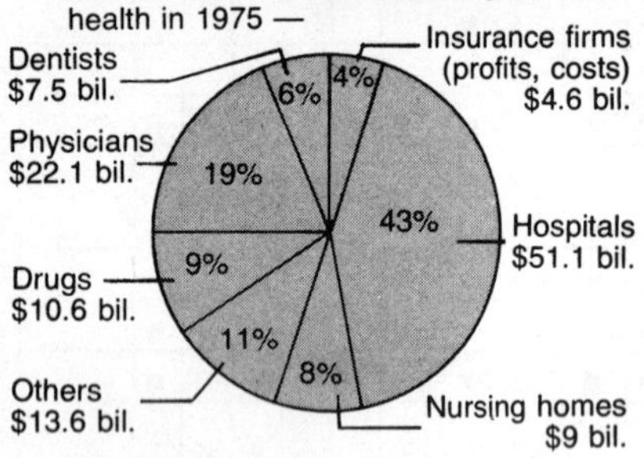

Average price increase since 1965 in cost-of-living index —

MEDICAL CARE	102%
ALL OTHER COSTS	76%

Two examples of rising medical costs, based on U.S. averages —

	1965	1975
Average stay in hospital	$311	$1,017
	1969	1974
Physician's fee, office visit	$13	$20

New technology and equipment, new types of treatment — usually providing better care — have driven up costs, particularly for complex procedures. Examples of average expenses —

	1964	1971
Treating a heart attack	$1,449	$3,280
Treating breast cancer	$1,559	$2,557

Source: President's Council on Wage and Price Stability, U.S. Dept. of Health, Education and Welfare; U.S. Dept. of Labor

Figure 16.9. Sample Graph and Pie Chart

The graph in Figure 16.9 shows the total spending, in billions of dollars, on health care. The line drawn upward from the lower left to the upper right of the graph marks the intersection points of the information listed horizontally and vertically in the graph. If you wanted to know how much money was spent on health care in 1969, you would read across the list of years at the bottom of the graph. You would then read up the 1969 column until you reach the line. Then, you would read across to find the amount of money ($60 billion) spent on health care in that year. Because the line does not always indicate the exact amount of money, you have to read some of the costs as "approximate." For example, the line crosses about halfway between $80 billion and $90 billion for the year 1972. So you would say the health care costs in 1972 were approximately $85 billion.

What was the approximate cost of health care in 1968? __________

Look in the Answer Key for the answer.

Another kind of drawing you may find in your books is called a **pie chart.** The pie, or circle, of the drawing stands for the whole amount of whatever is being explained. For example, the pie might stand for a whole dollar. In Figure 16.9, the pie represents the whole amount of money spent on health care in 1975. Each "slice" of the pie shows the amount and the part of the whole that went to that item or cost. In the chart, each slice represents the percentage of the total health care costs that went to hospitals, nursing homes, and so on. Look at the chart and answer the following questions.

1. What percent of the health care money was spent on dentists? __________
2. What percent of the health care costs was spent on drugs? __________
3. What amount of money was spent on dentists? __________
4. What amount of money was spent on drugs? __________

Look in the Answer Key for the answers.

Words and Terms to Know

survey
contents/table of contents
introduction
preface
foreword
overview
glossary
index
appendix
footnote
bibliography
chart
graph
pie chart

Concepts to Remember

1. Surveying a textbook means looking it over to find the study aids it contains.
2. The contents or table of contents lists the chapters and special information sections included in a book. It also gives the pages on which each chapter and section begins.
3. The introduction to a book may include sections called preface, foreword, overview, or introduction.
4. The introduction may contain such information as the objectives of the book, definitions of terms in the book, and explanations of the organization of the book.
5. A glossary is an alphabetical list of the special terms used in a book and their definitions.
6. An index is an alphabetical list of the words, ideas, or topics in a book. The index also gives the pages on which this information is discussed.
7. An appendix is a section at the end of a book that contains materials which supplement the information in the book.
8. Some notes tell you the documents in which the writer found the information used in the book. Other notes give you information that supplements the information in the book.
9. A bibliography is a list, alphabetically arranged according to the authors' last names, of the documents the writer used in preparing the book.
10. Charts and graphs represent information in a visual way.
11. Charts and graphs are generally read on two lines. One line runs horizontally, and the other runs vertically.
12. Pie charts are used to represent the parts of a whole, such as a whole dollar, that are assigned to certain uses or groups.

Assignment

1. Following the Answer Key, you will find a form to use in surveying textbooks. Choose three textbooks you are using in other courses or use three textbooks assigned by your instructor. Survey each book to find the information listed on the form. If a book does not have the information listed, write "none" or "not included" in the space on the form.
2. As your reading practice, your instructor will ask you to find certain information in a textbook. You should expect to read and answer questions about some charts and graphs.

Answer Key Task 16

pages 89–90

1. chapter number 1; section number 1-1
2. page number 1
3. chapter number 2; section number 2-7
4. page number 61

page 91

Objective 5 should be achieved through Task 16, "Reading and Study Aids."

page 91

The terms or concepts that are defined are *space, time, inertia,* and *force.*

page 91

1. pictures that summarize what the unit is about
2. a definition and background information (people and events) related to the topic of the unit

pages 95–96

1. 118
2. 124–127
3. 342–344 and 338–339

page 99

1. Overman, Michael. *Roads, Bridges and Tunnels.* Garden City: Doubleday, 1968.
2. Heilbrun, J. *Real Estate Taxes and Urban Housing.* New York: Columbia University Press, 1966.

page 101

1. If you were a computer specialist, the states in which you would be most likely to find work are Louisiana (La.), Montana (Mont.), and Virginia (Va.).
2. If you wanted to move to Florida, you would be most likely to find job openings for secretaries, bookkeepers, typists, and cashiers.
3. If you wanted to learn the occupation with the greatest number of openings expected in the next five years, you would become a bookkeeper.

page 104

The approximate cost of health care in 1968 was $52 billion. If you said $53 or $54 billion, your answer is correct. The line intersection shows that the cost was less than $55 billion but more than $50 billion.

page 105

1. 6 percent
2. 9 percent
3. $7.5 billion
4. $10.6 billion

Textbook Survey

NAME ____________________ DATE __________

Title of Textbook ____________________

____

1. *Table of Contents* (page numbers) ____________________

   Chapter Titles Only __________ *Section Headings Included* __________

2. *Introduction* (page numbers) ____________________

   Objectives of the Book Explained ____________________

   Special Terms Defined ____________________

   Other Special Information Included (list below)

   ____

   ____

   ____

3. *Glossary* (page numbers) ____________________

4. *Index* (page numbers) ____________________

5. *Appendix* (list items included and page numbers)

   ____________________ pages __________

   ____________________ pages __________

   ____________________ pages __________

   ____________________ pages __________

6. *Footnotes* (bottom of pages) ______ (end of chapters) ______ (end of book) ______

7. *Bibliography* (end of chapters) __________ (end of book) __________

8. *Charts and Graphs* ____________________

Textbook Survey

NAME ____________________ DATE __________

Title of Textbook ____________________

____

1. *Table of Contents* (page numbers) ____________________

   Chapter Titles Only __________ *Section Headings Included* __________

2. *Introduction* (page numbers) ____________________

   Objectives of the Book Explained ____________________

   Special Terms Defined ____________________

   Other Special Information Included (list below)

   ____

   ____

   ____

3. *Glossary* (page numbers) ____________________

4. *Index* (page numbers) ____________________

5. *Appendix* (list items included and page numbers)

   ____________________ pages __________

   ____________________ pages __________

   ____________________ pages __________

   ____________________ pages __________

6. *Footnotes* (bottom of pages) ______ (end of chapters) ______ (end of book) ______

7. *Bibliography* (end of chapters) __________ (end of book) __________

8. *Charts and Graphs* ____________________

Textbook Survey

NAME ______________________________ DATE ____________

Title of Textbook ______________________________

____

1. *Table of Contents* (page numbers) ______________________________
   Chapter Titles Only ____________ *Section Headings Included* ____________
2. *Introduction* (page numbers) ______________________________
   Objectives of the Book Explained ______________________________
   Special Terms Defined ______________________________
   Other Special Information Included (list below)
   ____
   ____
   ____
3. *Glossary* (page numbers) ______________________________
4. *Index* (page numbers) ______________________________
5. *Appendix* (list items included and page numbers)
   ______________________________ pages ____________
   ______________________________ pages ____________
   ______________________________ pages ____________
   ______________________________ pages ____________
6. *Footnotes* (bottom of pages) ________ (end of chapters) ________ (end of book) ________
7. *Bibliography* (end of chapters) ____________ (end of book) ____________
8. *Charts and Graphs* ______________________________

Task 17
Chapter and Section Ideas

The information included in a textbook is divided into units or **chapters.** Each chapter is based on a topic or division of the subject matter of the book. The information in a chapter is further divided into **sections.** Each section deals with an idea that is related to the topic of the chapter. In fact, even though a chapter may *look* different and may contain quite different information, a chapter is organized just like an essay. The following chart may help you see how the organization of an essay and the organization of a chapter are alike.

Essay	*Chapter*
Controlling idea	Chapter topic
Major point	Section idea
Supporting data	Supporting data
Supporting data	Supporting data
Major point	Section idea
Supporting data	Supporting data
Supporting data	Supporting data
Major point	Section idea
Supporting data . . .	Supporting data . . .

Each chapter of a textbook is usually organized according to the same plan. If objectives or special terms are listed at the beginning of the first chapter, the same information will probably be found at the beginning of every chapter. If questions, a summary, or other information is given at the end of a chapter, that same information will be found at the end of every chapter. Consequently, once you know the organization and contents of one chapter, you know the kind of information included in every chapter and where in the chapter the information can be found.

Titles and Headings

Like an essay, a chapter has a title that helps you determine what the chapter is about. Almost all textbooks have headings within the chapters. The headings are often in different kinds or sizes of type. Each different kind or size of type identifies a "level" in the information included in the chapter. For example, a very large type may be used for the section headings. A smaller or different kind of type may be used to show the divisions of information, or the supporting data, under the sections.

The subject of the textbook pages included here is helping handicapped and elderly people care for themselves. Notice that the title of the chapter tells you quite clearly what the chapter is about. Chapter titles are not always so detailed. Sometimes a title is only a word, such as "Memory," that tells you what the chapter is about.

In the pages of the example, two headings—"Easy-on, Easy-off Features" and "Easy-to-Fasten Features"—identify sections of information within the chapter. A different type is used to show the divisions under the "Easy-to-Fasten Features" section. In this section, the divisions are related to different kinds of fasteners: "Zippers," "Buttons," "Magnetic Fasteners," "Velcro," "Hooks and Eyes," and "Grippers."

Chapter 7 The Selection and Adaptation of Clothing to Suit Particular Needs for Men, Women, and Children

(1) Before clothing is purchased, the particular needs of the individual should be studied. Consider these questions: What will make dressing easier? What will help him to look his best? Will it be comfortable? Will it be easy to care for? Will it help to disguise his disability?

Easy-on, Easy-off Features

(2) Dressing is much easier when garments are easy to put on and take off, such as:

a. Garment openings that are large enough to slip in and out of without struggling.
b. Clothes amply cut through fitted areas, such as the armhole and waistline.
c. Fasteners that are easy to manipulate and located within easy reach.

Easy-to-Fasten Features

(3) The *type, size,* and *location* of fasteners on the garment determine how easily they can be managed.

(4) ZIPPERS are easy to pull up or down. Large zipper tabs are easy to grasp and may be made of a fabric loop or metal ring. It is possible to prevent catching by placing an extra piece of fabric to act as a guard under the zipper. Nylon coil zippers are pliable and less likely to snag. If something does get caught, it can be released by folding the zipper together and twisting it apart. Nylon zippers will melt easily and must not be touched with a hot iron.

(5) BUTTONS must be large enough to grasp and should not be sewed on tightly. A flat, smooth button slips through a buttonhole more easily than a fancy one.

(6) MAGNETIC FASTENERS are relatively new on the market and have been used primarily on children's clothing. They are sure to have more extensive use, since they require little skill to fasten. A tiny magnet snaps the fastener together and very little force is necessary to pull it apart.

(7) VELCRO—A type of tape fastener—requires a minimum amount of hand and finger dexterity to open or close the tape. Velcro is two strips of nylon with rough surfaces that stick together like burrs stick to clothing. One side of the tape is made of tiny nylon hooks and the other side has a looped surface. When the two strips come in contact with one another, they lock and hold

fast. They unlock by pulling the strips apart.
(8) Since Velcro is made of nylon, it should not be exposed to high temperatures in washing or ironing. Since the loops pick up lint, close the fastener before washing or dry cleaning the garment.
(9) HOOKS AND EYES are difficult to fasten unless they are large and sturdy. The type of metal hook and bar used on men's trousers is more manageable on skirts and slacks for anyone with hand limitations.
(10) GRIPPERS are usually easier to unfasten than they are to fasten. They require considerable pressure to close.
(11) The *location* of fasteners has a great deal to do with ease in dressing. They should be easy to see, easy to reach, easy to grasp. When located in the center front, they are usually easier to manipulate than on the side or on the back of a garment.

Key Words, Paragraphs, and Sentences

Since a textbook usually contains a great amount of information, you will find many key words, paragraphs, and sentences in each chapter. At the beginning of each chapter, for instance, you will generally find key words, paragraphs, and sentences that will help you decide what the chapter is about. However, a section generally contains important information too. Consequently, you may find key words, paragraphs, and sentences within each section.

Look back at the sample textbook pages again. In the first paragraph, you will find the key word *clothing.* The word is also found in the title of the chapter. The first paragraph is a key paragraph to the contents of the chapter. The first sentence is a key sentence to the chapter. The questions that follow it are key sentences to the sections you would expect to find in the chapter.

Within each section, you will find additional key words and sentences. You should notice the words *type, size,* and *location* at the beginning of the second section. The words are printed in italic to identify the kinds of information that will follow. In other books, words may be printed differently or underlined to call your attention to the special terms you need to know in the subject. The following chart shows you the key words, paragraphs, and sentences in the sample textbook pages.

Chapter 7 The Selection and Adaptation of Clothing to Suit Particular Needs for Men, Women, and Children

title — *key word (chapter)*

(1) Before clothing is purchased, the particular needs of the individual should be studied. Consider these questions: What will make dressing easier? What will help him to look his best? Will it be comfortable? Will it be easy to care for? Will it help to disguise his disability?

key word (chapter)
key sentence (chapter)
key sentences (section ideas)
key paragraph (chapter)

Easy-on, Easy-off Features

key word ... *key word*

(2) Dressing is much easier when garments

key words ... *key words*

are easy to put on and take off, such as: } key sentence (section)

a. Garment openings that are large enough to slip in and out of without struggling.
b. Clothes amply cut through fitted areas, such as the armhole and waistline.
c. Fasteners that are easy to manipulate and located within easy reach.

Easy-to-Fasten Features

key words ... *key word*

(3) The *type, size,* and *location* of fasteners on the garment determine how easily they can be managed. } key sentence and paragraph (section)

Read the paragraphs below. Then, answer the questions that follow the paragraphs.

CHANGES OF STATE

(1) When water reaches the freezing point it changes to ice (from the liquid to the solid state). When water boils, it changes from a liquid to a gas, steam. These are examples of matter changing from one state to another. Likewise, a piece of metal can be heated enough to melt it (change it from the solid to the liquid state). Further heating can change the liquid metal to vaporized metal, a gas. The reverse steps are also possible. Oxygen is a gas at room temperature. Upon sufficient cooling, it becomes a liquid. Further cooling then changes liquid oxygen to solid oxygen.

(2) In general, then, matter can usually be changed from one state to another merely by changing its temperature. Such changes are called *physical changes.* A physical change is one in which no new substance is produced although there may be a change of state or a change of color. Note that not all substances can be changed from solid to liquid to gas merely by changing the temperature. What about a piece of wood?

(3) The other type of change that matter can undergo is called a *chemical change.* A chemical change is one in which new substances are produced that have entirely different properties from the original substance. Burning a piece of wood is an example of a chemical change. New substances—ash and gas (smoke)—are produced. Note that these substances have properties different from those of the original piece of wood.

PROPERTIES OF MATTER

(4) One portion of matter can be distinguished from another by means of its properties. These distinguishing properties of matter may be classified into two main types—*physical properties* and *chemical properties.*

Physical Properties

(5) Physical properties include color, odor, taste, solubility in water, density, hardness, melting point, and boiling point. These physical properties can serve to identify a substance, although not all of these properties may be necessary for the identification. For example, when we say that the color of a substance is white, we automatically eliminate all substances that are not white. Next, if we say that the white substance is odorless, we can eliminate all white objects that have an odor, leaving a smaller number of substances that are both white and odorless. If we continue to eliminate in this manner by using additional physical properties, eventually only one substance will fit all of these properties—the substance we are trying to identify.

Chemical Properties

(6) Properties such as reacting (or not reacting) in air, or reacting (or not reacting) with an acid, or burning (or not burning) in a flame are chemical properties. An object can be identified by means of its chemical properties, but it is usually much simpler to do so by means of the physical properties.

Comparison of Physical and Chemical Properties

(7) A physical property tells what a substance *is*—it is white, or it is green; it is odorless, or it has a sharp odor; it is hard, or it is soft. A chemical property tells what a substance *does*—it burns, or it does not burn; it reacts with an acid, or it does not react with an acid, and so on.

Circle the letter of the correct answer.

1. The section headed "Changes of State" is about
   a. water changing to ice (from a liquid to a solid state)
   b. water changing to a gas or to steam
   c. matter changing from one state to another
   d. metal changing to a gas
2. The key sentence in the paragraphs under "Changes of State" is
   a. In general, then, matter can usually be changed from one state to another merely by changing its temperature.
   b. Note that not all substances can be changed from solid to liquid to gas merely by changing the temperature.
   c. The other type of change that matter can undergo is called a *chemical change.*
   d. Further cooling then changes liquid oxygen to solid oxygen.
3. The special terms related to "Changes of State" are
   a. water and metal
   b. solids and liquids
   c. physical changes and chemical change
   d. liquid and gas
4. The key paragraph of the section headed "Properties of Matter" is
   a. paragraph 7
   b. paragraph 4
   c. paragraph 5
   d. paragraph 6
5. The key sentence of the section headed "Properties of Matter" is
   a. One portion of matter can be distinguished from another by means of its properties.
   b. These distinguishing properties of matter may be classified into two main types—*physical properties* and *chemical properties.*

c. Physical properties include color, odor, taste, solubility in water, density, hardness, melting point, and boiling point.
d. Properties such as reacting (or not reacting) in air, or reacting (or not reacting) with an acid, or burning (or not burning) in a flame are chemical properties.

6. The special terms related to "Properties of Matter" are
   a. color and odor
   b. density and hardness
   c. physical properties and chemical properties
   d. substances and acids

Look in the Answer Key for the answers.

Topic Sentences

Generally, a paragraph in a textbook will have a topic sentence. Often, *but not always*, the topic sentence will be the first sentence of the paragraph.

The key sentence and key paragraph of the section below have been marked for you. Underline the topic sentences in the body paragraphs of the section.

THE ENGLISH SYSTEM OF MEASUREMENT

In any system of measurement, three basic units are necessary: units for length, weight, and volume. We need a unit of length so that we can define the distance between two points. We also need a unit to measure the weight of an object, how heavy it is. And we need a unit to measure volume, so that we can find the capacity of an object, or how much it can hold.

key sentence

key paragraph

In the English system, we use the *foot* as the unit of length, and we divide the foot into 12 units called *inches*. With these units we can measure long distances (using the foot), or short distances (using the inch). If we find that the foot is too small for the distance we are concerned with, the English system also provides us with the *yard* (which equals 3 feet), or the *mile* (which equals 5,280 feet).

The unit of weight in the English system is the *pound*. If we're weighing something that is less than a pound, we can divide the pound into 16 smaller units, each called an *ounce*. If we have to deal with larger weights, the English system has a unit called the *ton* (equal to 2,000 pounds).

In the English system as used in the United States today, the unit of liquid volume is the *quart*. If we are trying to measure smaller quantities, we use the *fluid ounce* (32 fluid ounces equal 1 quart). Other units of liquid volume are the *pint* (2 pints equal 1 quart) and the *gallon* (4 quarts equal 1 gallon). [Alan Sherman, Sharon Sherman, and Leonard Russikoff, *Basic Concepts of Chemistry* (Boston: Houghton Mifflin Company, 1976), p. 9. Copyright © 1976 by Houghton Mifflin Company. Used by permission.]

On the lines below, list the special terms you should probably know after reading this section of the textbook.

(Answers: The first sentence of each paragraph is the topic sentence. The special terms you should probably know are *foot, inches, yard, mile, pound, ounce, ton, quart, fluid ounce, pint,* and *gallon.*)

Transitional Paragraphs and Statements

Like an essay or article, a textbook may contain transitional paragraphs and statements. The examples below are from a sociology textbook. As in an essay or article, the paragraphs, sentences, and statements link the information by pointing back to what has been discussed and forward to what will be discussed.

> We have been discussing human groups throughout this part of the text. There remains one more feature of the general subject still to be examined: community. We shall proceed to this examination in the next chapter.
>
> We have noted that institutions have, in addition to procedures, particular belief systems that are associated with them. Such beliefs can be labeled *ideologies*—that is, idea systems that are subscribed to by persons who carry out the procedures linked with the institution.
>
> As we said earlier, an institution is not a group, as such. As we now can see, a group is an interaction setting, an association; an institution is a set of procedures and beliefs. [David Dressler with Donald Carns, *Sociology: The Study of Human Interaction,* second edition (New York: Alfred A. Knopf, 1973), pp. 389 and 423.]

information that has been discussed (human groups)

information that will be discussed (community)

transitional statement

transitional statement

transitional statement

Supporting Data

The ideas in a textbook, like the ideas in an essay or article, are explained through examples, facts, definitions, and so on. For instance, look back at the first paragraph of the section "Changes of State," which appears under the discussion of key words, paragraphs, and sentences. Water, metal, and oxygen are used as examples to explain the idea or concept of matter changing from one state (form) to another. In the second and third sentences of paragraph 2, the term *physical changes* is defined. In the second sentence of paragraph 3, the term *chemical change* is defined.

Burning a piece of wood (third sentence, paragraph 3) is an example of a chemical change.

Now look at the section "Properties of Matter." The classification word *properties* is divided into physical and chemical characteristics. In paragraph 5, an example is used to explain how a substance is identified through its physical properties or characteristics. In paragraph 7, the physical and chemical properties of matter are explained by contrasting them (telling you how the properties differ).

If you were studying for a chemistry course, you might not think about the *kind* of information used to explain the ideas or concepts in the paragraphs. You would of course be more concerned about remembering the *particular* information you read. However, understanding what you read depends, at least in part, on recognizing the information that explains or supports another idea. Also, when you are studying a subject, your instructor usually expects you to remember and be able to answer questions about the specific information in your textbook. In that case, the *kind* of information can be a clue to some of the questions you might be asked. For instance, you might be asked any of the following questions about the supporting data in the paragraphs on "Changes of State" and "Properties of Matter":

1. Define and give an example of a physical change of matter.
2. Define and give an example of a chemical change of matter.
3. How are the properties of matter classified?
4. Explain and give an example of the use of physical properties to identify a substance.
5. What is the difference between the physical and the chemical properties of matter?

To answer the questions correctly, you need to remember the *particular* information given in the paragraphs. But at the same time, you need to relate the *kind* of information you remember with the *kind* of information asked for in the question. For instance, to answer question 1, you need to remember the information that defines the term *physical change.* You must also recognize that the information is a definition. Therefore, it is the information that you need to use in answering the "define" part of the question. In the same way, you would need to remember and associate the information that is an example with answering the second part of the question.

Read the paragraphs below. Label the kinds of supporting data (definitions, examples, facts, and so on) that the author has used to explain *sole proprietorship.* Then, write five questions you might be asked about the information given in the paragraphs. Check your work with the answers and the suggested questions in the Answer Key.

> ***The sole proprietorship.*** The simplest form of business is the *sole proprietorship,* which as the name suggests is a business owned by one person who often manages it as well. Such owner-managers are often classified as self-employed. Generally, a sole proprietorship can be formed without the requirement of a written agreement, charter, or other legally binding document. The business is simply begun by an enterprising individual who

wants to follow a particular pursuit. The owner of a sole proprietorship assumes *unlimited liability*—that is, he is legally obligated, if necessary, to use his entire business and personal wealth to pay off any debts accumulated by the business.

Sole proprietorships range from a child's summer lemonade stand to a neighborhood laundry or shoe repair shop. Sole proprietorships are very numerous but usually small in size. In 1968 they numbered 9.2 million, representing 79 percent of all types of American business. However, their combined revenues of $222 billion accounted for only 13 percent of the total revenues of all business, and the average receipts of an individual sole proprietorship were only about $23,000. [From *An Introduction to Contemporary Business* by William Rudelius, W. Bruce Erickson, and William J. Bakula, Jr., p. 30; copyright, 1973, by Harcourt Brace Jovanovich, Inc. and reprinted with their permission.]

*Question 1*____________________________________

*Question 2*____________________________________

*Question 3*____________________________________

*Question 4*____________________________________

*Question 5*____________________________________

Transitional Markers

As in essays and articles, words and phrases are used in textbooks to link or make the transition from one idea to another. Quite often, you will find a series of ideas numbered. The numbers help you identify them easily. The different number words are also used frequently: one, two, three; first, second, third. A series of reasons or other ideas is sometimes marked with words like *for one thing, for another thing, in addition, moreover, furthermore,* or *finally.* Examples are often marked by the words *for example, for instance,* or *such as.*

Read the paragraph below. Circle the transitional markers. Then, answer the questions following the paragraph.

The psychological expectations of the teachers informally channel students into different achievement levels. In addition, there is the more formal channeling process, the *tracking system,* by which students are divided into curriculum tracks based on tests and other criteria. Since tracking often begins early in the child's school career, it tends to reinforce whatever disadvantages the child starts with. Belonging to the Bluebirds (slow readers) may destroy the student's self-confidence and does take him away from other children who might help him read better. Moreover, since middle-class children generally have a better home background for success in school than lower-class children, the tracking system tends to resegregate classrooms around social class and racial lines. Quite rightly, the tracking system is under heavy attack by civil rights advocates and educational reformers. [J. Victor Baldridge, *Sociology: A Critical Approach to Power, Conflict, and Change* (New York: John Wiley & Sons, 1975), p. 353. Copyright © 1975 John Wiley & Sons, Inc. Reprinted by permission of John Wiley & Sons, Inc.]

1. According to the paragraph, a *tracking system* is a method of dividing students into groups. The paragraph says the system is "in addition" to another process that divides students into groups. What is the other process named in the paragraph?

   ____

2. The paragraph says the tracking system is under attack by civil rights advocates and educational reformers. What four objections to the tracking system are mentioned in the paragraph?

   ____

   ____

   ____

   ____

Look in the Answer Key for the answers.

Words and Terms to Know

chapter
section

Words and Terms to Review

title
headings
key words
key sentences
topic sentence
transitional paragraphs and statements
supporting data
example
fact
classification and division
comparison and contrast
definition

Concepts to Remember

1. A chapter in a textbook is organized like an essay.
2. A chapter in a textbook is based on a topic or general idea.
3. The sections of information within a chapter explain the topic of the chapter.
4. The ideas within the sections are explained through various kinds of supporting data. The data may include examples, facts, cause and effect, classification and division, comparison and contrast, or definitions.

Assignment

Complete the worksheet at the end of this task according to your instructor's directions.

Answer Key Task 17

pages 119–120

1. *c*
2. *a*
3. *c*
4. *b*
5. *b* (The sentence under *a* could also be considered a key sentence. However, the information in sentence *b* gives you a more specific idea of the properties that are explained in the section.)
6. *c*

pages 122–123

In these paragraphs, the author has used definitions, examples, and facts as supporting data. *Sole proprietorship* is defined in the first sentence of the first paragraph. It means "a business owned by one person who often manages it as well." The term *unlimited liability* is defined in the last sentence of the first paragraph. The term means "the legal obligation to pay off any debts accumulated by the business." Examples of sole proprietorships are given in the first sentence of the second paragraph. They are a child's summer lemonade stand, a neighborhood laundry, a shoe-repair shop. Facts are used in the third and fourth sentences of the second paragraphs: the number of small businesses in 1968 (9.2 million), the percent of American businesses they accounted for (79 percent), their revenues ($222 billion), the percent of their revenues among all business (13 percent), and the average receipts ($23,000).

Suggested Questions

1. Define the term *sole proprietorship.* (Or: What is a *sole proprietorship*?)
2. Define the term *unlimited liability.* (Or: What is meant by *unlimited liability*?)
3. What is an example of a sole proprietorship?
4. In 1968, what percent of American businesses were sole proprietorships?
5. In 1968, what percent of business revenues were earned by sole proprietorships?

page 124

1. The other process that divides students into groups is "the psychological expectations of the teachers."
2. The four objections to the tracking system are as follows: First, it tends to reinforce the disadvantages the child starts with; second, it may destroy the student's self-confidence; third, it takes him away from other children who might "help him read better"; and fourth, it tends to resegregate classrooms on social and racial lines.

Task 17 **Worksheet**

NAME ______________________________ DATE ____________

Reading Practice

Read "Business Ownership and Private Enterprise" on the following page. Then, answer the questions based on the reading. After you have answered the questions, write a paragraph of five or more sentences in which you summarize what is said about forms of business ownership. You may use this page for your summary.

Business Ownership and Private Enterprise

(1) The modern American business system is usually described as a *mixed economy:* it includes a wide variety of organizations—business, government, labor, agricultural, and nonprofit—and is ruled according to no fixed ideology. Elements of capitalism, welfare-statism, and even socialism exist side by side, though sometimes uneasily.

(2) This chapter discusses three central aspects of the American business system: (1) major forms of business ownership, (2) the development of the modern corporation, and (3) the private enterprise system. A concluding section describes the principles on which the American economy's two main competitors, socialism and communism, are based.

FORMS OF BUSINESS OWNERSHIP

(3) In examining the modern American economy, it is useful to divide business ownership into two broad classes: nonprofit organizations and profit-making businesses.

Nonprofit Organizations

(4) There are several kinds of organizations in American business that do not normally seek profits as a primary goal. Two of the most important of these are the cooperative and the publicly owned business.

(5) ***The cooperative.*** A *cooperative* is a business chartered under state laws that seeks the economic betterment of its members through the achievement of common goals. It is owned by its members, who elect a board of directors. Each member has a single vote, but he may purchase shares in the cooperative up to a limit. Interest is paid to those providing capital in relation to the size of their investments. Profits of the cooperative are allocated to members in proportion to their purchases. The most common form of cooperative in the United States is the agricultural cooperative. Credit unions, many savings and loan associations, and mutual insurance companies are modifications of the cooperative concept.

(6) In the past five years numerous consumer cooperatives have sprung up near college campuses and in low-income areas across the United States. These organizations have sought to provide members with quality food at low prices; many have stressed "natural foods" that are grown and brought to market without artificial fertilizers or preservatives. Members of cooperatives divide up end-of-year profits and are often required to work at their store for several hours each month.

(7) ***The publicly owned organization.*** A *publicly owned organization* is a business established by the federal government or by a state government for the purpose of achieving a goal felt to be in the public good. Profits accruing to the organization are retained for use in its future operations; in the case of federally authorized organizations profits are returned to the U.S. Treasury. Publicly owned organizations and most other nonprofit organizations are frequently designated as nonstock corporations because they do not issue stock.

(8) The Tennessee Valley Authority (TVA) is an example of a publicly owned organization. It was created by the U.S. Congress in 1933 to provide for the systematic development of a variety of economic resources along the Tennessee River. Dams and other projects undertaken by the TVA have led to improved river shipping, reforestation, flood control, low-cost electric power, and better fertilizers. The TVA has provided an improved standard of living for thousands of Americans living in the area.

Profit-making Businesses

(9) The most important form of business ownership in the United States is the private business run for profit. The concept of business as a private profit-seeking enterprise was known even to the ancient Egyptians and Greeks. Two of the oldest forms of business organization are the sole proprietorship and the partnership. In the late eighteenth century the industrial revolution was instrumental in developing a type of business that neither the Egyptians nor the Greeks would recognize: the modern corporation.

Circle the letter of the correct answer in questions 1–11 and fill in the answer to question 12.

1. The key paragraph for the chapter is
   a. paragraph 1
   b. paragraph 2
   c. paragraph 3
   d. paragraph 4
2. According to the key paragraph, the chapter is about
   a. major forms of business ownership
   b. the development of the modern corporation
   c. the private enterprise system
   d. the principles on which socialism and communism are based
   e. all of the above (*a, b, c,* and *d*)
3. The key paragraph for the section headed "Forms of Business Ownership" is
   a. paragraph 3
   b. paragraph 4
   c. paragraph 5
   d. paragraph 6
4. The key paragraph of "Forms of Business Ownership" says that the two categories of business ownership are
   a. nonprofit and publicly owned
   b. nonprofit and cooperative
   c. profit-making and publicly owned
   d. nonprofit and profit-making
5. The kinds of nonprofit organizations discussed in the paragraphs are
   a. the Tennessee Valley Authority
   b. campus cooperatives
   c. cooperatives and publicly owned
   d. nonprofit and profit-making
6. The topic sentence of paragraph 5 is
   a. sentence 1
   b. sentence 2
   c. sentence 3
   d. sentence 4
7. The topic sentence of paragraph 7 is
   a. sentence 1
   b. sentence 2
   c. sentence 3
   d. sentence 4

8. A cooperative is owned by
   a. its members
   b. a board of directors
   c. savings and loan associations
   d. credit unions
9. Recently established consumer cooperatives have tried to provide their members with
   a. quality food at low prices
   b. health foods
   c. preservatives
   d. both *a* and *b*
10. The Tennessee Valley Authority is an example of
    a. a cooperative
    b. a profit-making business
    c. a publicly owned organization
    d. a sole proprietorship
11. The topic sentence of paragraph 9 is
    a. sentence 1
    b. sentence 2
    c. sentence 3
    d. sentence 4
12. Paragraph 9 is the key paragraph of the section headed "Profit-making Businesses." The rest of the section has not been included here. According to the information in the paragraph, what forms of a profit-making business would you expect to find discussed in the rest of the section? List them below.

    ____

    ____

    ____

Task 18
Reading Special Subjects: Mathematics and the Natural Sciences

Mathematics

The *particular* information included in a subject influences the way the information is organized and explained in a textbook. For instance, in mathematics you learn to use specifically defined numbers and symbols to solve problems. Thus, an idea or concept in mathematics will usually be explained in your textbook through definitions, examples, and problems to solve.

Quite often, you must use a table when you are solving a problem in mathematics. A math table gives you the values of certain numbers, such as square roots, or of certain measurements. When you survey your math textbook, you should become familiar with the tables included in the book. Usually, the tables are in the back of the book. Using the tables can simplify the figuring you have to do in solving a problem. In some cases, tables give the basic information you need in working a problem.

Answers to some or all of the problems may also be included in your textbook. The answers may be in the back of the book, at the ends of chapters, or even after each set of problems. When you survey your math textbook, you should find any answers that are given so you can check your own work as you study.

All math textbooks are not exactly alike, of course. However, math ideas are often organized and explained as shown in Figures 18.1*a-c* on pages 132–134. The notes in the margin tell you what information is given and explain how you would study the section.

2–10 Equivalent Measurements

section heading [equivalent means "equal"]

When Joe Hicks went out for basketball, the school doctor's report gave his height as 75 inches. A newspaper story on the team gave Joe's height as 6 feet 3 inches. Did the newspaper make a mistake? To find out, study the following example.

problem stated in words– facts given: 75 inches and 6 feet 3 inches → question to be answered: Is 75 inches the same as 6 feet 3 inches?

EXAMPLE 1

Express 6 ft. 3 in. as a number of inches.

example problem — *How many inches are there in 6 feet 3 inches?*

Solution. From the Table of Measurements on page 418, [page 134]

$$1 \text{ ft.} = 12 \text{ in.}$$

To compute the number of inches in 6 ft. 3 in., you work as follows:

$$\begin{array}{r} 12 \\ \times\ 6 \\ \hline 72 \end{array} \text{ (inches in 6 ft.)} \qquad \begin{array}{r} 72 \\ +\ 3 \\ \hline 75 \end{array}$$

Then 6 ft. 3 in. = **75 in.**

answer to problem

1. Find the number of inches in a foot.
2. Multiply 12 (the number of inches in a foot) by 6 (the number of feet given in the problem).
3. Add the result of 12×6 (72) and the 3 inches given in the problem.
4. The number of inches in 6 feet 3 inches equals 75.
5. Therefore, 6 feet 3 inches and 75 inches are the same or equal.

The example shows that Joe's height can be expressed either as 75 in. or as 6 ft. 3 in. The measurements 6 ft. 3 in. and 75 in. are **equivalent.**

The ability to convert a measurement from one form to another is a valuable skill. The exercises in this book will help you to gain this skill. In your work with measurements, you will usually be asked to give your answers in *basic form.*

Basic Form of a Measurement

A measurement is in basic form when the numbers used in stating it
(1) cannot be made smaller by the use of a larger unit of measurement;
(2) are whole numbers.

definition

Figure 18.1a. Sample Math Textbook Page

Lawrence Hyman, Irwin N. Sokol, and Richard L. Spreckelmeyer, *Modern Basic Mathematics* (Boston: Houghton Mifflin Company, 1975), p. 60. Copyright © 1975 by Houghton Mifflin Company. Used by permission.

example question to be answered

Thus, *none* of the following equivalent measurements are in basic form. (Why?)

56 in. 4 ft. 8 in. $4\frac{2}{3}$ ft. 1 yd. 20 in.

answer: 56 inches, 4 feet 8 inches, and 1 yard 20 inches are not in basic form because they can be made smaller by a larger unit of measurement. 4 2/3 is not in basic form because 2/3 is a fraction, not a whole number.

The basic form for these measurements is 1 yd. 1 ft. 8 in.

EXAMPLE 2

Express in basic form: **a.** 23 ounces. **b.** 135 minutes. *example problems*

Solution. **a.** From the table, 16 oz. = 1 lb.

$$16\overline{)23} = 1, \quad 23 - 16 = 7$$

23 oz. = **1 lb. 7 oz.**

answers to problems

b. From the table, 60 min. = 1 hr.

$$60\overline{)135} = 2, \quad 135 - 120 = 15$$

135 min. = **2 hr. 15 min.**

EXERCISES

A **Change to basic form. Use the table as needed.**

1. 12 inches
2. 14 days
3. 6 quarts (liquid)
4. 26 inches
5. 4500 pounds
6. 30 hours

problems to solve

answers to problems [from back of book]

ANSWERS

1. 1 ft. **2.** 2 wk. **3.** 1 gal. 2 qt. **4.** 2 ft. 2 in. **5.** 2 tons 500 lb. **6.** 1 da. 6 hr.

Figure 18.1*b*. Sample Math Textbook Page

Lawrence Hyman, Irwin N. Sokol, and Richard L. Spreckelmeyer, *Modern Basic Mathematics* (Boston: Houghton Mifflin Company, 1975), pp. 61, 62, and Answer Key, p. 2.

Table of Measurements

AMERICAN SYSTEM

LENGTH

12	inches	=	1 foot
3	feet	=	1 yard
$5\frac{1}{2}$	yards	=	1 rod
$16\frac{1}{2}$	feet	=	1 rod
320	rods	=	1 land mile
5280	feet	=	1 land mile
6076	feet	=	1 nautical mile

AREA

144	square inches	=	1 square foot
9	square feet	=	1 square yard
$30\frac{1}{4}$	square yards	=	1 square rod
160	square rods	=	1 acre
43,560	square feet	=	1 acre
640	acres	=	1 square mile

VOLUME

1728	cubic inches	=	1 cubic foot
27	cubic feet	=	1 cubic yard

WEIGHT

16	ounces	=	1 pound
2000	pounds	=	1 ton
2240	pounds	=	1 long ton

CAPACITY

Dry Measure

2	pints	=	1 quart
8	quarts	=	1 peck
4	pecks	=	1 bushel

Liquid Measure

16	fluid ounces	=	1 pint
2	pints	=	1 quart
4	quarts	=	1 gallon
231	cubic inches	=	1 gallon
$7\frac{1}{2}$	gallons	≈	1 cubic foot

To locate the measurement value you need, first determine the kind of measurement involved in the problem. Then, locate the specific measurement you need; for example, the number of inches in a foot.

MEASUREMENTS OF TIME

60	seconds	=	1 minute
60	minutes	=	1 hour
24	hours	=	1 day
7	days	=	1 week
52	weeks	=	1 year
12	months	=	1 year
365	days	=	1 year
366	days	=	1 leap year
100	years	=	1 century

Figure 18.1*c*. Sample Math Textbook Page

Lawrence Hyman, Irwin N. Sokol, and Richard L. Spreckelmeyer, *Modern Basic Mathematics* (Boston: Houghton Mifflin Company, 1975), p. 422. Copyright © 1975 by Houghton Mifflin Company. Used by permission.

Read pages 135 and 136. Answer the questions as you read. Then, work the exercises and the problems under "Applications." The answers to the problems are on page 136. The answers to questions 1 through 21 are in the Answer Key.

[page 62]

1. What is this section about?

2–11 Addition and Common Measurements

Suppose you want to know the combined length of two boards or the combined weight of two packages. To find out, you need to know how to add measures.

2. What facts are given?

3. What operation (addition, subtraction, multiplication, or division) is indicated by the word total?

4. What part of the table does the word weight tell you to look at?

5. Answer the question.

EXAMPLE 1

Mrs. Lopez bought some stew meat and some ground beef. The stew meat weighed 2 lb. 5 oz., and the ground beef weighed 3 lb. 6 oz. What was the total weight of the meat?

Solution.

lb.	oz.
3	6
+ 2	5
5	11

The total weight of the meat was **5 lb. 11 oz.**

Sometimes you will need to rename. When you are adding numbers of pounds and ounces, you rename 16 ounces as 1 pound. When you are adding numbers of hours and minutes, you rename 60 minutes as 1 hour. How do you rename when you are adding numbers of feet and yards? Example 2 shows how the renaming process works.

6. What operation is indicated by the words how much and in all?

EXAMPLE 2

Yesterday Tom Jenkins worked on his hot rod for 4 hours and 45 minutes. Today he worked 2 hours and 30 minutes more to finish the job. How much time did he spend in all?

Solution.

hr.	min.
4	45
+ 2	30
6	~~75~~
+ 1	15
7	15

Notice that 75 min. is renamed as 1 hr. 15 min.

Tom worked **7 hr. 15 min.** in all.

EXERCISES

[page 63]

7–11. Do the exercises. Check your answers on page 136.

A Add. Express your answers in basic form.

1.

lb.	oz.
5	7
+ 6	8

3.

gal.	qt.
6	2
+ 8	1

5.

yr.	mo.
14	8
+ 7	6

2.

hr.	min.
7	38
+ 9	15

4.

yd.	ft.
17	1
+ 29	1

APPLICATIONS

[page 64]

1. Mrs. Garcia bought two turkeys for her family's holiday dinner. If they weighed 12 lb. 15 oz. and 13 lb. 9 oz. dressed, how much did they weigh together?
2. A jet plane took 1 hr. 9 min. to fly from Cleveland to Chicago, and 3 hr. 58 min. to fly from Chicago to Los Angeles. Find the total flying time.
3. Mr. Dines has a board 9 ft. 6 in. long. He wants to make two shelves, one 4 ft. 9 in. long and the other 4 ft. 11 in. long. Is his board long enough to make both shelves?
4. On a vacation trip the Cort family drove for 6 hr. 45 min. the first day, 7 hr. 20 min. the second day, and 5 hr. 55 min. the third day. What was their total driving time?
5. A plumber needs three pieces of copper pipe having lengths of 8 ft. 6 in., 5 ft. 4 in., and 7 ft. 8 in. How much pipe does he need in all?

12. What words tell you to add?
13. What words tell you the table to look at?
14. What word tells you to add?
15. What word tells you the table to look at?
16. What word tells you to add?
17. What word tells you the table to look at?
18. What word tells you to add?
19. What word tells you the table to look at?
20. What words tell you to add?
21. What word tells you the table to look at?

22.-26. Work the "Applications" problems. Check your answers below.

ANSWERS

Page 63.

1. 11 lb. 15 oz. **2.** 16 hr. 53 min. **3.** 14 gal. 3 qt. **4.** 46 yd. 2 ft. **5.** 22 yr. 2 mo.

Page 64.

1. 26 lb. 8 oz. **2.** 5 hr. 7 min. **3.** 9 ft. 8 in. needed; no. **4.** 20 hr. **5.** 21 ft. 6 in.

Reading a math table of numerical values is like reading a chart. You need to read on two lines—horizontally and vertically. The number value you need is at the intersection of the two lines.

The table in Figure 18.2 gives the square root of numbers from 1 through 100. Suppose you needed to know the square root of 10. You would read down the number column until you found the number 10. Then, you would read across to the square root column. At the intersection of the

SQUARE ROOTS OF INTEGERS FROM 1 TO 100

Number	Square Root	Number	Square Root	Number	Square Root	Number	Square Root
1	1.000	**26**	5.099	**51**	7.141	**76**	8.718
2	1.414	**27**	5.196	**52**	7.211	**77**	8.775
3	1.732	**28**	5.292	**53**	7.280	**78**	8.832
4	2.000	**29**	5.385	**54**	7.348	**79**	8.888
5	2.236	**30**	5.477	**55**	7.416	**80**	8.944
6	2.449	**31**	5.568	**56**	7.483	**81**	9.000
7	2.646	**32**	5.657	**57**	7.550	**82**	9.055
8	2.828	**33**	5.745	**58**	7.616	**83**	9.110
9	3.000	**34**	5.831	**59**	7.681	**84**	9.165
10	3.162	**35**	5.916	**60**	7.746	**85**	9.220
11	3.317	**36**	6.000	**61**	7.810	**86**	9.274
12	3.464	**37**	6.083	**62**	7.874	**87**	9.327
13	3.606	**38**	6.164	**63**	7.937	**88**	9.381
14	3.742	**39**	6.245	**64**	8.000	**89**	9.434
15	3.873	**40**	6.325	**65**	8.062	**90**	9.487
16	4.000	**41**	6.403	**66**	8.124	**91**	9.539
17	4.123	**42**	6.481	**67**	8.185	**92**	9.592
18	4.243	**43**	6.557	**68**	8.246	**93**	9.644
19	4.359	**44**	6.633	**69**	8.307	**94**	9.695
20	4.472	**45**	6.708	**70**	8.367	**95**	9.747
21	4.583	**46**	6.782	**71**	8.426	**96**	9.798
22	4.690	**47**	6.856	**72**	8.485	**97**	9.849
23	4.796	**48**	6.928	**73**	8.544	**98**	9.899
24	4.899	**49**	7.000	**74**	8.602	**99**	9.950
25	5.000	**50**	7.071	**75**	8.660	**100**	10.000

Figure 18.2 Sample Math Table

From Mary P. Dolciani *et al.*, *Modern School Mathematics: Structure and Method*, Course 2, New edition (Boston: Houghton Mifflin Company, 1975), p. 474.

number 10 line and the square root column, you would find the number 3.162. That is the square root of 10. Look at the table and find the answers to the following questions:

1. What is the square root of 45? ____________________
2. What is the square root of 50? ____________________
3. What is the square root of 77? ____________________
4. What is the square root of 88? ____________________
5. What is the square root of 100? ____________________

Look in the Answer Key for the answers.

Chemistry

In chemistry, you learn to classify matter in various ways. Consequently, you will often find classification and division explanations in a chemistry textbook. In the paragraphs below, the term *elements* is explained. Read the paragraphs. Then, answer the questions that follow the paragraphs.

ELEMENTS

We can also classify matter according to the *elements* that go to make it up.

Elements are the basic building blocks of all matter. There are now 105 known elements, each with its own specific properties, and its own chemical symbol, which is a sort of shorthand you use to keep from having to write the name of a substance out in full every time. An element cannot be broken down physically or by ordinary chemical means.

Elements can be classified into three major groups: *metals, metalloids,* and *nonmetals.*

Examples of metallic elements are sodium (which has the symbol Na), calcium (Ca), iron (Fe), cobalt (Co), and silver (Ag). These elements are all classified as metals because they have certain common properties: they have luster (in other words, they are shiny), they conduct electricity well, and they conduct heat well.

Some examples of nonmetals are chlorine, which has the symbol Cl (and please note that the second letter of this symbol is a lowercase "el" and not the figure one), oxygen (O), carbon (C), and iodine (I). Again, the reason these elements are classified as nonmetals is that they have certain common properties: they don't shine, they don't conduct electricity well, and they don't conduct heat well.

The metalloids fall halfway between metals and nonmetals. Metalloids have some properties like those of metals and other properties like those of nonmetals. Some examples: arsenic (As), germanium (Ge), and silicon (Si). Metalloids are extremely important in our day-to-day life. For instance, they form the basis of transistors. Without them we couldn't have transistor radios, solid-state television sets, miniature hearing aids, and similar modern conveniences. [Alan Sherman, Sharon Sherman, and Leonard Russikoff, *Basic Concepts of Chemistry* (Boston: Houghton Mifflin Co., 1976), p. 35. Copyright © 1976 by Houghton Mifflin Company. Used by permission.]

Circle the letter of the correct answer in questions 1, 2, and 8 and fill in the answers to questions 3–7.

1. The paragraphs are about
   a. substances
   b. elements
   c. shorthand
   d. symbols

2. The kinds of elements discussed are
   a. metals
   b. metalloids
   c. nonmetals
   d. all of the above

3. List five examples of metallic elements, with their chemical symbols.

4. List three properties of metallic elements.

5. List four examples of nonmetals, with their chemical symbols.

6. List three properties of nonmetals.

7. List three examples of metalloids, with their chemical symbols.

8. The paragraphs say that metalloids are used in
   a. transistor radios
   b. solid-state television sets
   c. miniature hearing aids
   d. all of the above

Look in the Answer Key for the answers.

Biology

The paragraphs below are from a biology textbook. They also contain a classification and division explanation. The paragraphs tell you about the parts of a cell and the important chemical in the cell. Read the paragraphs. Then, answer the questions that follow the paragraphs.

WHAT IS A CELL?

Look about you. The people in the street, the birds sitting on the branch of a tree, and even the tree itself—all of these have something in common. They and all other living things are made up of tiny building blocks of life, called *cells.*

These cells are so small that you need a microscope to see them. And yet they are much more complicated than wooden building blocks.

Just as blocks can be used to build various structures—houses and bridges and tunnels—nature uses her building blocks, the cells, to make more than a million different kinds of living creatures. From tiny cells are made huge whales, larger than a house. But the cells in a timid little mouse, hiding in a dark corner, are just as large as the cells in the whale. For it is not the size of an animal's cells that makes it large or small, but how many cells it has.

Plants, too, are made of the same kind of building blocks. The giant redwood trees in California are made of tiny cells, and so is the grass on the front lawn.

But what *is* a cell? Just as the words of our language are made up of letters, our bodies are made up of cells, the basic units of life. And just as there are different letters in the alphabet, there are many kinds of cells. They have different sizes and shapes, and they have different functions.

Some cells look like tiny ice cubes; others are long and thin, and may stretch for inches or even a few feet. There are cells that look like little rods or balls, or doughnuts without the hole in the middle. Others look like kites or tadpoles. Some have no fixed shape at all, but merely look like blobs of jelly.

Some cells carry messages to and fro in our bodies. Others help us to walk and talk by pulling on our bones. Still others fight germs and help to keep us well.

Although most cells are smaller than the point of a pin, each is a busy factory. There are thousands of different chemicals in a cell, and each one seems to have a special job to do. Something is happening all the time. Chemicals are being freshly made, and other chemicals are passing in or out of the cell through a special wall called the *cell membrane.*

Just as a factory has a main office, which tells all the workers what jobs to do, the cell also has a "main office," called the *nucleus* (new-klee-us). In this small structure, often buried somewhere in the middle of the cell, are the "brains" of the factory. For the nucleus contains an amazing chemical called *deoxyribonucleic* (dee-ox-ee-rye-bo-new-CLAY-ic) *acid* or DNA for short. DNA is like a master set of blueprints, which holds the instructions for all the workings of the cell—all the chemicals that will be made and the reactions that will take place.

The nucleus is suspended in a sea of cell liquid, called *cytoplasm* (SYE-toe-plas-um). And in this sea there are many other structures as well. Some of them burn fuel and give the cell energy. Others manufacture chemicals.

There are still many unsolved mysteries about what a cell does. But scientists are constantly studying cells in their laboratories, and each day they are learning more about them.

The cells of our bodies work well together. We can walk and talk and play because the many different kinds of cells cooperate, each doing its share. But some cells in the living world live all alone. And they must do all their tasks by themselves.

It seems amazing that a tiny single cell, so small that it cannot be seen without a microscope, can do almost all the things that we can, with our trillions of cells, all working together. Cells that live alone can make or catch their food, and get rid of their wastes; some can move about; and they can even make new cells, just like themselves. [From the book *Cells: Building Blocks of Life* by Dr. Alvin Silverstein and Virginia B. Silverstein. © 1969 by Dr. Alvin Silverstein and Virginia B. Silverstein. Published by Prentice-Hall, Inc., Englewood Cliffs, New Jersey.]

Circle the letter of the correct answer in questions 1 and 2 and fill in the answers to questions 3 and 4.

1. The paragraphs say
   a. all cells are alike
   b. there are many different kinds of cells

2. The paragraphs say there are
   a. germs in a cell
   b. chemicals in a cell

3. List the three parts of the cell that are discussed in the paragraphs.

____

____

____

4. What is the name of the chemical that is the "brains" of the cell? (If you need to, look at the paragraphs to find the correct spelling of the chemical.)

____

Look in the Answer Key for the answers.

Words and Terms to Review

section heading
example
fact
definition
classification and division

Concepts to Remember

1. Mathematical ideas or concepts will often be explained in textbooks through definitions, examples, and problems to solve.
2. A math textbook will often contain tables that give you basic information you can use in solving problems.
3. A table of numerical values is read on two lines—horizontally and vertically. The information you need is found at the intersection of the two lines.
4. In the various natural science subjects, such as chemistry and biology, ideas or concepts are often explained through classification and division information.

Assignment

Complete the worksheet at the end of this task according to your instructor's directions.

Answer Key Task 18

pages 135–136

1. The section is about adding measurements.
2. The facts given are 2 lb. 5 oz. and 3 lb. 6 oz.
3. The word *total* indicates addition.
4. The word *weight* tells you to look at the weight section of the table.
5. You would rename in yards, with 3 feet equaling a yard.
6. *How much* and *in all* indicate addition.
12. The words *how much* and *together* tell you to add.
13. The word *weigh* tells you to look at the weight section of the table.
14. The word *total* tells you to add.
15. The word *time* tells you to look at the measurements of time.
16. The word *both* tells you to add.
17. The word *long* tells you to look at the measurements of length.
18. The word *total* tells you to add.
19. The word *time* tells you to look at the measurements of time.
20. The words *how much* and *in all* tell you to add.
21. The word *lengths* tells you to look at the measurements of length.

page 137

1. The square root of 45 is 6.708.
2. The square root of 50 is 7.071.
3. The square root of 77 is 8.775.
4. The square root of 88 is 9.381.
5. The square root of 100 is 10.

pages 138–139

1. *b*
2. *d*
3. sodium (Na), calcium (Ca), iron (Fe), cobalt (Co), and silver (Ag)
4. have luster, conduct electricity well, and conduct heat well
5. chlorine (Cl), oxygen (O), carbon (C), and iodine (I)
6. don't shine, don't conduct electricity well, and don't conduct heat well
7. arsenic (As), germanium (Ge), and silicon (Si)
8. *d*

page 141

1. *b*
2. *b*
3. cell membrane, nucleus, and cytoplasm
4. deoxyribonucleic acid (DNA)

Task 18 **Worksheet**

NAME ______________________________ DATE ____________

Reading Practice

1. Your instructor will ask you to read one or more of the selections in Unit Four. You should be prepared to answer questions based on the assigned readings.
2. Survey a math textbook (either your own or one assigned by your instructor) and list the tables you find in the book.

____

____

____

____

____

Are there answers to the problems ______ in the back of the book, ______ at the ends of the chapters, ______ after the sets of problems? (*Check the appropriate answer[s].*)

3. Examine a section of the math textbook. Does the section contain definitions of terms? Yes______ No______ If yes, list the terms that are defined in the section.

____

____

____

4. Does the section contain example problems and their solutions? Yes______ No______
5. Are there problems for you to solve, based on the information given in the section? Yes______ No______ If yes, where are the problems printed? ______ after the section? ______ at the end of the chapter?
6. Look through a chemistry textbook. Do you find any sections that contain mathematical explanations, like those in a math book? Yes______ No______
7. Look up the word *elements* in the index of the chemistry book. Read the explanation of elements in the book. Are elements classified in the same way as they are in the example in this task? (See page 138). Yes______ No______ If no, explain what is different about the two explanations.

8. Look up the word *cell* in a biology textbook. Read the explanation of the cell that is given in the book. Does the explanation include the same parts of the cell discussed in the example paragraphs in this task? (See pages 140–141.) Yes_____ No_____ If no, explain what is different about the two explanations.

9. Does the explanation of the cell in the biology textbook also refer to the chemical *deoxyribonucleic acid* (DNA)? Yes_____ No_____ If no, check the index of the book to see if the chemical is discussed on some other page(s). List the page number(s) _____

Task 19
Reading Special Subjects: Humanities and the Behavioral Sciences

English

Some of your English books explain the rules, or grammar, of written English. The *rules* are simply the ideas or concepts that your instructor usually expects you to follow in your own writing. These textbooks are often called *grammar handbooks* or *workbooks*.

In spite of the differences in subject matter, a grammar handbook is very much like a mathematics textbook. In a grammar book, an idea (rule or concept) is usually explained through definitions, examples, and corrections of the examples. In a workbook, there are also exercises for you to answer. As you can see, the method of explaining an idea is like the definition, example, solution, problems-to-solve arrangement of a math textbook. In both subjects, the purpose of the explanations is to teach you a principle or rule that you should use in your own work. In math, you must use the principle in solving problems involving numbers. In English, you must use the principle in writing sentences.

The paragraphs below are from a handbook. Notice that the section defines a sentence fragment, gives examples of fragments, and tells you how to correct them. This handbook does not contain any exercises, and so it is more like a reference book than a workbook. If you were using this book in a writing course, your instructor would expect you to correct any sentence fragments in your own writing by following the directions given in the paragraphs.

> FRAGMENTS
>
> A sentence fragment is a dependent clause, a phrase, or a sentence element (such as a verb or subject) that is treated and punctuated as if it were a complete sentence.
>
> The idea of conquering countries in southeast Asia.
> (a subject plus modifiers)
>
> Running the whole length of the field.
> (a participial phrase)
>
> Since the end of the first faculty meeting.
> (subordinate clause)
>
> To correct sentence fragments, simply add the missing sentence elements of clauses.
>
> The idea of conquering countries in southeast Asia is repugnant to many Americans. (addition of verb and object)
>
> Running the whole length of the field made me breathless. (addition of verb and object)

Since the end of the first faculty meeting, our sub-committee has accomplished a great deal. (addition of independent clause) [David L. Allen and Jane C. Parks, *Essential Rhetoric* (Boston: Houghton Mifflin Company, 1969), p. 142.]

Look at the section below from another grammar handbook. Notice that this explanation is numbered and gives an abbreviation or symbol in the section heading. In many grammar books, you will find the rules numbered. Your instructor may mark the errors in your writing according to these numbers. Your instructor may prefer, however, to mark your errors by an abbreviation, such as *frag* for sentence fragment, or a symbol, such as ¶ for a paragraph. In any case, the instructor's purpose is to tell you the material you should study to correct the writing problem. The numbers, abbreviations, or symbols used in the book are found inside the covers of the book or in a special section.

Read the following paragraphs. Mark the definitions, examples, and corrections that are given. Then, do the sentences in the exercise.

1. SENTENCE FRAGMENT *frag*

A *fragment* is a part of a sentence written and punctuated as if it were a complete sentence. It may be a dependent clause, a phrase, or any other word group which violates the accepted sentence pattern. Fragments usually reflect incomplete and sometimes confused thinking.

Compare the fragments on the left below with the revisions on the right.

FRAGMENTS	COMPLETE SENTENCES
A student *leaving* home for the first time, *entering* college, *facing* many new responsibilities. (No verb—only three verbals)	When a student *leaves* home for the first time and *enters* college, he *faces* many new responsibilities: (Now three verbs)
The arrangement of a schedule, the adjustment to new friends, the management of his budget. (No verb)	the arrangement of a schedule, the adjustment to new friends, the management of his budget. (Now series after colon)
No parents *calling* him several times before he gets out of bed each morning. (No independent clause)	*He cannot depend* on his parents to call him several times before he gets out of bed each morning. (Subject and verb added)
Teachers *who* merely make assignments without reminding the student to study. (Noun and "who" clause)	Teachers merely make assignments without reminding the student *to study* ("Who" omitted)
That he should spend a certain amount of time on each unit of work. (Dependent clause)	and *to spend* a certain amount of time on each unit of work. (Parallel infinitives)

FRAGMENTS	COMPLETE SENTENCES
Because the freshman must become a man, live independently, and think for himself. (Dependent clause)	The freshman must become a man, live independently, and think for himself. ("Because" omitted)

EXERCISE (Revise the following sentence fragments.)

1. The multitudes who never reason but only feel, who never consider but only act.

____

____

2. In a lonely village on the seacoast, where a man can still enjoy the primitive beauty of nature.

____

____

3. Some say that nonconformity has become a fad. Nonconformity for its own sake.

____

____

____

[Floyd C. Watkins, William B. Dillingham, and Edwin T. Martin, *Practical English Handbook* (Boston: Houghton Mifflin Company, 1971), pp. 3–4. Copyright © 1971 by Houghton Mifflin Company. Used by permission.]

Look in the Answer Key for the marking of the paragraphs and suggested revisions of the sentences.

In some of your English courses, you will use a textbook that teaches you the principles involved in writing themes. A *theme* is like an essay or article. It is called a theme to indicate that it is a student composition. Usually, a theme is shorter than a formal essay or magazine article.

A textbook that explains the way to write themes is often called a *rhetoric.* The word *rhetoric* refers to the study of the content, structure, and style used in literature or in speaking. Rhetoric also refers to the use of language to persuade a reader or listener. Since the principles of rhetoric apply to both writing and speaking, you may find some of the same principles explained in both your composition textbook and your speech textbook.

A textbook about writing themes will usually contain definitions of the different methods that writers use in organizing and explaining their ideas. You have already learned about many of these methods in Tasks 11, 12, and 13 of this module. However, in a writing course, you will be expected to *use* the techniques in your own writing. For instance, you will read the definition of a topic sentence and the explanation of the use of examples to develop that topic sentence. Then, you will write a paragraph that has a topic sentence and develop that paragraph by using examples.

As you can see, even though the subject matter is different, a textbook about writing is usually arranged like a grammar textbook and very much like a math textbook. In the three kinds of textbooks, ideas or concepts are usually explained through definitions, examples, and exercises or assignments that are based on using the concept you have learned. The only important difference, other than in subject matter, is in the examples. In grammar and writing textbooks, you may find both correct and incorrect examples used to explain an idea. The purpose is to show you the difference between the correct and incorrect use of a writing principle. In a math textbook, however, you will not usually find incorrect examples of solving problems.

Read the paragraphs below, which are from a writing textbook. Mark the definitions, examples, and exercises. Notice that the first part of the exercise asks you to analyze a paragraph in the same way you learned to analyze paragraphs in Tasks 12 and 13 of this module. Answer the two questions that follow the exercise paragraph. Think of the word *generalization* as meaning the "idea" of the paragraph. The word *thesis* has about the same meaning as the "topic sentence" of the paragraph. The word *illustration* means the same as "example." If your instructor asks you to, write a paragraph according to the directions under part B of the exercise. Space for your answers has been left after the paragraphs.

ILLUSTRATION

The simplest way to explain something is to say what it is and to give some examples of it. So the commonest and most useful pattern of organization consists of a general statement explained or illustrated by examples or details. This pattern is highly elastic—it can fill a sentence, a paragraph, or an essay of 4,000 to 5,000 words. The following takes one sentence:

Main idea followed by five examples

A trunk in the attic is often a treasure chest of things that once were deeply meaningful to someone—pictures of relatives no longer identifiable, faded newspaper clippings recording some triumph by one of the children, letters tied with ribbons or encased in boxes, old notebooks containing primitive stories or verses written in a child's hand, dresses that have been out of style for fifty years but are still lovely in a museum-like way.

The five details make a list: pictures, clippings, and so on—each an example of the opening general statement. . . .

EXERCISES

A. *Read the passage below and then answer the questions that follow it.*

There is always the miracle of by-products. Plane a board, the shavings accumulate around your toes ready to be chucked into the stove to kindle your fires (to warm your toes so that you can plane a board). Draw some milk from a creature to relieve her fullness, the milk goes to a little pig to relieve his emptiness. Drain some oil from a crankcase, and you smear it on the roosts to control the mites. The worm fattens on the apple, the young goose fattens on the wormy fruit, the man fattens on the goose, the worm awaits the man. Clean up the barnyard, the pulverized dung from the sheep goes to improve the lawn (before a rain in autumn); mow the lawn the next spring, the clippings go to the compost pile, with a few thrown to the baby chickens on the way; spread the compost on the garden and in the fall the original dung, after many vicissitudes, returns to the sheep in the form of an old squash. From the fireplace, at the end of a November afternoon, the ashes are carried to the feet of the lilac bush, guaranteeing the excellence of a June morning.[1]

1. What is the guiding generalization of this passage? Would you say that it is a thesis?

2. How many illustrations does the passage contain?

[1]From E. B. White, *One Man's Meat* (New York: Harper & Row, 1964).

B. *Write a paragraph developed with examples which illustrate one of the following generalizations or any other of your choice.*

1. People sometimes take affront when none was intended.

2. Some of the most valuable lessons are learned unconsciously.

3. Advertising often appeals to our vanity.

A. 1. ______________________________

____

____

2. ______________________________

____

____

B. ______________________________

____

____

____

____

____

____

____

____

____

____

____

____

In still other English courses, you will read essays and articles that analyze different kinds of literature. You will need to learn the meaning of the special terms that are used in analyzing literature, of course. However, even if you understand those terms, you may find the essays difficult because they refer to people, places, events, or pieces of literature that you do not know about. For example, in the paragraph below you will find the names William Dean Howells, Silas Lapham, and Horatio Alger. If you read the paragraph carefully, you will know the following information:

1. William Dean Howells was a major writer of the 1865 to 1920 period.
2. In his writing, Howells attacked the romantic writers.
3. Howells wrote a story about someone named Silas Lapham.*
4. In the story, Howells' attitude toward virtue and success differed from the attitude of popular novelists like Horatio Alger.

> During the period 1865 to 1920, major authors often wrote in direct attack on popular romancers. And it was relevant for a William Dean Howells to write the story of Silas Lapham with at least the partial motive of showing that popular novelists like Horatio Alger made an inaccurate association between virtue and success. [Max Westbrook, "Conservative, Liberal, and Western: Three Modes of American Realism," in *The Literature of the American West*, edited by J. Golden Taylor (Boston: Houghton Mifflin Company, 1971), p. 11.]

Until you have read a lot of literature and also a lot *about* literature, you will often find references to writers and to written works that you do not know. However, you can find information about many writers and their works in a dictionary, general encyclopedia, and literary encyclopedia. Read the following paragraph. Then, go to the reference room of your library and look up the authors who are listed below. Use a dictionary, general encyclopedia, and literary encyclopedia. Find and write down the following information about each of the writers: full name, birth and death dates (if no longer living), the title of at least one novel written by each of the writers.

> Even in a society remarkable for its self-criticism the major American writers have not succumbed to the temptation of making the machine into a Devil. Most of the novelists have amply expressed the frustrations of American life, and some (Dreiser, Dos Passos, Farrell and Algren come to mind) have mirrored in their style the pulse beats of an urban mechanized civilization. But except for a few isolated works, like Elmer Rice's *Adding Machine* and Eugene O'Neill's *Dynamo*, the writers have refrained from the pathetic fallacy of ascribing the ills of the spirit to the diabolism of the machine. The greatest American work on technology and its consequences—Lewis Mumford's massive four-volume work starting with *Man and Technics* and ending with *The Conduct of Life*—makes the crucial distinction between what is due to the machine itself and what is due to the human institutions that guide it and determine its uses. [Max Lerner, "The Culture of Machine Living," *America as a Civilization* (New York: Simon and Schuster, 1957).]

*The "story" is the novel *The Rise of Silas Lapham.*

NAME ______________________________ DATE ____________

Dreiser ______________________________

____

____

Dos Passos ______________________________

____

____

Farrell ______________________________

____

____

Algren ______________________________

____

____

Ask your instructor to check your work. On the lines below, list the titles of the dictionary, general encyclopedia, and literary encyclopedia that you used to find your information.

Dictionary ______________________________

____

General Encyclopedia ______________________________

____

Literary Encyclopedia ______________________________

____

History

In history, you study the events, decisions, people, and developments that have affected people's lives. As in any subject, the particular information influences the way the subject is explained. In a history textbook, information is generally explained in a chronological or time sequence. However, a history textbook will also discuss the cause and effect relations among the events and decisions that influence people's lives.

The paragraphs below are typical of the explanations you will find in history textbooks. The paragraphs follow a section about the migration of blacks from the rural South to the northern cities, during and after World War II. The paragraphs are about conditions in the 1960s. Be sure to read the marginal notes, which analyze the paragraphs for you.

The City Changes Black Attitudes — *section heading indicates section is about effect of cities on black attitudes*

(1) Urban life had profound effects on Afro-American attitudes. [*topic sentence*] Just making the move from an isolated farm house in Georgia to the teeming streets of Harlem is a profound psychological shock, similar to that made by millions of European peasants when they immigrated to America. Everything was changed. Most importantly, the ingrained pattern of submission to and dependence on whites, inherited from slavery and perpetuated on white-dominated southern farms, gave way. [*effect*] Young blacks could cheer a galaxy of heroes, from Willie Mays and Jimmie Brown in sports, to Sidney Poitier and Aretha Franklin in entertainment. Increasingly they realized that they were not inferior in talent, only in opportunity. [*effect*] The leaders of the black rebellion showed how to leave behind Amos 'n Andy and become Martin Luther King or Stokely Carmichael. The ghetto itself made blacks a community in a way they never were when they were scattered over the southern countryside. [*effect*]

(2) These huge new black communities in the North had the potential of becoming a fresh and vital civilization. [*topic sentence*] First, however, blacks faced the fact that the inner-city regions, within which they lived, were too often foul, decaying slums. The plumbing did [*cause of or reason for black communities not developing a "fresh and vital civilization"*] not work, and rats ran in the walls. Because the tax base was dwindling, schools were bad and garbage collection spotty. Stair

Robert Kelley, *The Shaping of the American Past*, © 1975, pp. 882–885. Reprinted by permission of Prentice-Hall, Inc., Englewood Cliffs, New Jersey.

wells, vacant lots, and side streets were choked with refuse. Rents were as high as in white residential areas, on the average, and

cause and effect

often higher. Bored, unemployed, and embittered residents often made a shambles of their living areas and preyed on one another by burglary, robbery, or drug peddling. For the last hundred years, crime and violence had been steadily dropping in American cities; despite common myths, they were much safer and more peaceful places to live

cause and effect

in than ever before. But in the 1960s, this trend reversed itself and blacks were everywhere held to blame.

cause and effect

(3) Since there was little money in the ghetto, there were few jobs. Factories were far away; employment was generally out in "white country." This required long rides on deteriorating, costly bus lines, if they even

cause and effect

existed. Since it was often impossible for black men to find jobs and support their families, many drifted aimlessly here and there, with disastrous effects on family life.

specific effects on family life

In the New York area alone, in 1960, one-fourth of the black families were headed by women, as against one in ten for white families. The harried mothers were miles from potential jobs, frequently had little education, and lived in hand-to-mouth desperation on welfare.

topic sentence

(4) When Martin Luther King began to lead the black revolution in the South, the tinder was dry in northern cities. Faced with

cause and effect

degrading lives, young black men were desperate for a means of realizing their manhood.

cause and effect

Fascinated by the rise of new black nations overseas and shamed by the fact that their southern brethren, whom they had long looked down on as crude country cousins saying "yas suh" to the white boss, were standing up with massive courage against white attacks, they sought to join in.

cause and effect

Pulled by their own version of the "revolution of rising expectations," northern and western blacks were ready to set off the greatest social explosion in American life since the Civil War.

The Flaming Cities

effects explained in preceding paragraphs become cause of riots

facts

(5) The beginning rumbles occurred in 1963, when 200,000 persons marched in Detroit to protest discrimination, 3,000 students boycotted Boston public schools to

riots explained in time sequence — note following dates: 1963, 1964, 1965, 1966, 1967

facts

protest segregation, and half the black children in Chicago—more than 200,000—did the same. Then, in the summer of 1964 came the first huge riots in northern cities. Harlem, as so often, led the way. For hours on end roaring multitudes smashed through the center of Harlem, shattering windows, frightening policemen, and looting stores—attacking the symbols of white domination within the ghetto. Then riots erupted in Brooklyn, Jersey City, and Paterson, then in Philadelphia and out west in Chicago. Everywhere the same deep feelings were displayed: despair, alienation, fierce anger—and, paradoxically, hopes for a better future. But these outbreaks were not religious in tone. Martin Luther King could lead a nonviolent crusade in the South, inspired by hymns and the Christian message of love; but northern cities held few "believing" blacks. Particularly among the young—and later studies found young male blacks, usually school drop-outs and unemployed, the leaders in the riots—there was little memory of what had been left behind in the South, only a consciousness of present unemployment and despair.

(6) In the summer of 1965 the flames mounted higher. In August an enormous riot raged for five days in Watts, a suburb of Los Angeles. Thirty-five people were killed, 600 buildings were looted and burned, and thousands were arrested. Then came three days of violence in Chicago's West Side, and another riot in North Philadelphia. In the summer of 1966, riots flared up again: in Atlanta, Chicago, Waukegan in Illinois, Lansing in Michigan, Omaha, Cleveland, New York City, and Dayton, Ohio. Then in Detroit, in July 1967, came one of the most massive of all the riots, lasting for weeks. More than forty people died. (As in all the riots, the dead were mainly black Americans, shot down by police or National Guardsmen.) Following this came more uprisings in Michigan, Indiana, Illinois, Wisconsin, and Connecticut.

If you were studying these paragraphs for a history course, you would probably not need to remember each fact given in paragraphs 5 and 6. Usually, you would need to remember only that there were violent and destructive black riots in many U.S. cities between 1963 and 1967.

However, you should be able to explain the effect of city life on the black migrant and the conditions that caused the riots.

Read the paragraphs below. The first paragraph discusses legislation (an act and a bill) that has helped give women equal rights. You should probably remember the particular acts or bills and understand their influence on the women's movement. Answer the questions that follow the paragraphs.

The Rise of Women's Liberation

(1) President Kennedy, responding to Eleanor Roosevelt's urgings, had already given the revived concern with women's problems a crucially important boost when, in 1961, he had established the Commission on the Status of Women. From its work came the Equal Pay Act of 1963, which covered all occupations except those of professional, executive, or administrative stature. Then, in one of history's more delightful ironies, the octogenarian chairman of the House Ways and Means Committee, Howard W. Smith of Virginia, stuck the word *sex* in the 1964 civil rights bill in order to make it even more ridiculous and unlikely of passage (its main concern was to outlaw job discrimination against black Americans and other minority groups). To his astonishment, he saw it not only remain in the bill through all subsequent debate, kept rooted there by determined advocates, but become the law of the land when the legislation, under Lyndon Johnson's urging, was enacted. The Equal Employment Opportunities Commission, thus created, at first ignored the existence of the word, but when forty percent of the complaints pouring in about job discrimination came from women, it began to take action. . . .

(2) Many court cases were filed that attacked issues such as differential rates of pay and promotion and the denial of jobs to mothers with small children. Everywhere demands were made that the government provide child care centers, so that women could escape the limitations of the home and find jobs. That the economic problem required persistent action was revealed in 1974, when the California Commission on the Status of Women reported that the gap between men's and women's incomes was increasing. This was so because women were still stuck in lower paying jobs, while men, who continued to monopolize managerial and executive posts, benefited from rising incomes. Some forty-three percent of American women of working age held jobs, as against thirty-seven percent in 1960, but while their average annual earning in 1960 was only $2,600 behind that of men ($3,600 as against $6,200), in 1974 they were $4,000 behind ($5,000 as against $9,000). California made divorce much simpler and less expensive by eliminating the question of fault. The fact of incompatibility, testified to by one party, became sufficient grounds for action. Laws preventing abortions were challenged in many states, and some were made so liberal that the number of abortions soared into the tens of thousands, thus becoming a significant factor in the continuing decline in the birth rate. . . .

(3) One clear result of the new attitudes among women was a changed notion about child-bearing. Consternation among demographers—and those who planned public facilities, such as schools—occurred when the "war baby" crop of young girls decided not to have so many children as their mothers when they reached child-bearing age in the mid-1960s. Polls showed that women wanted an average of 2.5 children in 1971, as contrasted with 3.03 in 1965, and about 3.7 in the era of the baby boom. During the 1960s, the number of children born to twenty-four-year-old women just out of college dropped by fifty-five percent. Furthermore, the num-

ber of young women remaining single rose significantly. Thus, though the number of possible mothers was at an all-time high, the actual number of births declined sharply. The sum result was that the birth rate reached the level of replacement in 1972, a fact that has created reactions of both approval and alarm.

Circle the letter of the correct answer in questions 1 and 3 and fill in the answers to question 2.

1. The following legislation helped improve the status of women:
   a. Equal Pay Act of 1963
   b. Civil Rights Bill of 1964
   c. House Ways and Means Committee
   d. both *a* and *b*

2. According to paragraph 2, five issues concerned women. List the five issues discussed in the paragraph.

____

____

____

____

____

3. One effect of the change in women's attitudes was
   a. an increase in the number of women
   b. a decline in the birth rate
   c. a larger percentage of women had babies
   d. couples had a larger number of children

Look in the Answer Key for the answers.

Psychology

In psychology, you learn about human behavior. As in other subjects, special terms are used to describe the ideas and concepts discussed. You will find definitions of many of the terms used in psychology in your psychology textbook. You should learn the meanings of the terms because they are necessary to your understanding of psychology.

Your psychology textbook will also discuss many different experiments involving animals or humans. The important ideas or concepts of psychology are based on the results of these experiments. Therefore, you should read the discussions carefully and understand how the results of the experiments are related to the basic ideas of psychology.

The following paragraphs are typical of the explanations you will find in a psychology textbook. Read the paragraphs and the notes in the margins. The notes will help you understand the paragraphs. Then, answer the questions that follow the paragraphs.

Classical Conditioning

section heading

Learning, as we have just seen, is not restricted to what happens in formal education. It is constantly influencing almost all phases of life. Generally, it is described as the process of having one's behavior modified, more or less permanently, by what he does and the consequences of his actions, or by what he observes. Learning is any change in behavior that results from experience—except changes which are due to injury or physiological adjustments, such as sensory adaptation and muscular fatigue.

transitional sentence

definition of learning

definition of learning

One type of learning is called conditioning, which is a relatively simple modification of behavior. This reference to its simplicity, however, does not imply a lack of importance in the broad spectrum of behavior. In fact, the example we have just cited can be interpreted as a form of classical conditioning. The term *classical* means "in the established manner," and *classical conditioning* refers to conditioning in the manner established by the Russian physiologist Ivan Pavlov, the first investigator to study this process extensively in the laboratory.

term to be learned definition

reference to example in preceding section of book

definition, term to be learned (classical conditioning), and name to remember (Ivan Pavlov)

HISTORICAL BACKGROUND

section subheading—refers to events that led to Pavlov's significant psychological work

Actually, Pavlov's investigations of conditioning arose partly by accident, for initially he was interested in studying gastric secretions and, in fact, received the Nobel prize for this work. In studying the dog's digestive processes, Pavlov obtained salivary secretions from a live subject by means of a tube inserted in the dog's cheek. As the experiments progressed, Pavlov and his assistants noted that the dog salivated not only at the sight of the food but also at the sight of the bowl, the experimenter, and eventually at the sound of the experimenter's footsteps. Pavlov at first called these responses "psychic secretions" in order to distinguish them from the original ones, elicited only when food entered the mouth.

Norman L. Munn, L. Dodge Fernald, Jr., and Peter S. Fernald, *Introduction to Psychology*, third edition (Boston: Houghton Mifflin Company, 1972), pp. 201–203.

This observation was not in itself of great significance, for it had long been known that one's mouth waters at the sound of the dinner bell or some other indication that food is nearby. Pavlov, however, with special capacity for grasping the significance of such an event, saw in this circumstance a controlled method for investigating mental phenomena. Consequently, he changed the focus of his research from physiological to psychological processes, and the results of his work are considered to have wide significance today (Pavlov, 1927).

sub-subheading
term to be learned

The conditioning process. Classical conditioning has been described as *stimulus substitution*. In this process, a new stimulus—previously a neutral one—is substituted for the stimulus which originally elicited the response. We could say, for example, that Pavlov's dog learned to make an old response (salivation) to a new stimulus (experimenter's footsteps). However, we shall see that such statements are somewhat oversimplified.

definition

example

In the Pavlovian method the subject is conditioned, or trained, to salivate in response to the sound of a bell, a flash of light, the ticking of a metronome, or some other previously neutral stimulus. Prior to the experiment, the subject is tested with this stimulus to discover whether it elicits the salivary response; if it does not, it is clearly a neutral stimulus for this response, though it may not be neutral for other responses, such as turning the head or pricking up the ears. Once this is established, classical conditioning procedures are used.

term explained

First, the sound of the bell is presented, followed by the food, which evokes the inborn salivary response. After repeated presentations of the sound followed by the food, the sound itself is adequate to elicit salivation. Conditioning (learning) has occurred when the sound of the bell alone, which was previously a neutral stimulus for salivation, elicits the salivary response. Then the bell is referred to as a conditioned stimulus and salivation in response to the bell is called a conditioned response. Pavlov had a special laboratory and apparatus for studying conditioning in this manner. . . .

conditioning method explained

term defined

term defined

sub-subheading

Basic terms. Our basic vocabulary in this area also originated with Pavlov. Salivation in response to food placed in the mouth is a natural, unlearned response—in short, a reflex. Thus, this response was called the *unconditioned reflex.* The food, because it elicited the unconditioned reflex automatically, was called the *unconditioned stimulus.* When Pavlov's repeated presentation of the bell followed by food led the dog to salivate in response to the bell alone, this salivation was designated a *conditional reflex,* which emphasized that arousal of the reflex was dependent upon a stimulus other than the natural one. Similarly, he referred to the bell or other previously neutral stimulus as the *conditional stimulus.*

term defined

term defined

term defined

term defined

In translation, however, the Russian word *ouslovny* became condition*ed* rather than condition*al,* hence the widespread adoption of the adjective *conditioned.* Also, it became apparent in later research that many conditioned responses are, strictly speaking, not reflexes. For these reasons, the following terms have come into general use: unconditioned stimulus (US), unconditioned response (UR), conditioned stimulus (CS), and conditioned response (CR).

summary of terms to know

Circle the letter of the correct answer.

1. Classical conditioning is a method of
   a. training behavior
   b. choosing different responses
   c. studying dogs
   d. observing eating habits

2. A natural or automatic reaction to a sound or other stimulus is called
   a. a conditioned response
   b. an unconditioned response
   c. an unconditioned stimulus
   d. a conditioned stimulus

3. If you put your finger in a baby's hand, the baby would probably grasp your fingers. In this case, your finger would be called
   a. an unconditioned stimulus
   b. an unconditioned response
   c. a conditioned stimulus
   d. a conditioned response

4. Suppose you bought a new electric can opener. The can opener makes a slight grinding sound when you use it. Each day, you use the opener to open the can of food that you feed your cat. After a few days, your cat runs to the kitchen each time you use the can opener. In this case, the cat's action is

a. an unconditioned stimulus
b. an unconditioned response
c. a conditioned stimulus
d. a conditioned response

5. The can opener described in question 4 is
   a. an unconditioned stimulus
   b. an unconditioned response
   c. a conditioned stimulus
   d. a conditioned response

Look in the Answer Key for the answers.

Sociology

In many of your textbooks, you will find explanations of the different opinions that experts have about even the most basic ideas in a subject. Such differences in opinions and ideas are usually explained through comparison and contrast.

In sociology, you study the various characteristics—the organizations, values, and so on—of different human societies. Sociology is concerned with understanding the similarities and differences among human societies. For this reason, you will often find comparison and contrast explanations in your sociology textbook.

Read the paragraphs below. They are from a sociology textbook. Then, answer the questions that follow the paragraphs.

Uniformity and Diversity in Culture

If we examine cultural systems throughout the world, it seems that everywhere there are *common* patterns and at the same time great *differences* built on that common base. In this section we will examine both the *universal* features of human culture and the *diversity* that makes every culture unique.

Cultural "Universals"

Human beings, whether they live in the jungles of South America or the jungles of a New York slum, face many of the same problems. They all have to get food, provide for their children, control violence, and work out a system of government. Although there are many differences among cultures, it is remarkable that societies have so many features in common. Many social scientists are convinced that there are basic patterns that all cultures share called cultural "universals."

As an example, all societies have cultural knowledge that helps them cope with the physical environment. Jungle rains, desert heat, Arctic cold, and mountain winds; tornadoes, hurricanes, ice storms, droughts, and floods; disease-carrying insects, maneating insects and animals, poisonous plants; are all part of life on this planet. Everywhere people must adapt to their environment, and they have developed elaborate systems of knowledge to help conquer the elements. Knowledge about housing, bridges, clothes, agriculture, tools, flood control, and road construction are all part of the cultural heritage that has been built up to deal with the physical environment.

There has been considerable debate about exactly what the universal aspects of culture are, but control of social violence and

J. Victor Baldridge, *Sociology: A Critical Approach to Power, Conflict, and Change* (New York: John Wiley & Sons, 1975), pp. 92–96.

war, the rearing and education of children, communication systems, political arrangements, and economic systems are problems that confront every society, and every society has constructed a large body of cultural knowledge to deal with these problems. . . .

Cultural Diversity: Cross-cultural Differences

The cultural universals mentioned above reveal some of the *similarities* in human cultures. But on these common bases wildly variant cultural systems have been built. It is probably true that for every attitude or behavior valued by any society, there is another society in which that attitude or behavior is considered absolutely inhuman and unthinkable. For example, modern Americans hold the value of private profit and material goods very highly, yet the Indians of the northwest coasts of British Columbia and Alaska had an elaborate ceremony called "potlatch," in which they gained social status by giving away as much material wealth as possible. For most modern societies the value of human life is extremely high and, except in time of war, the society spends huge amounts of time, energy, and money protecting even the smallest, weakest individuals. Yet this supreme value of human life has not by any means been a universal trait of man. Witness the slavery that prevailed over most of the world until lately; witness the human sacrifice customs of many ancient civilizations; witness the practice of killing female infants and old people among some Eskimo groups when the population was growing above the starvation level. . . . Without doubt, there are amazing cultural differences that give mankind an exciting diversity. Man is *one* human creature, yet he is *many* in his cultural variations.

Circle the letter of the correct answer in questions 1, 2, and 4, and fill in the answers to question 3.

1. The paragraphs are about similarities and differences between
   a. common patterns
   b. cultural systems
   c. jungles and slums
   d. Americans and Indians

2. The paragraphs say that all human beings have
   a. droughts and floods
   b. elaborate ceremonies
   c. inhuman attitudes
   d. many of the same problems

3. The paragraphs say that all societies have developed knowledge about dealing with certain problems. List the problems that are discussed as cultural "universals."

   ____

   ____

   ____

   ____

   ____

   ____

   ____

   ____

4. The paragraphs say that human societies have
   a. the same attitudes and values
   b. different attitudes and values
   c. a low value for human life
   d. a high value for human life

Look in the Answer Key for the answers.

Words and Terms to Review

definition
example
cause and effect
comparison and contrast

Concepts to Remember

1. In a grammar textbook, ideas (rules or concepts) are usually explained through definitions, examples, and corrections of the examples. Workbooks contain exercises.
2. In a composition textbook, specific writing methods are usually explained through definitions, examples, and exercises.
3. Textbooks about literature may refer to writers and to written works that you do not know. You can find information about writers and their works in a dictionary, general encyclopedia, or special literary encyclopedia.
4. In a history textbook, information is generally arranged in a chronological or time sequence. In addition, the cause and effect relation of the information is usually discussed.
5. In psychology, many special terms are used to describe the ideas and concepts related to human behavior. Therefore, a psychology textbook contains definitions.
6. Many important ideas and concepts in psychology are based on the results of experiments involving animals or humans. For this reason, various experiments are explained in a psychology textbook.
7. Sociology is the study of the institutions, habits, values, and so on, of different human societies. The different societies are often explained by comparing and contrasting their characteristics.

Assignment

Complete the worksheet at the end of this task according to your instructor's directions.

Answer Key Task 19

pages 148–149

The term *fragment* is defined in the first paragraph of the section. Examples of fragments are given in the left column, under the heading "fragments." Corrections are given in the right column, under the heading "complete sentences."

Suggested revisions of the fragments in the exercise:

1. The multitudes never reason but only feel, never consider but only act.
2. In a lonely village on the seacoast, a man can still enjoy the primitive beauty of nature.
3. Some say that nonconformity for its own sake has become a fad.

pages 150–151

The first paragraph explains or defines the method of developing an idea (general statement/topic sentence) by using examples. The second paragraph is an example of that method of developing or explaining an idea. The guiding generalization (main idea) of the exercise paragraph is *There is always the miracle of by-products.* The generalization is a thesis or topic sentence to the paragraph. The paragraph contains at least eight illustrations or examples. If you preferred, you could say that the fifth sentence (*The worm fattens on the apple. . . .*) contains three examples—not just one: *the worm fattens on the apple, the young goose fattens on the wormy fruit, the man fattens on the goose.* In that case, you could say the paragraph contains ten examples.

page 159

1. *d*
2. The five issues are different rates of pay, denial of jobs to mothers of small children, child-care centers, divorce, and abortions.
3. *b*

pages 162–163

1. *a*
2. *b*
3. *a*
4. *d*
5. *c*

pages 164–165

1. *b*
2. *d*
3. The problems discussed as "universals" are physical environment, control of social violence and war, rearing and education of children, communication systems, political arrangements, and economic systems.
4. *b*

Task 19 **Worksheet**

NAME ______________________________ DATE ____________

Reading Practice

1. Use a grammar handbook or workbook and look up *sentence fragment* in the index. Read the pages that discuss sentence fragments. Then, answer the following questions.

   a. Do the pages contain a definition of a sentence fragment?
   Yes______ No______

   b. Do the pages contain examples of sentence fragments?
   Yes______ No______

   c. Do the pages contain corrected examples of sentence fragments?
   Yes______ No______

   d. Do the pages contain exercises related to sentence fragments?
   Yes______ No______ If yes, work the exercises. Ask your instructor to check your work.

2. Use a composition textbook and look up *topic sentence* in the index. Read the pages that discuss topic sentences. Then, answer the following questions.

   a. Do the pages contain a definition of a topic sentence?
   Yes______ No______

   b. Do the pages contain examples of topic sentences?
   Yes______ No______

   c. Do the pages contain exercises or assignments in writing topic sentences? Yes______ No______ If yes, complete one of the exercises or assignments. Ask your instructor to check your work.

3. Look up the following writers in a dictionary, general encyclopedia, and/or special literary encyclopedia: F. Scott Fitzgerald, Ernest Hemingway, Truman Capote, and Gore Vidal. Find the following information about each writer: birth and death dates (if no longer living); the titles of at least two pieces of literature written by each author.

F. Scott Fitzgerald

Birth Date ____________________ *Death Date* ____________________

Titles of Two of Writer's Works ____

____

Ernest Hemingway

Birth Date ____________ *Death Date* ____________

Titles of Two of Writer's Works ____________

____

Truman Capote

Birth Date ____________ *Death Date* ____________

Titles of Two of Writer's Works ____________

____

Gore Vidal

Birth Date ____________ *Death Date* ____________

Titles of Two of Writer's Works ____________

____

4. Look in the index of an American history textbook for the following acts and bills: Equal Pay Act of 1963; Civil Rights Bill of 1964. Read the pages that discuss the acts. List the groups (women, blacks, minorities, and so on) that are mentioned in the pages in relation to the acts.

____

____

5. Look up *classical conditioning* and *Pavlov* in the index of a psychology textbook. Read the pages that discuss classical conditioning and Pavlov. (If you have trouble finding a discussion of classical conditioning, ask your instructor for help.) Then, answer the following questions.
   a. Is the term *classical conditioning* defined? Yes______ No______
   b. Does the discussion of classical conditioning refer to Ivan Pavlov? Yes______ No______
   c. If your answer to *b* is yes, does the discussion include an explanation of Pavlov's experiment with the dog? Yes______ No______

6. Look up *one* of the following groups in the index of a sociology textbook: Appalachians, Eskimos, Indians, Chicanos, blacks, ethnics. Read the pages that discuss the group's characteristics or problems. (If several page references are given for the group, ask your instructor to help you choose the pages to read.) Name at least two characteristics or problems of the group that are discussed in the pages.

____

____

____

____

____

Task 20
Reading Special Subjects: Business and Careers

Business

In business courses you learn about different forms of business ownership, methods of management, and the laws that regulate business and business transactions. As in other subjects, special terms are used. You will need to learn the meanings of the terms.

In the following paragraphs, the term *contract* is explained through definitions and examples. Read the paragraphs. Then, answer the questions that follow the paragraphs.

The Law of Contracts

Almost every transaction involves a *contract*—an agreement between two or more individuals or firms that is enforceable by court action. Many common transactions involve contracts of one kind or another. Examples are: using a credit card at a gas station; buying a ticket to a concert; paying a fare and riding a bus. Clearly an agreement does not have to be written and signed to be a contract. However, many states have enacted statutes of fraud requiring that certain types of contracts be written before they are considered enforceable. These include contracts for the sale of land, contracts for the sale of personal property valued in excess of some specified amount (usually $500), and contracts that are to be in force for more than one year.

To be enforceable, a written or an unwritten contract must meet several legal conditions:

1. There must be an offer.
2. There must be an acceptance.
3. There must be a consideration.
4. The parties must be competent.
5. The contract must have a lawful purpose.

An offer proposes a contract

There must be an offer. An *offer* is a proposal by one party (the offeror) to enter into a contract with a second party (the offeree). The offer must be made in definite terms and with the specific intention of creating a contract. For example, the courts have ruled that advertisements and store window displays are not offers because the terms they specify do not necessarily propose a contract with potential customers. Rather, advertisements are invitations to customers to offer to buy merchandise.

There must be an acceptance. An *acceptance* is an acknowledgment by the party to whom an offer is made that the terms of the offer are satisfactory and that the person is willing to be bound to a contract. The acceptance must conform to the terms of the original offer. If a party attempts to change the terms of the original offer after it is made, that party is actually rejecting the offer and making a counteroffer.

An acceptance consents to the offer

Offers and acceptances can be spoken, written, or in the form of an action. Thus, the presence of a bus on a city street is an offer by the bus company to carry passengers; the action of getting on the bus and putting money in the coin box is an acceptance of the bus company's offer.

The offer of a contract and its acceptance must be made voluntarily by both parties. A contract is not valid if one party is forced into the agreement. The contracts signed at gunpoint in the movies would never hold up in court. The agreement of both parties must also be based on a reasonable understanding of the facts. If one party signs the agreement under a mistaken impression of the situation, the contract may not be valid.

There must be consideration. For a contract to be enforceable, each party must give *consideration*—something of value in exchange for the agreement of the other party to the contract. Consideration may be in the form of money, goods, an action, or an agreement to refrain from an action. For example, if Mrs. Leary sells her dry-cleaning business, she may receive an additional $5000 for the "goodwill" associated with the business—the reputation the firm has earned over the years. In return she may agree to refrain from starting a similar business in the same city for five years so as not to draw old customers away from the firm she has sold. In this case, not starting a new business is the consideration that Mrs. Leary gives in return for the $5000.

A consideration involves something of value

The parties must be competent. Four classes of people are considered legally incompetent to enter into contractual agreements: minors (in most states, persons under 21 years of age), emotionally unbalanced persons, aliens, and intoxicated people. Most agreements made by such persons are voidable, although these people do have a legal right to contract necessities such as food, clothing, shelter, and medical care.

Legal contracts must be made by competent people for lawful purposes

The contract must have a lawful purpose. A contract is not enforceable if the parties have agreed to something that violates a statute or that is not in the best interests of society. Thus, contracts that restrain free competition or that involve unfair trade practices are illegal. In states where gambling is against the law, for example, contracts involving wagers or the payment of gambling debts are not enforceable. [From *An Introduction to Contemporary Business,* second edition, by William Rudelius, W. Bruce Erickson, and William J. Bakula, Jr., pp. 56–57; copyright © 1973, 1976, by Harcourt Brace Jovanovich, Inc. and reprinted with their permission.]

Circle the letter of the correct answer in questions 1 and 4 and fill in the answers to the other questions.

1. The paragraphs say a *contract* is
   a. a common transaction in the courts
   b. an agreement that the courts can enforce
   c. an agreement that involves more than $500
   d. an illegal agreement between individuals or firms

2. List the legal conditions that must be met for a contract to be enforceable.

3. An example of a contract is

4. An *offer* is
   a. a display in a store window
   b. an advertisement in a newspaper
   c. something you cannot refuse
   d. a proposal by one person for a contract with another person

5. An example of an *acceptance* is

6. An example of *consideration* is

7. Name the classes of people who are legally unable to make contracts.

8. Name two conditions or terms of agreement that would make a contract unlawful.

Look in the Answer Key for the answers.

Computer Programming and Data Processing

As in business and other subjects, special terms are used to describe the equipment and processes related to computer programming and data processing. In the paragraphs below, the term *memory*, as it relates to a computer, is defined through a classification and division explanation. Read the paragraphs. Then, answer the questions that follow the paragraphs.

(1) The capability of a computer to indefinitely store and retrieve information is one of its fundamental and most essential facilities. This facility is called its *memory.* What does the word "memory" actually mean? When a human being remembers something, he recalls it instantaneously from a storage area within his brain. In many respects, although this is still a strongly disputed point, the storage devices of a computer are similar to the storage area of a human brain. Instructions and data facts are stored in the computer's memory where they may be rapidly recalled whenever needed.

(2) There are two classifications of computer memory: *internal* and *auxiliary. Internal memory* is used to store instructions and data during processing. *Auxiliary memory* is used to supplement the internal memory.

(3) The internal memory of most modern-day computers consists of many thousands of small *magnetic cores.* A core looks like a little doughnut and is made of a metallic material (such as iron oxide) that is easily magnetized. The cores are strung like beads on insulated wires. When a current of sufficient strength is passed through a wire, the cores attached to it are magnetized in the direction of the current's flow. If the direction of the current flow is reversed, the magnetic state of the core is also reversed. This property makes it possible to represent two different states, the first by magnetizing the core in one direction and the second by magnetizing it in the other direction. Since these two states can be identified as the two binary numbers 1 and 0, the computer is enabled to perform all its calculations by binary arithmetic.

(4) A typical-size magnetic-core memory of a medium-size computer will include over a million cores.

(5) Auxiliary memories are used to supplement the computer's internal memory and ordinarily store considerably more information. Common devices used for auxiliary memory are magnetic drums, magnetic discs, magnetic cards, magnetic tapes, and large banks of magnetic cores. [Donald D. Spencer, *Computers in Society* (Rochelle Park, N.J.: Hayden Book Co., 1974), p. 9.]

Circle the letter of the correct answer.

1. The two classifications of computer memory are
   a. internal and magnetic
   b. internal and auxiliary
   c. auxiliary and magnetic
   d. magnetic and cores

2. A computer performs its calculations through
   a. recall of data
   b. storage of information
   c. binary arithmetic
   d. different magnets

3. A magnetic core of a computer is made of
   a. discs
   b. cards
   c. metallic material
   d. tapes

4. The auxiliary memory of a computer is used to
   a. supplement the internal memory
   b. store more information
   c. control the memory function
   d. both *a* and *b*

Look in the Answer Key for the answers.

Engineering Drawing and Drafting

In many of your textbooks, you will read about certain processes or activities. In many cases, the process must be carefully carried out according to specific directions. For example, in a nursing course, you must learn to prepare and give an injection or shot. If you do not follow the directions, your patient could be harmed. In a chemistry laboratory, you must follow directions for certain experiments. Again, mistakes can have serious results.

Of course, mistakes in following directions are not always serious. Even so, reading and following directions is an important skill. You must read and follow directions in taking examinations, in completing assignments, and in learning the processes related to particular occupations.

The paragraphs below are from a textbook of engineering drawing and drafting. Read the paragraphs. As you read, number the steps or procedures you should use in preparing to draw. Then, answer the questions that follow the paragraphs.

PREPARATION FOR DRAWING

The drawing table should be set so that the light comes from the left, and it should be adjusted to a convenient height, that is, 36 to 40 in., for use while sitting on a standard drafting stool or while standing. There is more freedom in drawing standing, especially when working on large drawings. The board, for use in this manner, should be inclined at a slope of about 1 to 8. Since it is more tiring to draw standing, many modern drafting rooms use tables so made that the board can be used in an almost vertical position and can be raised or lowered so that the draftsman can use a lower stool with swivel seat and backrest, thus working with comfort and even greater freedom than when an almost horizontal board is used.

The instruments should be placed within easy reach, on the table or on a special tray or stand which is located beside the table. The table, the board, and the instruments should be wiped with a dustcloth before starting to draw. [Thomas E. French and Charles J. Vierck, *A Manual of Engineering Drawing for Students & Draftsmen*, nineteenth edition (New York: McGraw-Hill Book Co., 1966), p. 28.]

1. The paragraphs are about the steps or procedures to use in ______________________________

2. List the steps or procedures that are discussed in the paragraphs.
____
____
____
____
____

Look in the Answer Key for the answers.

Foods and Nutrition

The paragraphs below are about the different methods of mixing cakes. The paragraphs explain the steps or procedures you should follow in each method. Read the paragraphs carefully. Be prepared to answer questions about the way the paragraphs are organized and the methods of explaining that are used. Be prepared, also, to answer questions about the directions given for the different mixing methods.

MIXING METHODS

(1) Several methods, which vary in the time required for mixing and in the quality of the cake produced, are now used for combining the ingredients of cakes. Any one of the methods must be followed carefully in all its details to insure success.

(2) One of the most rapid but least satisfactory methods of making cake with plastic shortening is the muffin method. The dry ingredients including the sugar are sifted together; the beaten egg, milk, and melted fat are combined, added to the dry ingredients, and beaten until smooth. Cakes made by this method are usually acceptable when warm, especially if they are served with a sauce, but do not keep so well as cakes made by some of the other methods.

(3) Oil can be used in cakes by a modification of the muffin method.[1] The flour, sugar, baking powder, and salt are sifted into a bowl; and the oil, egg yolks, liquid, and flavoring are added in the order mentioned. They are mixed thoroughly, and then the batter is folded into stiffly beaten egg whites. Sometimes only part of the sugar is sifted with the flour, while the remainder is beaten into the egg whites.

[1]H. B. Ohlrogge and G. Sunderlin. Factors Affecting the Quality of Cakes Made with Oil. *Journal of The American Dietetic Association*, 24: 213–216 (1948).

(4) The conventional method of mixing requires more time than the other methods discussed in this section. A solid fat such as hydrogenated fat is creamed until soft and plastic. Sugar is then added gradually with much creaming and mixing until the mass is light, fluffy, and of about the consistency of whipped cream. Many air bubbles are beaten into the mixture during this process. For yellow cake, either beaten eggs or egg yolks are added to and thoroughly blended with the creamed fat and sugar. The flour, baking powder, and salt are sifted together, and about one-fifth of these dry ingredients is added and mixed thoroughly for about half a minute. Flavoring is blended with the milk, which is added to the creamed mixture alternately with the dry ingredients in about four portions. After each addition of milk, the mixture is stirred slightly. After each addition of flour, it is mixed thoroughly but for no longer than about ten seconds. After the last portion of flour has been added, the mixture is beaten for about fifteen seconds if a tartrate or phosphate baking powder is used and for about one minute if a SAS-phosphate baking powder is used. If the eggs were separated or if white cake is being made, whites beaten stiff but not dry are folded into the batter after all the other ingredients have been added. The egg whites are mixed thoroughly for about one-half minute so that they will be well blended with the other ingredients. When an electric mixer is used, gradual addition of the ingredients is less important than in hand mixing. The fat, sugar, and eggs can be put into the mixing bowl at once and beaten together thoroughly, or the fat and sugar can be beaten together before the eggs are added. Sifted dry ingredients are added alternately with milk as when a cake is made by hand. Egg whites are folded into the batter by hand or for a short time at a low speed with a mixer. [Glayds E. Vail, Jean A. Phillips, Lucile Osborn Rust, Ruth M. Griswold, and Margaret M. Justin, *Foods*, sixth edition (Boston: Houghton Mifflin Company, 1973), p. 325. Copyright © 1973 by Houghton Mifflin Company. Used by permission.]

Fill in the answers to questions 1 through 9.

1. In the above paragraphs, the topic is *mixing methods.* The topic is treated as a classification in organizing the information in the paragraphs. Thus, *mixing methods* is the classification being discussed. What are the divisions of that term which are explained in the paragraphs? List the names or terms that identify the divisions.

____

____

____

2. If you were mixing a cake by the method explained in paragraph 2, list the steps or procedures (in order) that you would follow.

____

____

3. Why is the mixing method explained in paragraph 2 the least satisfactory mixing method?

4. If you were mixing a cake by the method explained in paragraph 3, list the procedures (in order) that you would follow.

5. If you wanted to know more about the mixing method explained in paragraph 3, what article could you read?

6. How does the method explained in paragraph 3 differ from the method explained in paragraph 2?

7. If you were in a hurry and wanted to make a cake that would keep for several days, what mixing method would you use?

8. If you found out late one afternoon that you were going to have company for dinner, what mixing method would you use if you wanted to have cake for dessert?

---

9. If you were not in a hurry and wanted to make a cake, what mixing method would you use?

Look in the Answer Key for the answers.

Words and Terms to Review

definition
example
classification and division

Concepts to Remember

1. In business courses, you learn about different forms of business ownership, methods of management, and laws that regulate business and business transactions.
2. There are special terms used in business, and you will need to learn the meanings of the terms. In business textbooks, the meanings of the terms are usually explained through definitions and examples.
3. Special terms are used to describe the equipment and processes related to computer programming and data processing. The terms are sometimes defined through classification and division.
4. In many subjects, you must learn to carry out certain processes. Textbooks often give specific directions for the processes. You will need to read and follow the directions carefully.

Assignment

Complete the worksheet at the end of this task according to your instructor's directions.

Answer Key Task 20

page 171

1. *b*
2. There must be an offer, an acceptance, a consideration, competent parties, and a lawful purpose.
3. Examples of contracts are using a credit card at a gas station, buying a ticket to a concert, paying a fare and riding a bus. You could also list the sale of land or of personal property. If you listed other examples, ask your instructor to check your answer.
4. *d*

5. An example of an *acceptance* is getting on a bus and putting money in the coin box. If you listed a different example, ask your instructor to check your answer.
6. An example of a *consideration* is money, goods, an action, or something of value given by one party in exchange for some agreement from the other party to the contract.
7. The classes of people unable to make legal contracts are minors, emotionally unbalanced persons, aliens, and intoxicated people.
8. Two conditions or terms of agreement that would make a contract unlawful are those that would restrain free competition or involve unfair trade practices.

pages 172–173

1. *b*
2. *c*
3. *c*
4. *d*

page 174

1. The paragraphs are about preparing for drawing (or drafting).
2. The steps or procedures in preparing to draw are (a) setting the drawing table so the light comes from the left; (b) adjusting the drawing table to a convenient height; (c) inclining the board for your working position; (d) placing the instruments within easy reach, on or beside the drawing table; and (e) dusting the table, board, and instruments.

pages 175–177

1. The divisions are the three mixing methods that are discussed: muffin method, modification of the muffin method, and conventional method.
2. In mixing a cake by the method explained in paragraph 2, you would (a) sift together the dry ingredients; (b) combine the beaten eggs, milk, and melted fat; (c) add the combined liquid ingredients (eggs, milk, and fat) to the dry ingredients; and (d) beat until smooth.
3. The mixing method explained in paragraph 2 is the least satisfactory method because cakes made by this method do not keep as well as cakes mixed by other methods.
4. If you were mixing a cake by the method explained in paragraph 3, you would (a) sift the flour, sugar, baking powder, and salt into a bowl; (b) add the oil; (c) add the egg yolks; (d) add the liquid; (e) add the flavoring; (f) mix thoroughly; (g) fold the batter into stiffly beaten egg whites. [Note: Although the paragraph does not tell you to do so, you would have to beat the egg whites before you could do the procedure under *g*.]
5. You could read the article listed in the footnote: "Factors Affecting the Quality of Cakes Made with Oil."
6. In the mixing method in paragraph 3, the liquid ingredients are added one at a time and in a particular order. In the method in paragraph 2, the liquid ingredients are combined and added to the dry ingredients all at the same time. Also, in the method in paragraph 3, the egg yolks and whites are beaten separately, and the batter is folded into the egg

whites as the last step in the method.

7. If you were in a hurry and wanted to make a cake that would keep for several days, you would use the method in paragraph 3.
8. If you were in a hurry and wanted to make a cake you could serve right away, you would use the mixing method in paragraph 2.
9. If you were not in a hurry and wanted to make a cake, you would use the mixing method in paragraph 4.

Task 20 **Worksheet**

NAME ______________________________ DATE __________

Reading Practice

1. Use a business textbook and look up *contract* or *contracts* in the index. Read the pages that discuss contracts. Then, answer the following questions.

   a. Do the pages discuss the legal conditions that must be met for a contract to be enforceable? Yes______ No______

   b. If the answer to *a* is yes, are the legal conditions the same five legal conditions you found in the paragraphs on pages 169–170? Yes______ No______

   c. If the answer to *b* is no, list the differences in the two explanations.

____

____

____

____

____

____

2. Look up the terms *software* and *hardware* in the index of a computer programming or data processing textbook. Read the pages that define the terms. If you cannot find the terms, ask your instructor for help. Then, answer the following questions.

a. *Meaning of* ***Software*** ______________________________

____

b. *Meaning of* ***Hardware*** ______________________________

____

Readings **Unit Four**

In this unit, you will find a collection of articles and textbook excerpts. Your instructor will want you to read some of them and use the reading skills you have learned in this module.

Reading 1 High Cost of Japanese School Exams

School exams in Japan take a harsh annual toll in disappointments, nervous breakdowns and suicides.

Through the months prior to exam season, hundreds of thousands of Japanese youngsters almost disappear from sight losing themselves in countless hours of preparation, depriving themselves—or being deprived by their parents—of almost every recreation.

Primary school children tell each other "four you pass; five you fail," meaning that those who sleep four hours a night or less during the pre-exam period will pass, while those who sleep five hours or more will fail.

Many students attend special schools where they are taught nothing more than how to take tests—there are about 650,000 such schools operating across Japan.

Millions of students and their parents go beyond the extra preparation time just in case—traveling to lucky temples and shrines throughout the country where they write prayers on small wooden plates and fasten them to altars or sacred trees.

Some who do not pass their exams end their lives, but suicides are not limited to those who fail. Excellent students have fallen victim because they couldn't stand the pressure any longer.

For several years, special classes have been treating children with "schoolphobia," a malady that apparently affects bright students more than dull ones.

There is talk in Japan about the need to convince the public that the anxieties of the exam season are not worth the human cost but it probably won't work because every student's future role is pretty much set by how he does in exams and thus, the ranking schools for which he can qualify.

Michael Berger, "Japan's Educational Rat Race." Reprinted with permission from *The New Leader*, March 15, 1976.

Reading 2 Why the Sky Looks Blue

Imagine that we stand on an ordinary seaside pier, and watch the waves rolling in and striking against the iron columns of the pier. Large waves pay very little attention to the columns—they divide right and left and reunite after passing each column, much as a regiment of soldiers would if a tree stood in their road; it is almost as though the columns had not been there. But the short

Sir James Jeans, *The Stars in Their Courses* (Cambridge: Cambridge University Press, 1948).

waves and ripples find the columns of the pier a much more formidable obstacle. When the short waves impinge on the columns, they are reflected back and spread as new ripples in all directions. To use the technical term, they are "scattered." The obstacle provided by the iron columns hardly affects the long waves at all, but scatters the short ripples.

We have been watching a sort of working model of the way in which sunlight struggles through the earth's atmosphere. Between us on earth and outer space the atmosphere interposes innumerable obstacles in the form of molecules of air, tiny droplets of water, and small particles of dust. These are represented by the columns of the pier.

The waves of the sea represent the sunlight. We know that sunlight is a blend of many colors—as we can prove for ourselves by passing it through a prism, or even through a jug of water, or as nature demonstrates to us when she passes it through the raindrops of a summer shower and produces a rainbow. We also know that light consists of waves, and that the different colors of light are produced by waves of different lengths, red light by long waves and blue light by short waves. The mixture of waves which constitutes sunlight has to struggle past the columns of the pier. And these obstacles treat the light waves much as the columns of the pier treat the sea-waves. The long waves which constitute red light are hardly affected but the short waves which constitute blue light are scattered in all directions.

Thus the different constituents of sunlight are treated in different ways as they struggle through the earth's atmosphere. A wave of blue light may be scattered by a dust particle, and turned out of its course. After a time a second dust particle again turns it out of its course, and so on, until finally it enters our eyes by a path as zigzag as that of a flash of lightning. Consequently the blue waves of the sunlight enter our eyes from all directions. And that is why the sky looks blue.

Reading 3 How the Mouse Motor Ultimately Failed and Other Tales

No article on strange inventions would be complete without the mouse-motor. The idea came to an eccentric New Yorker named Hatton from studying an unusual toy. It was a little drum which turned on an axle and in which there was imprisoned a mouse. The mouse ran around the circular walls trying to find its way out, with the result that the drum rotated faster and faster as the mouse increased speed.

Mr. Hatton studied the toy carefully and then copied it on a large scale and in quantity. In fact, he produced a number of drums and filled them with all the mice he could find—and attached to the drums a spinning contraption. Within a short time he announced that one mouse was capable of spinning 10 miles of thread a day, some superior workers raising their output as high as 15 miles. The whole thing was highly scientific and the mice were treated humanely.

They were well fed on a diet of bread and cheese and sugar. Each mouse was taken out of the drum at night to sleep in its own stable. They had an hour's break in the middle of the day and worked a six-day week.

In these ideal working conditions, the mice produced 4,500 miles of thread a year

Irwin Ross, *Passages, Northwest Orient Airlines Magazine* (May, 1975), p. 25. Reprinted by permission of the author.

each—or enough, claimed Mr. Hatton, to stretch right across the United States.

But Mr. Hatton, though in some respects he was not such a bad employer, had apparently never heard of the psychology of labor. He had not bargained with the fact that, with such a dull repetitive job, even mice would lose their enthusiasm and, indeed, their physical vigor, and furthermore that their speeds varied.

At the end of a year's trading, the results proved that Mr. Hatton, with his large and unpaid labor force, had only saved himself a few dollars compared with those who had wages to meet out of their profits.

His shareholders withdrew their support and Mr. Hatton was forced to advertise for mice, which, he said, he was going to train to work in his mills at a steady rate.

He rented an old warehouse and advertised for 15,000 mice. He was convinced that by installing mouse-drums all over the building he could produce hundreds of thousands of miles of thread and make a large fortune. But Mr. Hatton died before his great scheme had been put to the test.

Reading 4 The White Minority

After nearly 20 years of court-ordered integrated education, most Americans are aware of the problems of black students brought into a predominantly white school. But what happens when it is the other way around—when a few whites attend a black school? To find out, Gretchen Schafft, an anthropologist at Catholic University of America, conducted a year-long study of "Greentrees," the fictional name of a Washington, D.C., elementary school that has an enrollment of about 400 blacks and 50 whites. Recently, at the annual meeting of the American Anthropological Association in San Francisco, she presented her conclusion: the whites—most of them children of parents who moved into the neighborhood because they believed in integration—were usually anxious, fearful and isolated.

Although black and white pupils are together in the classrooms, Schafft found they are rarely together anywhere else. In fact, she says, white pupils, fearful of abuse from their black schoolmates, are reluctant to leave their classrooms. They seldom go into poorly supervised parts of the buildings, and the older they get, the closer they stay to their own rooms.

"While black children are vying for the privilege of carrying the teachers' messages," Schafft notes, "white children do not ordinarily raise their hands." As a result of the general reticence of the whites, at least one white Greentrees teacher considers them to be "uncooperative."

White children particularly shy away from the school bathrooms. Schafft says there are no records of physical attacks there, but "the verbal assaults are frightening enough to cause many children to avoid the bathrooms for the entire school year." Several whites admitted they went home for lunch solely to avoid using the school lavatory; one fifth-grade child wet his pants rather than venture into the toilet.

Separate groups. The racial separation extends to two school organizations. The courtesy patrol, which monitors halls and classrooms during lunch, is all black. The safety patrol, which supervises street crossing, is 60% white, and most of its officers are white; whites feel more secure outside.

After school black children play in the organized recreation program at the school, while whites tend to play at home. Whites avoid school sports. Says Schafft: "Not one white child belongs to or plays with neighborhood athletic groups. One senses an underlying anxiety on the part of white parents and children about competing with blacks in arenas where competence might be questioned." In other words, they are afraid that the blacks will outperform them. Yet Greentrees whites often imitate black mannerisms when playing with other whites. Reports Schafft: "Finger snapping and bottom twisting accompany a 'Hey, man, you're goin' get it!' or, looking at the floor, head tilted, a white child will do a short dance, just before the punch line of a joke."

During the year that she studied the school, Schafft asked one class to draw maps of the community, showing their homes, the school, and where their friends lived. Not a single black drew a white child on his map, and only one white drew a black. Concluded Schafft: "For this entire group of children, Greentrees is either black or white."

Schafft reports that many parents are not aware of the separation of blacks and whites in Greentrees. Thus while white parents hope for integration, the school experiences of their children point out what Schafft, in academic but accurate jargon, calls "the imperfect mesh between ideology and behavior."

Reading 5 The Buffalo

Early-day white explorers regarded the buffalo as a fearsome curiosity, but to the Indian the shaggy giant meant life itself. The whole economy of the plains tribes was based upon the buffalo; their very existence depended upon it. All parts of the animal were used; to discard any portion of the huge carcass was regarded not only as a sin against the Great Spirit but against the watchful spirit of the buffalo itself. Buffalo skins made up the Indian's winter clothing and his bed and blanket, his tepees, moccasins, leggings and shirts, and provided clothing for his family.

Boats were made from fresh hides stretched taut over green willow or cottonwood hoops; these later became known as the famous "bullboats" of the mountain men. Water buckets were fashioned from the lining of the paunch. Thread and bowstrings were made from the tough back sinews; spoons, bows, and ornaments came from scraped and polished horn. The massive ribs made excellent runners for dog-drawn sleds. Glue was made from the hoofs. The short, tasseled tails were used as fly swatters. Even the stones found in the gall bladders were used in making "medicine paint." Strangest of all, from the white man's point of view, the foetus, cooked in its own enveloping fluid, was esteemed a special treat or delicacy. Buffalo droppings, or "chips," furnished fuel in regions where there was no firewood.

Pemmican, the first concentrated meat ration, was the invention of the Indian. Buffalo meat was cut into thin strips and dried on racks in the sun. It was then pounded almost to a powder, mixed with boiling buffalo fat, and poured into lengths of buffalo intestines or rawhide *parfleche* boxes. An ideal diet—particularly when mixed with edible berries—it kept the Indian well nourished and free from scurvy. White explorers and later the mountain men learned to make pemmican for themselves. "Sticks to yore ribs without rilin' up yore guts," was Jim Bridger's inelegant but accurate description of the advantages of pemmican over white man's food.

French explorers gave the bison his classic misnomer, the word buffalo deriving from the French *le boeuf*—the bull. Through the years as English-speaking trappers, traders, and settlers poured onto the plains, the name became changed to "buff" and "buffler," finally ending up as "buffalo." Actually the American bison is not a buffalo at all, being of the family *Bovidae*, which also

Norman B. Wiltsey, "The Great Buffalo Slaughter," *Mankind* (April, 1968).

includes cattle, sheep, goats, and antelope. The name buffalo applies scientifically only to the water buffalo, or Philippine *carabao*, and the African buffalo. However, the name buffalo is too firmly affixed to the bison ever to be changed.

Reading 6 Sheep Die Near Nerve Gas

On March 13 a plane flew by. On March 14 the deaths began. Within the first week some 5,000 corpses lay on the rugged slopes of Utah's Skull Valley. The victims were sheep, who simply began dying one day with no advance warning except a sudden loss of muscular coordination, followed by collapse. Autopsies at first revealed practically nothing, and Federal, state, and university investigators were at a loss.

There was one fact: Bordering the grazing area is Dugway Proving Ground, the U.S. Army's main testing facility for chemical and biological weapons. The day before the sheep began to die, the Army had fired several 155-millimeter artillery shells containing Sarin, a U.S. variation of a nerve gas developed by Germany prior to World War II. That same afternoon, 160 gallons of an unnamed persistent nerve chemical were disposed of by burning in an open pit, and 320 gallons of a similar persistent agent were sprayed from a "high-performance" aircraft flashing along 150 feet above the ground. The spraying took place some 27 miles from the nearest sheep kill.

At first the Army said it "definitely was not responsible" for the deaths, which by the beginning of last week had topped 6,400. Then it changed to the view that "no definite cause of death" had been established. As investigators chipped away at other possible causes, the official statements backed off even further. "We are still saying that as far as has been determined, we had nothing to do with it," an Army spokesman said a week after the first report.

Science News (April, 1968), pp. 327–328. Reprinted with permission from *Science News*, the weekly news magazine of science, copyright 1968 by Science Service, Inc.

Meanwhile, the dead and dying sheep were confounding doctors and scientists from the Federal and State Departments of Agriculture, the U.S. Public Health Service, the University of Utah and the Army itself; the bodies revealed hardly any symptoms of anything, let alone nerve gas.

"We've pretty well ruled out contagious disease," reports Dr. Jordan Rasmussen, chief USDA veterinarian in Utah. Painstaking examination of a vast variety of tissues from the sheep showed no abnormalities.

Nor did poisonous plants seem to be to blame. Investigators, looking for culpable flora, combed Skull Valley in vain. One noxious weed called halogeton has taken a heavy toll in the past, according to Utah State Agriculture Commissioner David Waldron, but it could never fit the killer's description. It is usually fatal only if the animal drinks water soon afterward, causing bloat, and the symptoms would be obvious. In addition, thousands of acres of the plant have been plowed under; there is not enough left in Skull Valley to do such terrible damage.

Adding to the mystery was the fact that the affected sheep seemed to be limited to a fairly well-defined area. "There are sheep to the north and sheep to the south," says Waldron, "and they're doing fine." Even more curious is the fact that sheep were the only animals affected. People—Skull Valley has a population of about 55—horses, cattle, rabbits, birds, rodents and other creatures showed no symptoms at all. Almost the only difference between the sheep and everybody else was that sheep are natural snow-eaters.

This seemingly innocuous fact again suggested Dugway as the source of the killer. State officials theorized that wind carried the droplets of nerve gas spray over the low Cedar Mountains then allowed it to settle on the snow that had fallen on previous days.

By this time the Army was just about ready to indict itself. "We fully recognize, with this occurring right on our doorstep . . . that we are highly suspect," admits Brig. Gen. William W. Stone, in charge of research and laboratories for the Army Materiel Command.

Yet the Army couldn't even make its own rap stick. The reason, says Gen. Stone, was that it simply could not isolate its own nerve gas from the bodies of the sheep. By this time, after some 10 days of sleuthing, scientists had managed to determine from urine and tear samples that the deaths were apparently due to an organo-phosphate compound similar to those used in nerve agents, as well as in several insecticides. Such compounds kill by blocking the action of a blood chemical called cholinesterase, whose job is to suppress another chemical that causes muscular action. Without this suppression, the muscle operates continuously, causing convulsions. Unfortunately, this was not enough to pin down the Army compound. Traces from the spraying were easily found and identified by the Army on its own test range, and should, officials say, have been just as easily identifiable in the sheep.

Another possibility raised last week was that the poison might have come from a chemical preservative used on seed grain that may have been fed to two herds of rams in the valley. A similar incident reportedly occurred in Turkey a few years ago. Even if such feed was used in the valley, however, it would have been virtually inaccessible to the sheep, which were at least six miles from one of the buck-herds and 20 miles from the other. Waldron writes the idea off entirely. "I've heard quite a few ideas that I thought were silly," he says, "but I'd have to put that at the top of the list."

So Dugway still looks like the culprit. If it is, the Skull Valley incident is one of the biggest chemical-warfare-agent disasters in U.S. history.

Reading 7 When Driving, Speak Up!

The horn aside, your car has a voice. Use it.

Dr. Jekyll walks mildly to his garage and Mr. Hyde comes storming out in the car.

There are various theories to explain why perfectly nice people turn into wild beasts at the slam of a car door. The very ones with a mouthful of "Excuse me" and an automatic "After you" gesture while afoot take to dark mutterings and fender-to-fender infighting on wheels.

"Territoriality" is one currently voguish explanation. The driver, now expanded to the size of his car, feels more keenly the possible encroachment on his space and acts accordingly.

Maybe. But I think most of the fuming and fussing behind the wheel stems from sheer frustration—the frustration at not being able to cope with the problems of communication created by the interfering enclosures of metal and glass.

Because we are highly verbal creatures, we tend to believe that we communicate our meaning only through words. Not so. Anthropologists tell us that meaning comes out of a melange of nonverbal cues—gesture, tone, stance—as well as words. What communicates meaning are culturally agreed-upon symbols, and drivers have at their disposal an impressive array of these symbols. Stir in a little syntax and you have a road language in which all drivers—if only for the sake of their blood pressure—should be fluent.

There are five basic ways for a driver to communicate with other road users: lights, horn, hand signals, eye contact, and car position. Here is a guide to the effective use of each of these:

Denise McCluggage, *Sky* Magazine (January, 1977), p. 9.

Lights. Headlights flicked from dim to bright and back again have long been an accepted nighttime means of asking an oncoming driver to dim his brights or to inform a car ahead that you are about to pass. But why should daylight "silence" this voice? It's easier if your car comes equipped with a handy fingertip lever that turns on your lights or allows you to flash them with a touch. Flash-flash a warning to a car edging into your path that you are closer than he thinks. Flash-flash an alert to an oncoming car that a danger awaits him just over the hill or around the curve. Your flashing lights cannot spell out precisely that a hay wagon is on the shoulder of his lane or a string of bicyclists is causing detours in yours, but it does—in comic-strip terms—put a balloon with a question mark over his head. And that prepares him for *something.*

Brake lights glow red when you put your foot on the pedal. Learn to play your brakes to make that red glow more expressive. Particularly at night when other visual clues are limited and you have to stop suddenly, tap-tap-tap your brakes rapidly to flash a sense of urgency to following cars. A more leisurely cadence is for more leisurely slowing.

Turn signals are much abused, both by drivers who leave their signals blinking pointlessly for block after block, and by those who don't use theirs soon enough for you to choreograph a smooth path around them.

"Soon enough" is defined by law in some states, by common sense in all of them. Keep in mind: Information is ambiguous if sent too soon and is not information at all if sent too late to be acted upon.

Another gross grammatical error in road language is slowing down to make a turn—particularly in fast-moving traffic—before signaling your intention to turn. *Always signal your turn direction before braking for it.* Braking first communicates only the maddeningly incomplete information, "I'm slowing down." There could be a dog in the road, a bee in your car, or a sudden realization that you've left your credit card at the last gas station. However, signaling your turn first tells others: (1) that you are planning to turn; (2) which way you plan to turn; and (3) that you are going to brake soon. How satisfyingly complete.

Four-way flashers are generally called hazard lights, with good reason. Use them when your car represents a hazard either because it is stopped near ongoing traffic or is moving slowly *compared to other traffic.* Many drivers have chosen to turn the highway into what looks like a firefly orgy when everyone is creeping along on icy pavement, for instance. There is no dangerous confusion here, but it does erode the precision of meaning that hazard lights can have.

Horn. The only audible voice of the car is illegal to use in many instances and considered rude in others. Some of the horn's ill repute can be blamed on the manufacturers. To make a horn audible above traffic sounds and through air-conditioned isolation they have found it necessary to give it a strident and unpleasing tone. What it communicates best, therefore, is stridency and displeasure. Unnecessary. More musical tones can be every bit as penetrating. Still, what you have can be modulated with sensitive use. Tapping at your horn can make it say, "Excuse me; don't overlook my presence," before a hard push makes it blast, "Stupid! Watch it!" Teach your horn a more varied vocabulary and use it more often where it is allowed.

Hand signals. The old waving about outside the window has largely given way to lights, but don't ignore the use of your hands to underscore your intentions. For instance, if you are turning off a highway onto a minor road shortly before a main intersection, a mere direction signal might be complacently read as your intention to turn at the intersection. If a car is following so closely that such a misunderstanding could mean a trip up your tail pipe, add a hand signal to your light signal. Point even. You might be taken for someone who wears both a belt and suspenders, but more likely you will have impressed your road companion that there's something special about this turn.

Motioning other cars—or pedestrians—on their way with a sweep of your hand (motions should be onstage large to be sure they are seen) can also make your intentions immediately clear and cut down on that what's-he-going-to-do hesitation, which causes traffic to congeal.

Eye contact. This is a most neglected means of communication between cars. Indeed, drivers seem to avoid it, as if afraid they might suddenly be perceived as mere human beings instead of giant machines. That's the whole idea. Human beings are still generally more polite to each other one-on-one than they are when machines mediate. Looking another driver directly in the eye says, "I see you." That's often a valuable piece of information.

Car position. A clear bearer of information, rarely used to its greatest effect, is where your car is on the road. If you are following another car on the highway and its turn signals blink on, immediately drop back. Your car's position tells the other driver you have received his message. Similarly, when approaching a main thoroughfare from a lesser one, don't charge right up to the brink, casting doubt into the minds of those approaching as to your intent. Hold back early. Let them see, by where your car is, that you intend to yield. That hesitant catch in the traffic flow is eliminated, and everyone's progress, including yours, is smoothed.

The point in all this is that you and your car are communicating something all the time whether you know it or not. An awareness of the semantics of road language can enable you to communicate information of value instead of frustrating contradictions.

Speak up.

Reading 8 Water? There's Plenty Under Us

Drinking water. Mention it today and emotions begin to boil. Newspaper stories of dwindling resources stir the cauldron. Add "cancer scare" to the recipe, as in the flap over New Orleans water from the Mississippi, and we all grow apprehensive over who to believe and what to do about it. Let me attempt to ease your thinking and offer some suggestions for action.

First, there is plenty of water in the ground beneath us. U.S. Geological Survey scientists estimate a ground water reserve in the United States of over 7,000 years duration, at our present rate of consumption.

Second, ground water is as pure as any water available today. The earth is a highly efficient sanitary filter.

Third, drawing on ground water reserves is far less expensive than treating and distributing surface water. Most surface systems cost 10 times [as much as] the average ground water system.

Jay H. Lehr, *House Beautiful* (March, 1975), pp. 10, 14. Reprinted from *House Beautiful*.

If, as the U.S. Geological Survey tells us, 90% of our water resources is underground, doesn't it seem ironic that only 20% of our water supplies is drawn from this reserve? Approximately 80% of the water we use comes from less abundant surface water sources. Often, surface water is used simply because it is more visible. Yet, it is a fact that there are single wells in the country that yield more than 10 million gallons of water every day of the year.

Admittedly, this vast reservoir of ground water is not evenly distributed throughout the United States. Some of the west central states are not as richly endowed as other areas. Yet, there is an ample quantity of water for normal domestic use everywhere in the nation. In some localized areas in the West, there is not a sufficient supply of ground water for both normal domestic use and agricultural or industrial use. But it is true that even this kind of shortage can be minimized by judicious distribution of the existing water resources.

With surface water purity being challenged ever more, it is time to consider using ground water for safety's sake. For the first time, private and public scientists alike have openly recognized the potential dangers which exist in the ingestion of surface water, even though it has been processed through standard water supply treatment systems.

When I say that 99% of ground water is pure, I'm speaking of the present. The danger flag is up for underground sources as well. Underground disposal of industrial wastes, including noxious chemicals, is a growing practice today requiring deep wells. If this continues, we can expect the purity of our underground sources to decline. By the year 2000, only 60% of our underground water supply may be totally unpolluted. Still, no organized specifications or criteria exist for even evaluating potential impact on underground water supplies. To sweep our wastes underground may create unsolvable future problems.

Many cities in the United States already are served by municipal water wells. Let me give a cost comparison between ground water and surface water in two cities in Ohio.

In Dayton, there are two well fields, covering 1,700 acres with about 60 wells producing $3^1/_2$ million gallons a day each for a total potential production of 210 million gallons a day serving 375,000 people. Construction costs were low over the years, but at today's prices of $30,000 a well and $1,000 an acre, we would have a capital investment of $1,800,000 for wells and $1,700,000 for land or a total of $3,500,000. If we are very conservative and assume an average output of only 125 million gallons a day, which is Dayton's normal water usage, we have a $3.5 million expenditure for 125 million gallons a day or a ratio of $28,000 per million gallons a day.

But now let us look at what a city might have been willing to spend on surface water. The city of Columbus has long been pushing for the construction of the Alum Creek Dam in Ohio, a multi-purpose structure for flood control, recreation, and water supply to be built by the Army Corps of Engineers for a cost of $40 million (calculated back in 1964; obviously, the price will go up). For the use of the water supply made available from this projected reservoir, the city of Columbus agreed back in 1964 to pay up to $12 million of the $40 million cost, then predicted by the Corps of Engineers. For the city's $12 million, they would receive a total water supply calculated at 40 million gallons a day or a capital input of *$333,000 per million gallons a day made available.*

So, you see, for at least three good reasons (ample supply, purity and low cost) ground water has advantages in most areas over surface water. If your community needs more water, you'd be wise to voice an opinion in favor at least of investigating the potential of tapping ground water resources.

Reading 9 Money and Wages

Reducing dollars to cents. Sometimes we find it desirable to change a number of dollars and cents all into cents. To do this, merely remove the decimal point from between the dollars and cents and you will have the number of cents. Everyone knows that:

$1.00 is 100 cents
$1.25 is 125 cents
$ .25 is 25 cents

Likewise:

$ 12.75 is 1275 cents
$ 247.86 is 24786 cents
$1000.00 is 100000 cents

What we have really done in making these changes is to multiply the dollars by 100 to get the equivalent cents. We have taken a mixed number and multiplied it by 100 because there are 100 cents in a dollar. This operation is performed by moving the decimal point two figures to the right, or placing it after the cents, where it is, of course, useless and is seldom written.

In many problems it is very desirable to change the dollars to cents and carry the work through as cents. The following example shows clearly such a case.

Example:

During one month a foundry turned out 312,000 lb. of iron castings. The total cost of the iron used, including the cost of melting and pouring, was $3900. What was the cost, in cents, of 1 lb. of iron, melted and poured?

$$\$3900 = \$3900.00 \quad = \quad 390{,}000 \text{ cts.}$$
$$390{,}000 \div 312{,}000 \quad = \quad 1\frac{78}{312} = 1\frac{1}{4} \text{ cts., } \textit{Answer.}$$

Explanation: Since the cost of iron per pound melted and poured is but 1 or 2 cts., we might as well change the total cost to cents before we divide by the number of pounds. Then we will get the cost directly in cents per pound, as we want it.

Reducing cents to dollars. The reduction of cents to dollars is really performed by dividing the number of cents by 100, since there are 100 cents in 1 dollar.

$$217 \text{ cents} = \frac{217}{100} \text{ dollars} = \$2\frac{17}{100} = \$2.17$$

Hence, 217 cents = $2.17

This shows us that the following simple rule can be adopted for this reduction:

To reduce cents to dollars, place a decimal point in the number so as to have two figures to the right of the decimal point.

Earle B. Norris and Kenneth G. Smith, *Shop Mathematics* (New York: McGraw-Hill Book Company, 1913, 1924), pp. 30–31.

Reading 10 The Addition Process

The modern method of naming numbers is sometimes called the *Hindu-Arabic System* of numeration in honor of the people who invented it. The Hindu-Arabic system uses *digits* and *place values* to name numbers. The ten **digits** are 0, 1, 2, 3, 4, 5, 6, 7, 8, and 9. Each digit names a number, called the **face value** of the digit. Each place in a Hindu-Arabic numeral also has a value, shown by the name of the place. The names of the first twelve places in a standard Hindu-Arabic numeral are given below.

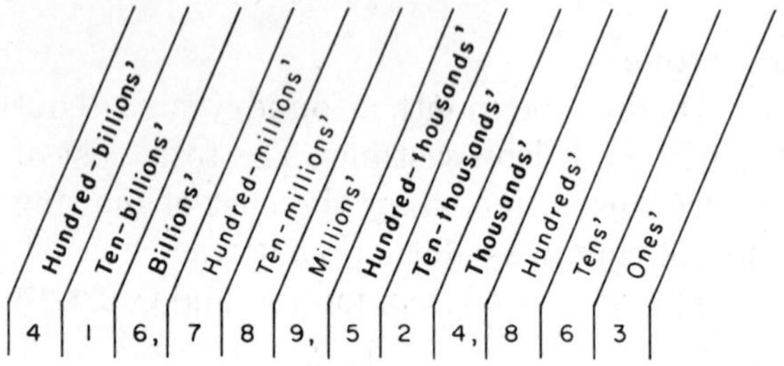

Notice that the **place values** (1, 10, 100, 1000, and so on) increase from right to left. The **total value** of a digit in a numeral written in standard form is found by multiplying the *place* value of the digit by the *face* value of the digit. For example, the total value of the digit 2 in the numeral above is 2 × 10,000, or 20,000.

Expanded forms of numerals are based on place values. The expanded form shows the total value of each digit in a numeral, as illustrated in Example 1.

Example 1

Standard Forms	*Expanded Forms*
24,863	20,000 + 4,000 + 800 + 60 + 3
385	300 + 80 + 5
17	10 + 7
5,603	5,000 + 600 + 00 + 3

Lawrence Hyman, Irwin N. Sokol, and Richard L. Spreckelmeyer, *Modern Basic Mathematics* (Boston: Houghton Mifflin Company, 1975), pp. 38–39.

The expanded forms help to explain the process of addition.

Example 2

Find the sum for 36 + 42.

Solution 1. First express each number in expanded form. Then add the ones and the tens separately, using the expanded forms, and put your answer into standard form.

$$\begin{array}{rcl} 36 &=& 30 + 6 \\ +\ 42 &=& 40 + 2 \\ \hline & & 70 + 8 = 78 \end{array}$$

Solution 2. Here the work is shown in stages. Notice that you only *think* of the expanded forms; you need not write them.

$$\begin{array}{cc} \text{Stage 1} & \text{Stage 2} \\ \begin{array}{r} 3\ 6 \\ +\ 4\ 2 \\ \hline 8 \end{array} & \begin{array}{r} 3\ 6 \\ +\ 4\ 2 \\ \hline 7\ 8 \end{array} \end{array}$$

Stage 2 shows how your written work will appear.

Many addition problems require a renaming process, illustrated by the following examples.

Example 3

Find the sum for 36 + 47.

Solution 1. First express each number in expanded form. Then add ones and tens separately to get 70 + 13. Rename 13 as 10 + 3 and use the associative property: 70 + (10 + 3) = (70 + 10) + 3, or 80 + 3.

$$\begin{array}{rcl} 36 &=& 30 + \ \ 6 \\ +\ 47 &=& 40 + \ \ 7 \\ \hline & & 70 + 13 = 80 + 3, \text{ or } 83 \end{array}$$

Solution 2.

$$\begin{array}{rl} 36 & \\ +\ 47 & \\ \hline 13 & \leftarrow\ 6 + 7 \\ +\ 70 & \leftarrow\ 30 + 40 \\ \hline 83 & \end{array}$$

Solution 3.

$$\begin{array}{r} 1 \\ 36 \\ +\ 47 \\ \hline 83 \end{array}$$

Solution 3 shows how your written work might appear.

Many persons do not actually write the digit at the top of the tens' column (Solution 3); they simply *remember* to use it when adding.

Reading 11 Systems of Measurement, or Sizing Things Up

LEARNING GOALS

After you've worked your way through this chapter, you should be able to:

1. Solve problems of area for geometric shapes like the square, rectangle, circle, and triangle.
2. Solve problems of volume for geometric shapes like the cube, other rectangular solids, the cylinder, and the sphere.
3. Convert units of mass, length, and volume within the metric system using the factor-unit method.
4. Convert from a metric unit to the corresponding English unit using the factor-unit method.
5. Convert from an English unit to the corresponding metric unit using the factor-unit method.
6. Distinguish between the mass of an object and the weight of an object.
7. Calculate the third one when you are given any two of the following: density, mass, and volume.
8. Write numbers in scientific notation.
9. Find the number of significant figures in a measurement.
10. Do calculations using the rules for significant figures.
11. Convert temperatures from the Celsius to the Fahrenheit scale and vice versa.

Alan Sherman, Sharon Sherman, and Leonard Russikoff, *Basic Concepts of Chemistry* (Boston: Houghton Mifflin Company, 1976), pp. 6–9.

INTRODUCTION

Everything we touch and everything we see has dimensions. So we must have a way to describe these dimensions. If you can't measure something, you can't describe it.

Today we take our systems of measurement for granted. When we buy a quart of milk, four square yards of cloth, or five pounds of sugar, we know exactly how much we're going to get. We can't argue with the salesperson about the amount we are purchasing because we are dealing with defined quantities.

In early England, if you wanted to buy one foot of wooden planking, you couldn't be sure how long a piece you were going to get. A foot was taken to be the length of the king's foot, and with each new king the length of the foot would change. Since every country had its own king, the length of the foot also varied from country to country. Having a unit of length that was not defined must have caused a lot of problems in both domestic and international trade. Eventually a fixed unit of length was developed, and standardized measurement began.

FORMULAS AND MEASUREMENT

Suppose you want to know the area of a tennis court. Flat surfaces have just *two* dimensions: length and width. So you can describe any area with just these two measurements, abbreviated l and w.

Volume, now, is a different affair. It takes *three* measurements to describe the volume of a thing, because the thing you are measuring has three dimensions. For example, a cereal carton has length, width, *and* height. These three dimensions describe the carton's volume. A soup can also has volume, but since its shape is a cylinder, we have to figure out its volume in a different way. . . .

Table 2-1 lists the various geometric figures that you will come across often, and gives formulas for finding their dimensions. Let's practice using one of these formulas by doing a sample problem.

Example 2-1
Suppose that a soup can has a height of 4 inches and a radius of 1 inch. What is the volume of the can?

Solution. From Table 2-1 we find that the formula for the volume of a cylinder is $V = \pi r^2 h$. Now write down what's given in the problem.

Given: $\pi = 3.14$, $r = 1$ inch, $h = 4$ inches

Substitute the numbers into the formula and solve for V. Remember that the units of volume are cubic inches (sometimes written as in^3).

$$
\begin{aligned}
V &= \pi r^2 h \\
&= (3.14)(1 \text{ in.})^2(4 \text{ in.}) \\
&= 12.56 \text{ in}^3
\end{aligned}
$$

This means that the can will hold 12.56 cubic inches of soup, which is about two servings.

Table 2-1 Formulas for various geometric figures

Areas (Note that areas are always given in square units: in^2, ft^2, and so on.)

1. Square	Area = side × side $A = s \times s$
2. Rectangle	Area = length × width $A = l \times w$
3. Circle	Area = π × (radius)^2 $A = \pi \times r^2$
4. Triangle	Area = ½ × base × height $A = \frac{1}{2} \times b \times h$

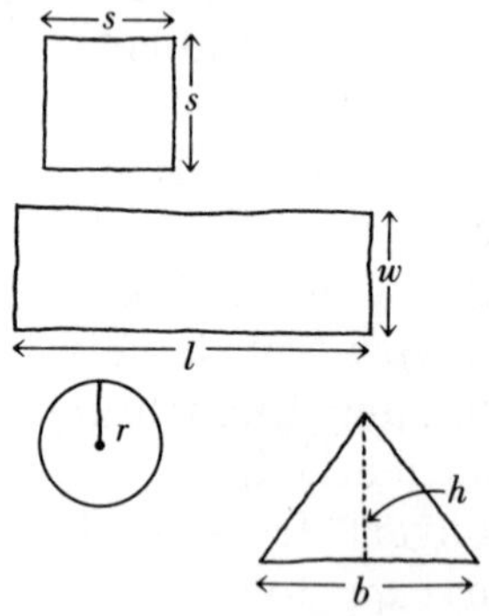

Volumes (Note that volumes are always given in cubic units: in^3, ft^3, and so on.)

5. Cube	$V = s \times s \times s$
6. Carton	$V = l \times w \times h$
7. Cylinder	$V = \pi \times r^2 \times h$
8. Sphere	$V = \frac{4}{3} \pi \times r^3$

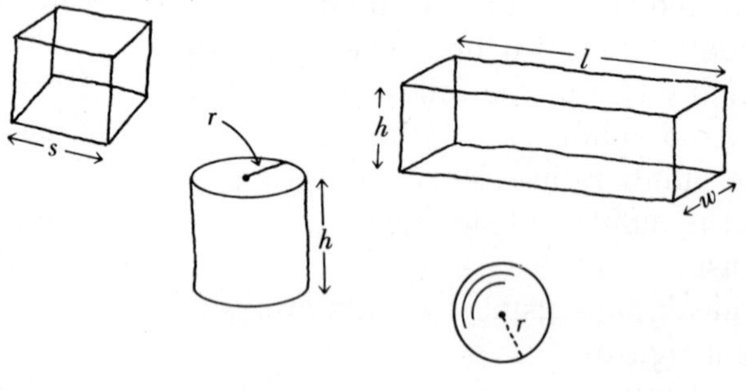

Reading 12 The Stream of Life

As you read the lines on this page, your eyes are moved by sets of tiny muscles. It isn't heavy work, but the cells of your eye muscles, like all your cells, must have a steady supply of oxygen. It is brought to them in the blood, along with many other substances they need. The blood also carries away wastes that the cells produce. Let's see how this exchange is carried on.

HALF LIQUID, HALF SOLID

About half of your blood is a liquid called *plasma*. The rest of the blood is made up of cells (mainly *red blood cells*) that are carried by the plasma as it flows through the arteries, capillaries, and veins.

Blood in the capillaries is very close to the body cells. The capillary walls are composed of flat cells. . . . The flatness is important, for the oxygen carried by the red blood cells and much of the material dissolved in the plasma must diffuse through the walls of the capillaries. Much, but not all, because some plasma seeps through the places where one capillary cell joins another. . . . The escaped plasma, called *tissue fluid*, surrounds all the body cells. Bone cells in a finger, nerve cells in the brain, muscle cells in the leg—all are bathed in tissue fluid. Like the single-celled ameba surrounded by water, each one of your trillions of body cells gets its supplies from the fluid and passes its wastes back into the fluid.

Tissue fluid changes slowly. As fluid escapes from the capillaries, some of the old fluid seeps back in. Some fluid also diffuses into a special kind of tube called a *lymph capillary*. Tissue fluid that is inside these tubes is called *lymph*. Later we will see how the lymph, passing through a series of bigger lymph tubes, gets back into the blood stream. First, let's learn something about the blood itself.

WHAT'S IN PLASMA?

As part of a physical examination, the doctor may take a small sample of blood for chemical tests. It is usually drawn from a vein in the arm into a small test tube. The blood we see in the tube is called *whole blood*. It is a red liquid, rather thick (viscous) compared with water. The color and most of the viscosity are caused by the red blood cells. If a chemical to prevent clotting is added and the blood is allowed to stand for a while, you will see it separate into two almost equal parts.

The part on top, a clear yellowish liquid, is the plasma. The bottom part, made up of the blood cells, is red. You can't see through it. When chemical tests of the blood are needed, it is usually the plasma that is tested, for it is a very complex liquid. About 90 percent of the plasma is ordinary water. The other 10 percent comes from a big variety of substances dissolved or suspended in the water. Listing all these substances would take pages, but let's glance at just a few.

Dissolved nitrogen, carbon dioxide, and a little oxygen are here.

Dozens of substances obtained from the digestion of food are carried by the plasma to the body cells.

Substances called *salts* (table salt is just one of them) are dissolved in the water.

There are wastes from the cells, being carried for disposal.

Iron, iodine, and other minerals are here.

Hormones are carried. We'll learn more about them, and the glands that produce them, in Chapter 4.

Antibodies are carried. They form one of our lines of defense against invading germs.

Many kinds of protein are carried. We'll give three of these our special attention in a moment.

You can see that the plasma is a treasure house of the chemicals of life. This is why transfusions of blood are so important in saving the lives of many sick or injured patients. At one time only whole blood was used for transfusions, even if the patient needed only a particular part or *fraction* of the blood. Today . . . we know how to separate blood into fractions. Instead of whole blood, the doctor can order a transfusion of just the fractions that are needed.

Reading 13 Beginning and Ending Sentences

There is only one way to begin a sentence—a *capital letter.*

There are three ways to end a sentence—a *period,* an *exclamation point,* or a *question mark.*

PERIOD [.]

- Use a *period* at the end of a sentence that makes a statement.

Example: I went to the same movie eight times this week.

EXCLAMATION POINT [!]

- Use an *exclamation point* at the end of a sentence that commands or expresses a strong emotion.

Example: Get out!
Wow!

(Use the exclamation point sparingly.)

QUESTION MARK [?]

- Use a *question mark* at the end of a sentence that asks a question.

Example: Where are you going?

Practice 1
Begin and end these sentences properly.

1. how are you feeling
2. please sit down immediately
3. the students gave the instructor a gift
4. did the instructor give the students a present
5. too much soda rots your teeth
6. get out of there right now
7. he has often wondered how a question mark is used
8. autumn in this part of the country is colorful
9. where are my beige sneakers
10. writing is one way to learn about yourself

Practice 2
Write 5 sentences ending with a period, 5 ending with a question mark and 5 ending with an exclamation point. Make sure that you begin the sentences correctly.

1. ______________________________
2. ______________________________
3. ______________________________
4. ______________________________

5. ______________________________

6. ______________________________

7. ______________________________

8. ______________________________

9. ______________________________

10. ______________________________

11. ______________________________

12. ______________________________

13. ______________________________

14. ______________________________

15. ______________________________

Reading 14 Classification, Definition, Causation

After studying this chapter and completing the applications that follow it, you should be able to do the following:

1. To identify and differentiate three supporting forms of development: *classification, definition,* and *causation.*
2. To identify and write *classification* correctly.
3. To identify and write several kinds of definition: *synonym, derivative, subjective or personal, basic or classical,* and *extended.*
4. To identify and write correctly logical relationships in *causation.*
5. To identify and write controlling sentences that allow or require development by *definition, classification,* or *causation.*
6. To write supporting paragraphs of *definition, classification,* or *causation.*
7. To write *definition, classification,* or *causation* in developing the supporting paragraphs of a full-length composition.

Joseph P. Dagher, *Writing: A Practical Guide* (Boston: Houghton Mifflin Company, 1976), pp. 221–222, 235–236.

The human mind constantly seeks order, and it has developed certain clear ways of finding or imposing it. Enumeration, exemplification, analysis, and synthesis are some of these ways. Three others which we shall consider in this chapter are *classification, definition,* and *causation.*

CLASSIFICATION

Classification is sorting related items and placing them in groups, classes, or categories. Almost everything we do requires some sort of classification. We classify our clothing according to the kind of material it is made of, its purpose, cost, fashion, and so on. We classify people by appearance, age, personality, sex, and the jobs they do. Every occupation requires classification. Plumbers, electricians, doctors, lawyers, or professors classify supplies, tools, laws, medicines, or students in various ways depending upon the standards or criteria required by their classification at a given time. Even writers must classify; their outlines indicate how they classify ideas.

Applying a name to a person or an object is a form of classification. When we call a person a *man* or a *woman,* an *American,* a *New Yorker,* or a *carpenter,* we are classifying that person in one way or another. Even a proper noun classifies a person. Judge Elmer Gribbs, for example, is classified by name and title as to occupation, age, sex, and blood relationship to other members of the family of Gribbs.

The class in which we place an object or an idea will always depend on the criterion and the need upon which the classification is based. This criterion is the kind of relationship which exists between one item and others in the same category. Nothing exists which fits in only one class. Whenever we use any noun, the name of anything—*boy,* for example—we are classifying the person so described in one of several ways. Perhaps the standard is physical structure; a boy is similar in many ways to other boys, and he is certainly different from girls. To say "John is a tennis player" is placing John in a class with other persons who play tennis. Students can be classified according to many different standards; following are only a few of them.

Academic achievement
Attitude toward war, politics, and so forth
Mannerisms
Age
Race
Class—freshman, for example
Club
Physical dimensions, height, weight, and so forth
Interests: hobbies, sports
Sex

Here is a supporting paragraph developed by placing the same subject—the modern college student—in different classes based on different roles performed.

College students in the twentieth century have many roles in which they must demonstrate their expertise if they want to be acclaimed "successful students." They must be logical and critical thinkers, attentive readers and lucid writers, careful experimenters, responsible campus citizens, sympathetic roommates, and adequate test-takers. This skimpy list could be expanded if I did not at this precise minute have to read a chapter in history and outline my paper for sociology before I dash to Drama Club (and I haven't finished my treasurer's report). Then between five and six o'clock I will just barely have time to take my roommate to the bus and get a bite to eat before my six o'clock class in Chicano Literature. . . .

Application 12-3

The following paragraphs are developed by classification. Read them carefully and answer the questions that follow each.

A. The three main types of arrows are cedar, fiberglass, and aluminum. The aluminum arrow is commonly thought of as the ultimate arrow for target or tournament shooting. The close manufacturing tolerances for the aluminum tube add uniformity and accuracy to the arrow, thus creating this common opinion. Many people have begun using aluminum arrows for hunting, as well as target or tournament shooting. This is quite impractical though, because the aluminum arrow will bend if it should happen to strike something a little too solid while in the field. The cost of aluminum arrows is quite high. The cedar and fiberglass arrows are designed for more abuse, both in structure and cost. Although neither of these arrows are considered really good for target or tournament shooting, they are both favorites for hunting. The cedar arrow is considered especially good for hunting because it will ordinarily break after it enters the animal's body; it is then impossible for the animal to work it out. The fiberglass arrow is prized for its ability to endure both abuse and climatic conditions, unlike cedar arrows which warp if they happen to be exposed to rain or extremely humid weather. Everyone has his own opinion as to which one is the best all-around arrow. I choose fiberglass.

1. What is the subject or term? ________

____

____

2. What are the standards or criteria? ____

____

3. List the classes. ____

____

B. Sneezing, the involuntary spasmodic expirations caused either by direct or reflexive irritations of the sensory nerves of the nasal mucous membrane may be broadly divided into two classes, depending upon their causes. These are extrinsic causes and intrinsic causes.

Extrinsic causes are those which originate outside of a person's body. Many bits of foreign matter continually enter a person's nasal passage with the air he breathes. Fumes, smoke, dust, pollen are only a few of the kinds of particles which are inhaled, causing direct nasal irritations, resulting in sneezing. External causes also cause reflexive sneezing. The most common of these is the sneezing which results from the excessive stimulation of the optic nerve by strong light.

The intrinsic causes for sneezing are numerous. Any of the many changes within the body which cause an inflammation of the mucous membranes in the nasal passage are in this classification. Many of these intrinsic causes for sneezing are often lumped under the heading of colds.

1. What is the subject or term? ____

____

2. What are the standards or criteria? ____

____

3. List the classes. ____

____

C. There are four basic seismic waves: two preliminary "body" waves which travel through the earth, and two which travel only at the surface. Combinations, reflections, and diffractions produce a virtual infinity of other types. The behavior of these is well enough understood that wave speed and amplitude have been the major means of describing the earth's interior. In addition, a large earthquake generates inelastic waves which echo through the planet like vibrations in a ringing bell, and which actually cause the planet to expand and contract infinitesimally.

1. What is the subject or term? ____

____

2. What are the standard or criteria? ____

____

3. List the classes. ____

____

Reading 15 *from* Euphemisms, the Fig Leaves of Language

. . . Freedom of the press includes freedom to print ideas that may antagonize certain individuals, since naturally we do not all agree as to what is good and proper and desirable. Except for pornography, we must allow free expression of attitudes and ideas divergent from our own, or we may find that ultimately we are not allowed free expression of our ideas either. One of the first acts of any dictatorship is to burn books that challenge its tyranny. Socrates and Aristophanes were put to death for discussing or writing about ideas offensive to Grecian politicians. (Today some radical reactionaries still want to ban Socrates and Plato.) The medieval church imprisoned Roger Bacon for fourteen years because of his scientific writings. Savonarola, the Florentine reformer of the fifteenth century, burned the works of Dante and many other poets and philosophers, only to have his own writings banned in turn and himself put to death by the authorities. William Tyndale was strangled at the stake and his body burned for his translation of part of the Bible into English. The Puritan William Prynne had his ears cut off and was fined and imprisoned for criticizing in print the court revels of Charles I, who was in turn beheaded by the Puritans. Voltaire had to go into exile to save his life from the French censors. In the late nineteenth century, Zola's English publisher was sent to prison for printing such "pernicious literature" and emerged so broken that he died shortly after his release. The Nazis burned the works of Helen Keller, Stefan Zweig, Sigmund Freud, Jack London, Ernest Hemingway, John Dos Passos, Thomas Mann, Alfred Einstein, Erich Maria Remarque, and others, and the Communists have banned many besides Pasternak.

Reading 16 Chicano Activism

In the 1960s a new generation of young Mexican-Americans began for the first time to make the Mexican-American voice heard on the national scene. They had earlier formed a number of organizations, notably the G.I. Forum, which has been strongly political in its tactics, and the Mexican American Political Association, largely responsible for the immensely popular Viva Kennedy clubs, which helped to place John Kennedy in the White House. More and more Mexican-Americans were moving into cities; significant numbers were rising to middle-class status in income and professional position; and increasingly they were no longer ready to accept the inferior roles they had long played in American society. It was now that "Chicano" became a popular term that spread swiftly through the Mexican-American community. The older generation had counselled a passive role, but the newer leaders urged activism. As so often has been true in the history of American ethnic groups, the new world prominence of leaders and movements drawn from their own cultural tradition inspired a sense of emulation among Chicanos. Fidel Castro and Ernesto "Che" Guevara seemed eloquently to demonstrate that the Spanish-speaking need no longer be passive toward Anglo-America. Especially among Chicano students, cultural identity and cultural pride led to demands that prejudiced teachers and administrators be discharged and course offerings be changed to emphasize the Chicano past, present, and future. The Brown Berets were organized in the 1960s, consisting primarily of high school and college age Chicanos in the southwestern states. Their goal was to unite the Chicano community by their own example of brotherhood and self-sacrificial discipline. While for black Americans the adversary has been, within their own community, the Uncle Toms who would acquiesce in second-class status, for activist Chicanos the adversary was the *tio taco:* the Mexican-American who clung to the old stereotype and role.

Robert Kelley, *The Shaping of the American Past,* © 1975, pp. 892–894. Reprinted by permission of Prentice-Hall, Inc., Englewood Cliffs, New Jersey.

The most activist Chicanos came from among Mexican-Americans in rural areas, where living conditions were the most pitiable. One Chicano leader, Reis Lòpez Tijerina, led a demand for the reversion of millions of acres of southwestern land to direct heirs of those who, under the Treaty of Guadalupe Hidalgo (1848), had their land rights guaranteed but subsequently taken away by American courts. A true visionary (and a convert to fundamentalist Protestantism), Tijerina formed in 1963 the Alianza Federal de Mercedes (Federal Alliance of Land Grants), which envisioned the recapturing of immense lost territories for Chicanos and the building of a confederation of free city-states based on utopian principles. In 1967 he led an occupation of a courthouse in the New Mexican town of Tierra Amarilla. During the ensuing brief warfare with local authorities, men were wounded, and a massive manhunt with tanks and helicopters finally captured the fleeing Tijerina. Jailed in 1969 after an unsuccessful appeal following conviction for various crimes, Tijerina served two years and emerged to find his movement fading.

Far more lastingly effective was the campaign launched by César Chavez for the organization of farm workers. The first Chicano to achieve a truly national standing and to become a unifying symbol for Mexican-Americans in the manner of Martin Luther King for black America, he was also, like King, an apostle of Gandhi's nonviolence policy. Deeply spiritual in his motivations, a gentle and thoughtful man, since 1962 he had been working in Delano, California, to form a union among grape workers. Director of the AFL-CIO United Farm Workers Organizing Committee, he had himself emerged from the extreme poverty of a family caught in the migrant farm worker cycle of constant movement, illiteracy, and low wages. Keenly aware of the need to mobilize the support of national opinion, he attracted students, ministers, and civil rights workers to Delano and by 1968, during which year Robert Kennedy gave his cause prominent support, had successfully organized a nationwide boycott of table grapes. In 1970 his long struggle came to an apparent end when the grape growers signed a three-year contract with his union. Later on, however, the growers began signing contracts instead with the Teamsters Union, apparently an organization more palatable to them in its objectives, leading to a new eruption of turmoil and protest in 1973. Furthermore, in the background was the sobering fact that the increasing cost of farm laborers was stimulating landowners to turn to machines for the cultivation and picking of row crops. In the decade of the 1960s, migrant farm workers in the United States as a whole dropped in numbers from 400,000 to 250,000. Whatever the outcome, however, the figure of César Chavez provided lasting inspiration to the Chicano community.

Meanwhile, urban Chicanos, notably through the Brown Berets, were joining in the mass uprisings of the late 1960s. When some were jailed in Los Angeles in 1968 for staging a demonstration, Joanne Gonzales in *La Raza Yearbook* proclaimed their cause as "seeking Chicano Power for our people so that we can have control over our environment; control over our schools so that our children can receive a better education; control over the agencies which are supposed to be administering to the needs of our people; control over the police whose salaries we pay but who continually brutalize our people." Mexican-American leaders demanded an educational process that was both bilingual and bicultural, thus reviving the equality of treatment guaranteed in the Treaty of Guadalupe Hidalgo. Teachers of Mexican ancestry were urged to retain and emphasize, with pride, their "Mexicanism," and authentic Mexican arts experienced widely enhanced prominence. The image of the Mexican-American in Anglo-American eyes, long summed up in the figure of a somnolent peasant under a large sombrero, was beginning to be replaced with a fresh understanding of Latin civilization as urban as well as rural, progressive as well as traditional, sophisticated as well as uncomplicated.

Nevertheless, Mexican-Americans found it hard to achieve unity. Their very identity was difficult to crystallize. "To start a long discussion among Angelenos of Spanish-Mexican descent," observed Paul M. Sheldon in *La Raza: Forgotten Americans* (1966), "simply introduces the . . . question, 'Who are we?'" Spanish, Mexican, or completely Americanized? Chicano culture, he wrote, carried with it an intense individualism that discourages unity; an intense family consciousness that places the focus of concern elsewhere than in politics; and traditional values often opposed to the hard-driving success ethic of the American urban world. However, the very entrance of Mexican-Americans into the mainstream of American life made it increasingly difficult for them—as for the American Indians who had also become increasingly urban—to retain a hold on ways of life that for many had become remote. Without question, the days of a quiet rural past, in which passiveness and political quiescence was the distinguishing mark of Mexican-Americans, had irrevocably disappeared.

Reading 17 Drives and Motives

HOSTILITY

This is a motive that most of us do not like to admit but that all of us possess. Evidence of it first appears in the child at about the age of two. Up to then, all that he has seemed to want from other people is their presence and the stimulation, help, and approval they provide. But at this stage he begins to want something else from them. He wants—at times—to see them display signs of worry, fears of discomfort, actual pain. Later he may hope that misfortune will befall them and that he will have the gratification of knowing about it.

Some scientists, as has been said, consider hostility to represent a biological trait that makes aggressive behavior as inevitable a part of the human condition as fighting over territories is for baboons and other animals. Others, probably a majority, believe that the hostility motive is learned and that it stems from the fact that the child cannot have everything he wants. Some of his desires are bound to be frustrated by the rules of society and by the conflicting desires of other people. He cannot always eat when he wants to. He has to learn to control his drive for elimination except when he is in the bathroom. He cannot have the toy that another child owns and is playing with. His mother cannot spend all her time catering to his whims. Other children, bigger than he, push him around.

From *Psychology: An Introduction*, 2nd ed., by Jerome Kagan and Ernest Havemann, pp. 349–351;

AGGRESSION

The aggression that often results from hostility may take such varied forms as argumentativeness, scorn, sarcasm, physical and mental cruelty, and fighting. Yet, while most people are motivated at some time by hostility, not everyone displays aggression. Boys and men are more inclined to do so than are girls and women, for society approves of a certain amount of aggression in the male but discourages it in the female. Just as dependent behavior is peculiarly a female prerogative in our society, so is aggression largely a male prerogative.

In recent years there has been considerable debate on the question of whether watching aggressive behavior in movies or on television encourages aggression. Some psychologists have taken the view that it does just the opposite—that it has a cathartic effect that tends to purge tendencies toward hostility and therefore to discourage actual aggression. Among the experimental evidence that supports this viewpoint is a study of the dreams of boys aged six through eleven. The boys, who were volunteers, slept for two nights in a laboratory, were wakened each time they displayed REM sleep, and were asked to report if they could remember having been dreaming. On one night just before going to bed they watched a baseball film, on the other night a violent scene of an Indian attack on a frontier settlement. Although one might suppose that the violent movie would result in numerous bad dreams, actually the boys had fewer dreams of any kind after watching it—and of the dreams they did have fewer were hostile or otherwise unpleasant.

A number of other studies, however, seem to dispute the theory that viewing aggression has a cathartic effect, except perhaps under rather special conditions. It is important to note that people are more likely to behave aggressively when they are feeling frustrated or angry, such as when they have been subjected experimentally to situations in which they fail at a task or receive ridicule. Some recent evidence indicates that a combination of some kind of angry arousal plus the observation of aggression is especially likely to result in aggressive behavior.

Six groups of adolescent youths in a California penal institution volunteered for what they thought was a learning experiment. Three groups were made angry by disparaging remarks from a confederate of the experimenter, while the other three groups were not. All the groups then watched one of three short movies. For all the groups, the first half of the movie was the same—two boys shooting baskets. The last half, however, was different. In one case the boys merely went on to play a friendly game of basketball; this was the film called "neutral." In another they got into a fight, in which one boy's angry facial expressions, shouts, and blows were emphasized; this was the "aggression" film. In the third the boys again got into a fight but this time the emphasis was on the beating one boy appeared to be taking and the pain he was supposedly suffering; this was the "pain" film. Afterward the subjects were asked to help in a learning study by giving feedback to another person in the form of an electric shock every time he made a mistake. The intensity and duration of the shocks were left to the subjects' own judgment. (Actually no shocks were delivered; the "learner" was again a confederate of the experimenter and only pretended to be suffering pain.) The lowest amount of pain was inflicted by subjects who had not been angered and had not watched the neutral film, the highest amount by subjects who were angered and had watched the pain film.

Reading 18 An Example of Scientific Management: Increasing a Bricklayer's Output

The use of scientific management to increase productivity is illustrated by a bricklaying study conducted by Frank Gilbreth. While working as a bricklayer's apprentice, Gilbreth was puzzled by the innumerable ways that experienced bricklayers laid bricks. He reasoned that since bricklaying dated back to biblical times, trial and error should have produced a "best method" for laying bricks, but this was not the case.

Gilbreth analyzed each phase of the bricklaying process: the bricklayer, the tools, the physical positions of the bricklayer and the bricks to be laid, how the worker selected the bricks to be used, and the mortar. Then, taking the best elements of the various methods bricklayers used, Gilbreth developed his own system. For example, he designed a scaffold that placed the bricklayer, the bricks, and the mortar at three different levels, so that they were always properly positioned relative to the structure being built. Traditionally, bricklayers obtained their own bricks and then studied each brick to find its best side before laying it. Gilbreth specialized this function by having a separate worker carry the bricks to the bricklayer and place each brick with its best face up. Finally, to insure consistency in construction, Gilbreth developed a standard formula to be used for the mortar.

As a result of Gilbreth's changes, the number of movements made by a bricklayer decreased from 18 to 5, and individual output increased from 120 to 250 bricks per hour. Thus, Gilbreth's scientific approach accomplished in several weeks what the trial-and-error method had failed to achieve in over 2000 years.

Implementing plans: the use of scientific management. As a result of the pioneering efforts of Frederick W. Taylor, Frank and Lillian Gilbreth, and Henry L. Gantt, the scientific management approach to developing and implementing plans for individual projects is widely used today. *Scientific management* is an entire school of thought that emphasizes ways to increase productivity through the careful planning and execution of corporate objectives. The four key principles of scientific management, as applied by Frank Gilbreth to increasing the output of bricklayers . . . are listed below:

1. *Develop an ideal or best method:* Analyze each job to determine the best way of doing it. Once a best method has been determined, set a standard for average performance and an incentive to be paid for work beyond that standard. Thus, analysis might show that under Gilbreth's method of laying bricks an average

bricklayer could lay 200 bricks per hour. A rate of 4 cents per brick might be established, so that the typical bricklayer would earn $8 per hour. Workers who achieved a level of 250 bricks per hour would receive hourly wages of $10.

2. *Select workers properly:* After identifying the best method for a given task, a manager should find the right workers to do the job. Thus, those considered for the job of bricklayer would be screened to determine if they had the necessary manual dexterity and strength. The same would apply to the job of brick carrier.
3. *Train workers to use the best method:* This principle emphasizes greater specialization of and collaboration among workers rather than individual effort. Under Gilbreth's plan, some workers would be trained to lay bricks and others to carry and stack the bricks properly. If one brick carrier served two bricklayers, cooperation could be encouraged by relating the brick carrier's incentive pay to the number of bricks laid by the two bricklayers.
4. *Separate the planning and the preparation of work from the actual execution of the task:* In essence, this extends the third principle to managers as well as to workers. Taylor reasoned that each group would perform the duties to which it was best fitted—managers would plan and workers would carry out the plans—with an attendant increase in efficiency. Although workers would not be allowed to choose their own methods, close cooperation between management and workers would be assured because of the greater incentive earnings workers would receive. Hence, under Gilbreth's plan, bricklayers would be able to increase their income with the incentive pay they received when they surpassed bricklaying standards.

In summary, Taylor's ideas reduced wasted effort and developed standards of performance, better methods for selecting and training workers, and greater specialization, including planning by someone other than the worker.

Reading 19 The Purpose of a Data Processing System

Data processing systems are used to collect, manipulate, and store data for reporting and analyzing business activities and events. Data is organized into *files* to achieve these purposes.

A file is an organized group of associated *records* which relate to a particular area of a business. Each record generally contains information about a single unit in the file such as an inventory item, a customer, or an employee. For example, a payroll file . . . contains a record for each employee, and each record contains *fields* of information such as the employee's number, name, pay rate, and address. A field is a specified area reserved for data of a specific nature. It is the smallest element of a file that is processed.

A *character* is actually the smallest subdivision of a file. It consists of a single alphabetic, numeric, or special character. Generally, a single character within a field is not dealt with as an entity; rather, the entire field is manipulated when processing a record.

Files are usually divided into two classifications: master and detail. *Master files* contain permanent data, as does the payroll file. *Detail* (or *transaction*) *files* contain data of a temporary nature; an example is a file of weekly employee time cards.

Most data processing involves file manipulation. When it is determined that there is a need for information concerning some area of a business, a file may be *created* to provide that information. Once a file has been created, it often is necessary to *add* records to it. For example, when an employee is hired, a new record must be added to the payroll file. When a record is no longer useful, say, when an employee leaves a company, it is usually *deleted* from the file. It is sometimes necessary to change fields in a record, such as when an employee's pay rate or job classification is changed. In this case, a record is *updated.*

In most files, records are arranged in some sequence or order. At times, if the purpose or nature of a file is altered, it is necessary to change this sequence. For example, if employee records in a payroll file are organized by department, but at a later date it is necessary to organize them by division, it is necessary to *resequence* the file.

The process of updating, adding, and deleting records in a file to reflect changes is referred to as *file maintenance.* When a file is updated on a periodic basis or reports are created, the action is usually referred to as *file processing.*

Reading 20 How to Make White Sauces

Several methods can be used for preparing smooth white sauces. In each method the separation of dry starch granules is accomplished by coating the granules with fat or by suspending them in cold liquid. Probably the most used method is to melt the fat and stir in the flour or starch until all particles are coated with fat. The hot or cold liquid is then added. If hot liquid is used it should be added gradually with constant stirring until gelatinization occurs. The thickened mixture is then heated until no raw starch taste remains. If cold liquid is used it may be added as described for hot liquids or the starch-fat mixture may be removed from the heat, liquid added all at once, heating resumed with constant stirring and the sauce completed as when hot liquid is used. In a second method, flour is mixed with a small amount of cold milk, the remaining milk and fat are heated together in a double boiler, and the flour mixture is added gradually with stirring. The mixture is then boiled for two minutes with constant stirring over direct heat or cooked for a longer time in the top of a double boiler. In a third method, the flour and fat are combined, added to the hot liquid, and the cooking is finished as in the second method.

Another way of making white sauce is from a mix that can be prepared easily at home. One cup of all-purpose flour, 1 cup of table fat, 4 teaspoons of salt, and $2^1/_2$ cups of nonfat dry milk are mixed with a pastry blender or fork until crumbly. The mixture is stored in a covered jar in the refrigerator. To make white sauce, 1 cup of liquid is combined with $^1/_4$ cup of mix for thin sauce, $^1/_2$ cup of mix for medium sauce, or $^3/_4$ cup of mix for thick sauce. The liquid can be water, broth, or the liquid in which vegetables have been cooked. The mix is put into a saucepan and the liquid is added slowly with constant stirring. It is cooked until thickened and seasoned to taste.

Gladys E. Vail, Jean A. Phillips, Lucile Osborn Rust, Ruth M. Griswold, Margaret M. Justin, *Foods,* sixth edition (Boston: Houghton Mifflin Company, 1973), p. 267.

The Ideas Module Tasks **Unit Five**

Task 11: Controlling ideas

You should be able to determine the controlling idea of an essay by prereading the title, lead, headings, key words, key paragraphs, and key sentences.

Task 12: Major points and body paragraphs

You should be able to determine the major points in an essay by reading the body paragraphs for topic sentences, transitional paragraphs, digressions, single-sentence paragraphs, transitional sentences and statements, and key words.

Task 13: Supporting data and body paragraphs

You should be able to determine the supporting data in an essay by reading the body paragraphs for examples, facts, reasons, cause and effect, classification and division, and definitions.

Task 14: Determining the meaning of ideas

You should be able to determine the meaning of ideas by using your knowledge of sentence patterns and problem sentences.

Task 15: Expressing the meanings of ideas

You should be able to express the meaning of the ideas you find in your reading by paraphrasing and summarizing the ideas.

Task 16: Reading and study aids

You should be able to survey a textbook for its table of contents, introduction, glossary, index, appendix, footnotes, bibliography, charts, and graphs. You should be able to use the reading and study aids to find information.

Task 17: Chapter and section ideas

You should be able to determine the ideas in a chapter of a textbook by reading the title and headings; key words, key paragraphs, and key sentences; topic sentences; transitional paragraphs and statements; supporting data; and transitional markers.

Task 18: Reading special subjects: mathematics and the natural sciences

You should be able to use your knowledge of definitions, examples, facts, classification and division, tables and charts, and other methods of explaining to determine the meanings of the special terms and the ideas and concepts in your mathematics and natural science textbooks.

Task 19: Reading special subjects: humanities and the behavioral sciences

You should be able to use your knowledge of definitions, examples, cause and effect, comparison and contrast, reference sources, and other methods of explaining to determine the meanings of special terms and the ideas or concepts in your English, history, psychology, and sociology textbooks.

Task 20: Reading special subjects: business and careers

You should be able to use your knowledge of definitions, examples, classification and division, and other methods of explaining to determine the meanings of the special terms and the ideas or concepts in textbooks on the subject of business or other careers.

Inferences Module

Contents

Unit One Overview 219

Inferences 219
The Inferences Module Instruction 219
The Inferences Module Objectives 220

Unit Two Making Inferences 221

Task 21 Implied Meanings 223
Inferences from Varied Amounts of Information 224
Inferences from Different Kinds of Information 226
Answer Key *235*
Task 22 Opinions 249
Task 23 Generalizations 263

Unit Three Readings 285

1 The Bandanna 287
2 The Basis of Capital 288
3 The Industrial Revolution Begins 288
4 *from* Death in Miami Beach 289
5 The Man Who Drew the Boundaries of a New Nation's Capital 290
6 Single Man in 1776 Could Have Survived for a Year on Less Than $1,000 in 1976 Dollars 292
7 The Bad-Paper Vets 292
8 Assimilation 293
9 The Hundred Days 294
10 National and Regional Preferences for Foods 296
11 Old-Style Occupations That Still Pay 297
12 Occupational Profile 300
13 The U.S. Labor Force in 1990: New Projections 304

14 Educational Attainment of Workers, March 1976 305

15 Students, Graduates, and Dropouts in the Labor Market, October 1975 312

16 Families and the Rise of Working Wives—An Overview 318

Unit Four The Inferences Module Tasks 321

Overview **Unit One**

Inferences

An **inference** is a conclusion based on facts or indications. Making inferences is an important reasoning skill that you use every day, in many different situations.

Some inferences are quite easy. For example, if you read the sentence *The children had a snowball fight,* you would make the inference that the fight took place in the winter. You would associate snowballs with the known information that, generally, snow falls in the winter.

Sometimes inferences are complicated. For example, suppose that you read the following account of an accident:

> The sun was really bright that morning, and it glared in his eyes and blinded him as he drove out from under the trees. That's why he ran over the dog that was crossing the street.

The sentences do not tell you in what direction the man was driving. However, you can infer that he was driving east. You would associate the word *morning* with the statement about the sun glaring in the man's eyes. You would then use the information, which is generally believed, that the sun rises and is in the east in the morning. If the sun was in the man's eyes, the indications are that he was driving east.

When you are reading, you may need to make inferences to learn the meaning of a word, the topic of a paragraph, or the important ideas in a book. Making inferences is particularly necessary to understanding fiction and poetry. However, in this module, you will work with making inferences from expository writing—the kind of writing you find in essays, articles, and textbooks.

The Inferences Module Instruction

In Unit Two, "Making Inferences," you will learn to work out the **implied meanings** in various reading selections. You will learn to form reasoned **opinions** based on the information you read and the information you already know. You will also learn to make **generalizations** based on the information in several different reading selections. In Unit Three, "Readings," you will find articles and textbook excerpts. You will use some of the readings in completing the objectives of the module, which are explained below. The tasks of the *Inferences Module* are listed in Unit Four.

The Inferences Module Objectives

A. Objectives
To achieve the objectives, or learning goals, of the *Inferences Module,* you should show that you are able to do the following:
1. Determine implied meanings in reading selections
2. Form reasoned opinions related to information in a reading selection
3. Develop generalizations based on information in two or more reading selections

B. Conditions of performance
1. The reading selections should be assigned by your instructor.
2. You should read and make inferences from the readings according to your instructor's guidelines.

C. Criteria for evaluation
1. You should show you are able to determine the implied meanings in reading selections by
   a. Answering the questions in the Task 21 reading practice
   b. Stating the implied meanings in assigned readings
2. You should show you are able to form reasoned opinions by
   a. Answering the questions in the Task 22 reading practice
   b. Answering questions based on assigned readings
3. You should show you are able to make reasoned generalizations by
   a. Completing the Task 23 reading practice
   b. Stating and developing a generalization based on the information in two or more readings

Making Inferences **Unit Two**

Suppose that you are standing at the corner of two streets. You see a car coming very fast down one of the streets. You see another car racing down the other street. A big truck is parked at the corner, blocking the drivers' view of the intersection. You think, for a moment, about what you see. Then, you say to yourself, "Those two cars may run into each other." You have just made an **inference.** You have drawn a conclusion based on the facts, or the indications, that you observed.

Perhaps you have heard the expression "reading between the lines." When you read between the lines you make an inference. You infer a meaning that is not directly stated. For example, a writer may *imply,* or indirectly indicate, the idea of a paragraph. You *infer,* from the information in the paragraph, the meaning that the writer has only implied (said indirectly). In this module, the term **implied meanings** refers to meanings that writers indirectly indicate through the information in their writing. You must determine those meanings by making inferences.

You may also need to make inferences to answer some of the questions your instructors ask about the readings they assign. For example, suppose you read an article that said scientists had found a way to produce frogs with identical characteristics. According to the scientists, the same process could be used to produce, if you chose, other human beings who would be exactly like you. In a sociology class, you might be asked to discuss or write an answer to the question, "How would the reproduction of identical human beings affect our society?" In science, government, or philosophy, you might be asked, "Should we reproduce human beings who are identical to us? Why or why not?" or "Who should decide which human beings to reproduce?"

To answer such questions, you must form an opinion. To form an opinion, you must make inferences. You would use the information you read and other information you know to decide answers to the questions. In this module, such answers are called opinions. An **opinion** is a conclusion that you have based on evidence but that you may not be able to prove absolutely.

A **generalization** is a broad idea or conclusion that is based on a number of facts or ideas. In this module, the term **generalization** means an inference that is based on the information in two or more reading sources. Making a generalization from different sources is something like looking in your cupboards and refrigerator to decide what you will have for dinner. You will choose only some of the foods stored in the different places. But the foods you choose go together to make a meal. In this same way, you choose only some of the information you read in different sources. But you put that information together to make a generalization.

Words and Terms to Know

inference
implied meaning
opinion
generalization

Concepts to Remember

1. An inference is a conclusion that is based on facts or indications.
2. An implied meaning is a meaning that is indirectly indicated. You determine that meaning by making an inference.
3. An opinion is a conclusion or inference that you have based on evidence but that you may not be able to prove absolutely.
4. A generalization is a broad idea, conclusion, or inference that is based on the information in two or more reading sources.

Task 21
Implied Meanings

To **imply** means to hint, suggest, or say something indirectly. Sometimes writers do not actually state their meaning directly. Instead, they give you information that implies their meanings. They expect you to have the information you need to make a logical association between what they say and what they mean. In other words, they count on your ability to determine their meaning by making an inference based on the information they state.

An example should help you see how the process works. Read the following sentence. If you make certain inferences while you read the sentence, you can find the meaning of the word *thanatology.*

> There is a thanatology boom in colleges and in print and there are random reports from the lecture circuits that the subject of death is now outdrawing the perennials—sex and politics. [Daniel C. Maguire, *Death by Choice* (New York: Doubleday & Company, 1974).]

To learn the meaning of *thanatology,* you would first associate the words "subject of death" with *thanatology* and infer that *thanatology* has something to do with death. You would then understand the meaning of the word well enough to determine the meaning of the sentence. However, you would have a more precise understanding of the word if you knew that the suffix *-logy* means "the science or study of," as in biology, psychology, or sociology. You would then infer that *thanatology* means the "study of death." You could also associate the word *college* with a place where you study or take courses. You could infer from that knowledge that *thanatology* is the study of death.

Now read the paragraphs below and determine the meaning of the word *persuasion.* Answer the questions that follow the paragraphs.

> So far in this book we have been dealing with expository writing—that is, with writing chiefly concerned with explaining a subject or a thesis through illustration, comparison, process, or causal relation. We now turn to persuasion, a more complex form of communication, and socially the most important form. . . .
>
> Throughout the discussion of exposition we emphasized the importance of keeping your reader in mind. This requirement is even more important in persuasion, because it is your readers you are trying to persuade and your whole effort is concentrated on bringing them into agreement with you. This task is easiest when they are already predisposed to agree with you, and most difficult when they have compelling reasons for not agreeing. For example, it would be relatively easy to persuade your class that

students should have a greater voice in deciding what courses they should take and how those courses should be conducted. It would probably be much harder to persuade them that the number of essays required in English should be doubled. [James M. McCrimmon, *Writing with a Purpose,* fifth edition (Boston: Houghton Mifflin Company, 1972), pp. 268–269.]

Circle the letter of the correct answer in question 1 and fill in the answers to question 2.

1. In the paragraphs, *persuasion* means
   a. keeping the reader in mind
   b. a kind of expository writing
   c. arguing about the number of essays to write
   d. writing about a subject by using comparison

2. On the lines below, list the information from the paragraphs that you used to find the meaning of *persuasion.*

____

____

____

____

____

____

Look in the Answer Key for the answers.

Inferences from Varied Amounts of Information

Almost any idea or meaning can be implied, rather than stated directly. The amount of information that the writer actually states can vary widely. Because you depend on that information, it is sometimes easy and at other times difficult to determine the writer's implied meaning. In the above paragraphs, the stated information makes finding the meaning of *persuasion* fairly easy. In the examples below, less information is stated, and you may find it harder to learn the implied meanings.

A. THE INVENTION OF THE COKE BOTTLE

Coca-Cola has been bottled since 1891, but originally the bottles were nothing special. There was an astounding variety—some were white, some amber, some had arrow designs blown into their sides—and they all had diamond-shaped paper labels that quickly sweated off the bottles. Company executives argued about the design of the bottle until one of them issued a proclamation: the bottle should be uniform in design and so recognizable that if a person saw only a fragment of one he would be able to identify it immediately.

The company decided to run a contest for new designs among its bottle suppliers. One of these was the Root Glass Company in Terre Haute, Indiana. Alex Samuelson, the plant superintendent, thought that the design should have something to do with the two most famous ingredients in Coke, the cola nut and the coca leaf. He sent Earl R. Dean, the principal bottle designer, to the library for appropriate pictures, but he mistakenly brought back a drawing of a cocoa pod. Samuelson saw that its shape could be adapted to a workable design and promptly ordered a bottle to be molded with a cocoa-pod pattern. The Coca-Cola company adopted this prototype, and, after some modifications, it went into production in 1916. [Larry Dietz, "The Invention of the Coke Bottle." Copyright © 1975 by *Harper's Magazine*. All rights reserved. Reprinted from the April, 1975 issue by special permission.]

Circle the letter of the correct answer in questions 1, 3, and 6 and fill in the answers to questions 2, 4, and 5.

1. The paragraphs imply that
   a. Coke bottles are not recognizable from their design
   b. the Coke bottle shape does not indicate the ingredients of Coca-Cola
   c. Coca-Cola company executives designed a bottle in 1891 that shows the ingredients of the drink
   d. the cocoa pod is one of the ingredients of Coca-Cola

2. On the lines below, list the stated information in the paragraph that you used to answer question 1.

B. While walking along the river, he saw some berries in the water. He dived down for them, but was stunned when he unexpectedly struck the bottom. There he lay for quite a while, and when he recovered consciousness and looked up, he saw the berries hanging on a tree just above him. [Paul Radin, "Manbozho and the Berries," *Memoirs of a Geological Survey of Canada: Anthropological Series, II* (Ottawa: Information Canada, 1914).]

3. The paragraph implies that what the man saw was
   a. berries that grow in the water
   b. a tree growing in the water
   c. the bottom of the river and a tree above him
   d. the reflection of the berries in the water

4. On the lines below, list the information in the paragraph that you used to answer question 3.

5. What did you have to know about water and about how berries generally grow to answer question 3?

6. Paragraph B also has an implied moral or lesson. Such morals are often expressed in sayings we use. Which of the following familiar sayings describes the implied moral or lesson of paragraph B? Circle the letter of each appropriate saying. More than one answer may be appropriate.
   a. Look before you leap.
   b. Think twice before you act once.
   c. Willful waste makes woeful want.
   d. A fool and his money are soon parted.
   e. Things are not always what they seem.

Look in the Answer Key for the answers.

Inferences from Different Kinds of Information

Writers may use different kinds of information to imply a meaning. For example, they may use figures of speech, such as similes and metaphors. They may use irony and allusions. Implied meanings may even be made through examples, facts, causes, or other information.

A *figure of speech* is an expression that is usually not meant to be taken literally, or as meaning exactly what it says. Generally, the figure of speech associates unlikely characteristics with a person or object. The figure of speech implies that the person or object has those characteristics. *Similes* and *metaphors* are examples of figures of speech.

Similes

A **simile** is a comparison of unlike items. The simile says the items are *like* or *as* each other. A common expression such as *She's as pretty as a picture* is a simile. Although a simile names the items being compared, there is an implied meaning in the comparison. For example, the expression *She's as pretty as a picture* implies that *she* is very pretty and also that pictures are always pretty.

Decide the implied meanings in the similes below. More than one answer may be appropriate. Then, circle the letter of each appropriate answer.

1. His smile was as shallow as a saucer.
   a. He was really friendly.
   b. His smile didn't mean anything.
   c. He was not being honest.
   d. His teeth didn't show when he smiled.

2. Her room looked like a junk heap.
   a. Her room was very large.
   b. Her room was a mess.
   c. Her room had an old car in it.
   d. Her room was very untidy.

Look in the Answer Key for the answers.

Metaphors

A **metaphor** is an expression that implies a similarity between persons or items that are not alike. In a metaphor, the comparison is not identified by the words *like* or *as*. Instead, the characteristics of one item are used to describe the other item.

Some metaphors are quite clearly indicated in what the writer states. Sometimes, however, the metaphor is implied in only a word or two. The paragraph below has two clearly indicated metaphors. A third metaphor is implied in only a few words. Read the paragraph and answer the questions that follow it.

> In 1900, electric cars were a common sight on city streets. They were high, boxy, and heavy—those early electric cars—and they couldn't get up much speed. Nor could they be driven very far before the battery had to be recharged. So by the 1930s, the electric car was a curiosity piece that now and then sailed out of a carriage house, usually with a stern-faced matron sitting at the steering tiller. Car and driver were somehow suited to each other: heavily built, elegantly appointed, and quietly majestic. They were quality products. They didn't guzzle fuel, raise their voices above a murmur, or become a public problem. But they both disappeared in favor of slimmer-lined, stripped-down models that drink high-powered fuels, shout in the streets, and cost a lot to keep going. Now maybe only a few people would like to see that old-style matron stage a comeback. But these days, most of us would like to have a car that didn't use gas, was quiet, and was inexpensive to operate. That's why, as soon as our engineers can solve the battery problem, we'll probably have electric cars again.

Circle the letters of the appropriate answers. More than one answer may be appropriate.

1. The paragraph implies that
   a. electric cars and older women of the 1930s were alike
   b. electric cars were carefully manufactured
   c. older women of the 1930s had been carefully raised
   d. older women of the 1930s spoke softly
   e. electric cars didn't use gasoline
   f. older women of the 1930s didn't drink
   g. older women of the 1930s didn't create disturbances in public

2. The paragraph also implies that
   a. new cars and today's women are alike
   b. today's women are thinner than women were in the 1930s
   c. today's women do not wear as much clothing as women did in the 1930s

d. today's women drink alcoholic beverages
e. today's women are noisy in public
f. today's women need a lot of money

3. The paragraph also implies that an electric car was like a
   a. carriage
   b. ship
   c. model
   d. stage

4. On the lines below, list the words and expressions in the paragraph that you used in deciding the answer to question 3.

____

____

____

____

Look in the Answer Key for the answers.

Irony

Irony is an expression that implies a meaning that is the opposite of what is actually said. Irony is sometimes conveyed by understatements. An understatement makes the situation or event appear less ridiculous or impossible than it really is. Irony may also be conveyed in a straightforward account of facts. The writer expects you to infer from the facts that the situation is contrary to what is expected.

In the first example below, the irony is achieved through the understatement, *The state says it is difficult to administer the program.* To say that it is only "difficult" to administer the program understates the problem. A program that has been changed so often and has such detailed rules would be almost impossible to administer.

> The State of California last week filed a suit against the U.S. Department of Agriculture, asking a Federal judge to ban any more changes in food-stamp regulations unless they bear on constitutional rights.
>
> The state says the food-stamp manual was rewritten every year from 1965 to 1968, rewritten again in 1972, modified 89 times over the next two years, rewritten again last December and revised 27 times since then. There have been 500 individual regulatory changes in 1975 alone. The rules are both sweeping and detailed; one regulation stipulates when to use paper clips and when to use staples on food stamp files.
>
> The state says it is difficult to administer the program. irony
> [*Newsweek* (December 15, 1975), p. 44. Copyright 1975 by Newsweek, Inc. All rights reserved. Reprinted by permission.]

The paragraphs below contain several ironies. Read the paragraphs. Then, answer the questions that follow them.

> RESIGNATION IN IOWA
>
> Old Town, Iowa, is neither very old nor very much of a town. It was incorporated 40 years ago so that its only business, a

nightclub, could get a liquor license; today it's a hamlet of 24 souls with no sewer or water facilities and one dead-end street to its name. But it does have its full share of bureaucracy.

Under Iowa law, Old Town is required to have a mayor, a town clerk, a treasurer, a five-person city council and a planning and zoning commission. It's too small to qualify for Federal revenue sharing, but Mayor O.E. Humphrey, 60, still has to fill out all the proper forms. Humphrey also had to go to two days of classes to be taught how to report the town's annual budget—$500 this year. "We can't do a thing without filling out a form," he complains. "If we want to make a repair on our dead-end street we have to file a report with the state for road-use money."

It was too much to cope with, and anyway the nightclub burned down ten years ago, so the city council decided last July to close the town down. But again it wasn't that easy. Humphrey announced his intentions to state officials; after three months he was told to file a formal petition at the proper state office. A hearing had to be held last week so that the townspeople could voice objections—nobody did. A referendum must be held at the end of this month. The whole process, says the mayor, is going to cost about $250. But the council has already resigned, and the six street lights have been turned off. [*Newsweek* (December 15, 1975), p. 45.]

Complete the questions below by identifying the statements that point out the irony in the situation described in the above paragraphs. The first question has been completed for you, as an example.

1. Old Town was incorporated so its nightclub could get a liquor license. The statement that makes the incorporation of the town ironic is ___the nightclub burned down ten years ago___

2. The town has only 24 residents. The statement that makes the irony is ________________________________

____

3. The town is too small to qualify for Federal revenue sharing. The statement that makes the irony is ________________________________

____

____

4. The town has an annual budget of $500. The statement that makes the irony is ________________________________

____

____

5. The town was required to have a hearing and a referendum to close it down. The statement that makes the irony is ________________________________

____

Look in the Answer Key for the answers.

Allusions

An **allusion** is a reference to a person, event, literary work, or fact. When a writer makes an allusion, the writer expects the reader to know about the person or other information and to associate the allusion with the idea being discussed.

Sometimes allusions refer to information you do not know. Such allusions may keep you from understanding what you are reading. In fact, to understand the writer's meaning, you may have to look up the person or other information the writer alludes to. You can generally find the information in a dictionary or encyclopedia.* But even then, you may have to reason through more than one possible association to find the relationship the writer implies.

In the paragraph below, the writer discusses the blood lust that, he says, makes Americans love to watch boxing matches. By *blood lust* he means a thirst for or enjoyment in seeing blood. He alludes to some Americans being "Roman" enough to admit that they enjoy and need the sport of boxing. He expects the reader to associate the word *Roman* with early Roman citizens who enjoyed watching Christians and other enemies of the Roman Empire being fed to the lions.

> In America, we give maximum expression to our blood lust in the mass spectator sport of boxing. Some of us are Roman enough to admit our love and need of the sport. Others pretend to look the other way. But when a heavyweight championship fight rolls around, the nation takes a moral holiday and we are all tuned in—some of us peeping out of the corner of our eye at the square jungle and the animal test of brute power unfolding there. [Eldridge Cleaver, *Soul on Ice* (New York: McGraw-Hill Book Company, 1968).]

Now read the paragraph below, which is from an article about making pottery. Answer the question that follows the paragraph.

> By many accounts, the first potter was the Lord and the first pot was Adam. Certainly, shaping things out of clay is a very ancient human activity, one that was already highly developed in China and the Sumer 7,000 years ago. [Beth Gutcheon, "Not So Common Clay," *New York Times Magazine* (July 25, 1976), p. 34. © 1976 by The New York Times Company. Reprinted by permission.]

Explain what is meant by the allusion "the first potter was the Lord and the first pot was Adam."

____

____

____

____

*Dictionaries are discussed in Task 8 of the *Vocabulary Module.*

Look in the Answer Key for the answers.

Examples

An **example** is an illustration that is used to explain or prove an idea.* In the paragraph below, the term *deviant label* is explained by examples of such labels: *criminal, hoodlum,* and so on. The examples illustrate and, consequently, imply the meaning of the term. In the second paragraph, an example is used to illustrate the reaction of society to a person who has been labeled a criminal. The example implies that we should not attach labels to people. It also implies that we treat people according to the labels given them, even when they do not deserve the labels. After reading the paragraphs, you should know that the authors feel that labeling a person is very undesirable.

> *(1)* When the deviant label is applied to persons whose behavior or thought is or is presumed to be deviant, they are then deviant persons. Familiar among such labels are *criminal* or *hoodlum, delinquent* or *punk, psychotic* or *nut, alcoholic* or *drunken bum, drug addict* or *drug fiend, prostitute* or *whore, homosexual* or *fag. Whenever response to a person is governed mainly by the perception that the person acts or thinks in deviant ways, that person is a social deviant.*
>
> (2) For example, a person charged, tried, convicted, and sentenced to prison for committing a crime is involved in a long, complex process of social definition controlled by powerful segments of society and their agents. He is henceforth a *criminal.* In his contacts with the police, lawyers, the courts, and the officials and officers of the prison, he is deeply and effectively stigmatized . . . as a deviant person. Even after he leaves prison he will continue to face reminders of this defining process. He may have to report at intervals to his parole officer. The police may keep a close watch on him. The chances are that he will have trouble getting a job, or holding one if his being a deviant becomes known. [Alan P. Bates and Joseph Julian, *Sociology: Understanding Social Behavior* (Boston: Houghton Mifflin Company, 1975), p. 288. Copyright © 1975 by Houghton Mifflin Company. Used by permission.]

Read the paragraphs below. Then, answer the question that follows the paragraphs.

> *(1)* Helen, a 30-year-old homemaker, had been plagued for five years by migraine headaches. They were relieved only by heavy doses of pain-killing medication. Finally, her internist referred her to a hypnotist, and after eight weeks of treatment and instruction Helen no longer suffered from migraines.

*The use of examples as supporting data is explained in Task 13 of the *Ideas Module.*

(2) Louise, a 42-year-old teacher, was 40 pounds overweight. She had tried diet after diet, but any weight loss had always been temporary. She was then treated, over a two-month period, by a hypnotist. She lost 40 pounds. Her hypnotherapy ended five years ago and Louise has been able to maintain her ideal weight ever since. [William A. Nolen, M.D., "How Doctors Use Hypnosis," *McCall's* (March, 1975), p. 66.]

Circle the letter of each correct answer.

The examples imply that
a. Helen was cured of headaches by taking pain-killers
b. Helen was cured of headaches by hypnotism
c. Louise was able to lose weight and not gain it back after she dieted
d. Louise was able to lose weight and not gain it back after being treated by a hypnotist
e. hypnotism can cure some people of headaches
f. hypnotism can cure some people of being overweight

Look in the Answer Key for the answers.

Facts

A **fact** is a figure, statistic, or other information that can be checked for its accuracy.* Facts are generally used to make a direct statement of meaning. However, facts sometimes have implied meanings. In the example below, the statistics are stated, and you must infer their meaning. Read the paragraphs. Then, answer the question that follows the paragraphs.

From a national poll conducted in 1964 and again in 1974 by Market-Opinion Research Co.:

Q. How much of the time do you think you can trust the government in Washington to do what is right?

	1964	*1974*
Always	14%	2%
Most of the time	62%	30%
Some of the time	22%	64%
Don't know	2%	4%

[*Newsweek* (December 15, 1975), p. 44.]

Circle the letter of each correct answer.

The facts imply that in 1974
a. people trusted the government less than in 1964
b. a small percentage of people trusted the government all the time
c. about a third of the people trusted the government most of the time
d. almost two-thirds of the people trusted the government sometimes
e. the percentage of people who trusted the government most or some of the time had increased over the percentage in 1964

Look in the Answer Key for the answers.

*The use of facts as supporting data is explained in Task 13 of the *Ideas Module.*

Cause and effect

A **cause** explains why a certain effect, or result, occurs or exists. An **effect** is the result or consequence of certain causes. Cause and effect explanations are found in many kinds of articles and textbooks. A writer may explain the cause of a social condition, a disease, an event in history, a decision, or other situation. The explanation may be based on several causes for one effect, or on a single cause for several effects.*

A cause and effect explanation has a stated meaning. The explanation may also have an implied meaning or even more than one implied meaning. Read the paragraph below. As you read, think about possible meanings that seem to be implied.

ILLEGAL DRUGS AND CRIME

In the last half century a strange situation has arisen from the value conflict among Americans over the use of drugs. Those who have most feared certain drugs have attempted to control their use or abolish them by law in disregard of the fact that others have not shared their view. Under Prohibition, the millions who wanted alcoholic beverages had the choice of going without or breaking the law to get them since they could not be had legally. A major consequence of this situation was that organized crime took over the liquor business and prospered mightily. Much the same thing has happened in more recent years with other drugs. Americans thus have a major dilemma. When they attempt legal control of behavior in areas where there are major value conflicts, their efforts to reduce one problem increase the incidence of another: crime. [Alan P. Bates and Joseph Julian, *Sociology: Understanding Social Behavior* (Boston: Houghton Mifflin Company, 1975, p. 298. Copyright © 1975 by Houghton Mifflin Company. Used by permission.]

The paragraph seems to imply that Prohibition was a bad idea. Prohibition refers to the constitutional amendment that forbade the manufacture, sale, or transportation of intoxicating liquors. The paragraph also seems to imply that laws to control the use of drugs are equally bad. Perhaps your instructor will want to discuss the paragraph and its implied meanings with you. On the lines below, note any other implied meanings you thought of as you read the paragraph. You may want to discuss the meanings you found with your instructor.

____

____

____

____

____

____

The article below tells how food became contaminated and caused passengers on an airplane to suffer food poisoning. The account is a cause

*The use of cause and effect as supporting data is explained in Task 13 of the *Ideas Module*.

and effect example of food poisoning and is based on facts. Even though the article is a straightforward account of the incident, you can make several inferences from the stated information. Read the article. Then, answer the question that follows the article.

(1) The classic pattern of cause and effect in an outbreak of mass illness is often postulated but not proven. Recently, the actual sequence involved in food poisoning on an international jet flight was traced by epidemiologists, and their findings fit the textbook pattern. Here is what took place:

(2) On the weekend of Feb. 1, a cook in Alaska preparing ham and omelet breakfasts for International Inflight Catering has blisters on two fingers. The blisters are infected with staphylococcus, a common contagious bacteria. The cook handles at least 205 portions of ham, which are kept at room temperature for 6 hours during preparation of the food trays.

(3) The 343 passengers board a Japan Air Lines jumbo jet in Tokyo. While the plane flies to its scheduled refueling stop in Anchorage, the contaminated food trays are stored overnight at 50 degrees. Staph multiply at temperatures over 40; as they multiply, they produce a toxin which is a common cause of food poisoning.

(4) Food trays are loaded on the 747 at Anchorage. The trays have been labeled for distribution on the plane. The contaminated trays go to Galley 1, which serves 40 first class seats, and Galley 2, which serves 93 seats in the forward portion of the coach cabin; 72 of them go to Galleys 3 and 4 to the rear. A fresh crew boards, and the plane takes off for Copenhagen, the next refueling stop on its polar route to Paris.

(5) Six to seven hours later, the passenger breakfasts are heated in 300-degree ovens for 15 minutes, treatment which cannot inactivate the toxin. The passengers are served. For the crew it is dinner time and only one stewardess takes a ham and omelet tray. As the plane approaches Copenhagen, those who ate contaminated food begin to experience staph food-poisoning symptoms: nausea, vomiting, cramps and diarrhea.

(6) The sick, 144 of them, disembark at Copenhagen the morning of Feb. 3. The rest, 51 of whom later become ill, go on to Paris.

(7) The pattern of contagion was reconstructed through laboratory analysis that matched bacterial samples from the cook's blisters, uneaten tainted food, and the victims' vomit and stool. Dr. Mickey S. Eisenberg, the U.S. Public Health Service officer in Anchorage who had pinpointed the probable source of infection, completed the picture by comparing passenger interviews with the galley plan. ["A Textbook Case," *New York Times* (February 16, 1975), 7-E. © 1975 by The New York Times Company. Reprinted by permission.]

Circle the letter of each correct answer.

The paragraphs imply that

a. people who prepare food should be free of contagious bacteria
b. ham and eggs should be kept stored at temperatures below 40°
c. ham and eggs should not be kept warm for long periods of time

d. the plane was flying at night between Anchorage and Copenhagen
e. some of the passengers on the plane did not develop food poisoning
f. there were not enough of the contaminated food trays to serve all of the passengers
g. the passengers were served breakfast before the plane landed in Copenhagen
h. symptoms of food poisoning develop at different rates in different people
i. all of the people who developed food poisoning may not have eaten at the same time

Look in the Answer Key for the answers.

Words and Terms to Know

imply
simile
metaphor
irony
allusion
example
fact
cause
effect

Concepts to Remember

1. An implied meaning is an idea or opinion that is hinted, suggested, or indicated indirectly.
2. An implied meaning is determined by making an inference from the information that is stated.
3. Implied meanings may be based on different amounts of information.
4. Implied meanings may also be based on different kinds of information.
5. Some of the kinds of information used to imply meanings are similes, metaphors, irony, and allusions. Implied meanings may also be found in explanations based on examples, facts, cause and effect, or other information.

Assignment

Complete the worksheet at the end of this task according to your instructor's directions.

Answer Key Task 21

page 224

1. *c*
2. ". . . we have been dealing with expository writing. . . . We now turn to persuasion, a more complex form of communication. . . ." You could also

list "the importance of keeping your reader in mind" in persuasion. The reference to "your reader" indicates that you are writing. The words *expository* and *exposition* indicate that persuasion is a form of expository writing.

pages 225–226

A. 1. *b*

2. ". . . the design should have something to do with the two most famous ingredients in Coke, the cola nut and the coca leaf"; ". . . the principal bottle designer . . . *mistakenly* brought back a drawing of a cocoa pod"; "Samuelson . . . ordered a bottle to be molded with a cocoa-pod pattern"; and "The Coca-Cola company adopted this prototype and . . . it went into production. . . ."

B. 3. *d*

4. ". . . he saw the berries hanging on a tree just above him."

5. To answer question 3, you would have to know that water reflects an image of what is over it and that berries do not generally grow in water.

6. The most appropriate sayings are *a, b,* and *e.* You would associate "Look before you leap" with the man diving into the water without looking carefully or thinking about what he thought he saw. You would associate "Think twice before you act once" with the idea that the man should have given more thought to whether the berries were actually in the water before he dived in after them. You would associate "Things are not always what they seem" with the idea that although the berries seemed to be in the water, they were not.

pages 226–227

1. *b* and *c*
2. *b* and *d*

pages 227–228

1. All of the answers are appropriate inferences.
2. All of the answers are appropriate inferences.
3. *b*
4. The words *sailed* and *steering tiller* can be associated with a ship. A ship sails through the water and is steered by a tiller, as an electric car was. You might also associate the word *majestic* with a ship. Ships are sometimes said to be "majestic" or to "sail majestically through the water."

page 229

2. "Old Town is required to have a mayor, a town clerk, a treasurer, a five-person city council and a planning and zoning commission."
3. "Major O. E. Humphrey, 60, still has to fill out all the proper forms."
4. "Humphrey also had to go to two days of classes to be taught how to report the town's annual budget. . . ." You might also have listed the statement, "The whole process [of shutting down the town] . . . is going to cost about $250." There is irony in the fact that the cost of shutting the town down would cost half as much as the town's entire annual budget.

5. "But the council has already resigned, and the six street lights have been turned off."

pages 230–231

According to the Bible, the Lord fashioned or shaped the first man, Adam, out of earth. The allusion implies that the first person to make something out of clay (or earth) was the Lord and that the first pot (or piece of pottery) was Adam.

pages 231–232

b, d, e, and *f* are correct answers.

page 232

All the answers are correct. You need to make the following inferences for each of the answers.

a. Between 1964 and 1974, the percentage of people who trusted the government all the time declined from 14% to 2%. The percentage of those who trusted the government most of the time declined from 62% to 30%. The figures indicate a considerable drop in trust. The increase in persons who trusted the government only some of the time (from 22% to 64%) and in those who "don't know" (from 2% to 4%) had to come from the group that previously trusted the government always or most of the time. Thus, the statistics imply that the people trusted the government less in 1974 than in 1964.

b. 2% is a small percentage.

c. 30% is a little less than "about a third of the people."

d. 64% is almost two-thirds of the people.

e. The total percentage of people who trusted the government most or some of the time had increased to 94% over 84% in 1964. If you did not know the declines in trusting the government always or most of the time, you might believe that the increase was a positive finding.

pages 234–235

All the answers are correct. You need to make the following inferences for each of the answers.

a. The contagious bacteria on the food handler's hands caused food poisoning. Therefore, people who handle food should be free of contagious bacteria.

b. The staphylococcus bacteria multiplied at temperatures over 40 degrees. Therefore, the food should have been stored below 40 degrees.

c. The food was stored at temperatures over 40 degrees for a long time (probably 24 to 35 hours before it was served). At over 40 degrees, toxin developed and caused food poisoning. Therefore, ham and eggs should not be kept warm for long periods of time.

d. The contaminated food was served as breakfast, six to seven hours after the plane left Anchorage. Therefore, you can infer that the plane was flying at night between Anchorage and Copenhagen.

e. Paragraph 6 says a total of 196 persons developed food poisoning. But paragraph 3 says 343 passengers boarded the plane. Therefore, some of the passengers did not develop food poisoning.

f. Paragraph 2 says 205 portions of ham were prepared, but paragraph 3 indicates there were 343 passengers. Thus, there were not enough contaminated trays for all the passengers.

g. Paragraph 5 says some of the passengers had symptoms of food poisoning as the plane approached Copenhagen. Therefore, these passengers must have been served before the plane landed in Copenhagen.

h. Paragraph 6 says that 144 people were sick by the time the plane landed in Copenhagen, but that 51 more passengers became ill later. Therefore, if everyone was served at the same time, you can infer that the symptoms develop at different rates in different people.

i. On the basis of the same information as used in *h,* it would also be reasonable to infer that the passengers ate at different times.

Task 21 **Worksheet**

NAME ______________________________ DATE ____________

Reading Practice

Read the paragraphs below. Remember, you are reading for implied meanings—meanings that are only suggested by the information that is stated.

Answer the questions that follow the paragraphs. Some of the questions may have more than one correct answer. Circle the letter of each answer that is correct. You will also need to explain the information you use in determining your answers to the questions.

A. A CHEYENNE BLANKET

The Cheyennes, like other Indians, do not speak to each other when they are away from the camp. If a man goes away from the village, and sits or stands by himself on the top of a hill, it is a sign that he wants to be alone; perhaps to meditate; perhaps to pray. No one speaks to him or goes near him.

Now, there was once a Pawnee boy, who went off on the warpath to the Cheyenne camp. In some way he had obtained a Cheyenne blanket. This Pawnee came close to the Cheyenne camp, and hid himself there to wait. About the middle of the afternoon, he left his hiding place, and walked to the top of the hill overlooking the village. He had his Cheyenne blanket wrapped about him and over his head, with only a little hole for his eyes. He stood there for an hour or two, looking over the Cheyenne camp.

They were coming in from buffalo hunting, and some were leading in the pack horses loaded down with meat. A man came along, riding a horse packed with meat, and leading another pack horse, and a black spotted horse that was his running horse. These running horses are ridden only on the chase or on war parties, and are well cared for. After being used they are taken down to the river and are washed and cleaned with care. When the boy saw this spotted horse, he thought to himself that this was the horse that he would take. When the man who was leading it reached his lodge, he dismounted and handed the ropes to his women, and went inside.

Then the Pawnee made up his mind what he would do. He started down the hill into the village, and walked straight to this lodge where the women were unloading the meat. He walked up to them, reached out his hand, and took the ropes of the spotted horse and one of the others. As he did so the women fell back. Probably they thought that this was some one of the relations of the owner, who was going to take the running horse down to the river to wash it. The Pawnee could not talk Cheyenne, but as he turned away he mumbled something—*m-m-m-m*—as if speaking in a low voice, and then walked down toward the river. As soon as he had gone down over the bank and was out of sight, he jumped on the spotted horse and rode into the brush, and pretty soon was away with two horses, stolen out of the Cheyenne camp in broad daylight. [Gerald W. Haslam, *Forgotten Pages of American Literature* (Boston: Houghton Mifflin Company, 1970), pp. 30–31. Copyright © 1970 by Houghton Mifflin Company. Used by permission.]

1. The paragraphs imply that the Cheyenne Indians particularly valued their
   a. women
   b. horses
   c. blankets
   d. village

2. On the lines below, write the information you used to determine your answer to question 1.

____

____

____

____

____

____

3. The paragraphs imply that the Cheyenne women
   a. did not know all the Cheyenne men
   b. were expected to do heavy work
   c. took care of the horses
   d. were not considered equal to men

4. The paragraphs imply that Indian tribes
   a. spoke different languages
   b. had no customs in common
   c. wore different kinds of blankets
   d. expected women to care for the horses

5. On the lines below, write the information you used to answer question 4.

____

____

____

____

____

____

6. The paragraphs imply that Indian blankets were
   a. woven in bright colors
   b. representative of a tribe
   c. worn for hunting trips
   d. very warm

7. On the lines below, write the information you used in answering question 6.

B. TURNING THE TIDE OF PAPER

Everybody agrees there's too much paper work demanded by government, and the government is doing something about it. The Commission on Federal Paperwork held its first meeting in October and went to work right away, recommending the abolition of the Internal Revenue Service's Form 941, the quarterly report of wages paid by businessmen. The commission's staff said the reports cost the government $20 million a year and businessmen $200 million, and could be consolidated into a single yearly report.

All told, the staff says, Federal agencies produce 10 billion sheets of forms, applications, reports and the like each year, at a cost of $40 billion to the economy. No one can really be sure of such totals, but the Office of Management and Budget is fairly precise about the actual number of forms required: 5,146 last year, not counting an estimated 4,400 more for the Internal Revenue Service, the regulatory commissions and bank supervisory agencies. OMB calculates that business spent 35.6 million person-hours filling them all out. The government's curiosity is all-embracing; last year it received 4,200 returns of the weekly and monthly Turkey Hatchery Report.

There is, of course, a catch to the notion of reducing paper work: the new commission is itself generating a tidy bit of paper, with a staff now grown to 36 and a budget set for next year at $4.6 million. But it is wrong, says chairman Frank Horton, a New York congressman, "to suppose that there will be any significant reduction in Federal paper work without detailed prior analyses of Federal paper work policies and practices. We cannot wish paper work away."

The commission plans to phase itself out within two years—but not before it issues a report. [*Newsweek* (December 15, 1975), p. 44.

8. The irony in the article is that the Commission on Federal Paperwork
   a. held its first meeting in October
   b. went to work right away
   c. recommended abolition of an income tax form
   d. is adding to the paperwork

9. On the lines below, write the information you used in answering question 8.

____

____

____

____

____

____

C. WHO WAS HORATIO ALGER?

Horatio Alger Jr. epitomizes the American success story. But was Alger a real person or a fictitious character? Most Americans probably don't know.

Alger was not only a real person—born 1832, died 1899—but the most widely read writer in the history of America. More than 100 of his melodramatic works about stereotyped heroes like Phil the Fiddler and Ragged Dick were serialized in such popular magazines as *Munsey's* and *Argosy,* then published as books, of which some 250 million copies were sold. Two long-lost novels have even come to light in the past three years and have been published with forewords by Ralph D. Gardner, a New York advertising man who is the leading expert on Alger's life.

One of five children of an impoverished minister in rural Massachusetts, Alger knew first hand about the mortgages and foreclosures that played so big a part in his fiction. But he somehow scrambled through a Harvard education and became in turn an editor, a teacher and a minister before he began living by his prolific pen. Later, settled in a furnished room in New York City, he tutored the sons of the Lehman and the Harriman families.

Like his innocent heroes, for whom hard work and honesty invariably brought success, Alger made the journey from rags to, not riches, but financial comfort. Just over five feet tall and shy, he never married, was awkward around women and wrote clumsily about romance. Some people suspect he was a homosexual.

His major influence, in any case, was as supersalesman of the Great American Dream. Among his avid readers were Ernest Hemingway, F. Scott Fitzgerald, Carl Sandburg, Alfred E. Smith and Cardinal Francis Spellman. [*Dun's Review* (July, 1976), p. 16. Reprinted with the special permission of *Dun's Review,* July 1976. Copyright, 1976, Dun & Bradstreet Publications Corporation.]

10. If you read *Ragged Dick,* one of Horatio Alger's stories, would you expect the hero, Ragged Dick, to be
    a. honest
    b. hardworking
    c. poor
    d. rich

11. The article implies that the Great American dream means
    a. anyone who really tries can succeed in life
    b. writers make a lot of money by writing stories
    c. being married is not important to success
    d. going to Harvard will make you a success

D. "LOVE"

For a long time many psychologists thought that the origins of love in childhood were bound up with the fact that a mother provides nourishment to the newborn infant. According to this idea, the bond between an infant and his mother develops from the infant's associating the source of food (his mother) with the satisfaction of his nutritive needs. Even Freud echoed this view in his description of the first or "oral" stage in infant development.

In the middle 1950s, it occurred to [Harry F.] Harlow that the touch and contact that an infant receives from his mother might be at least as important as feeding. His problem was to verify this idea. How could he pit the value of feeding to the infant against the value of physical contact?

Let him choose! Harlow raised two groups of infant monkeys with artificial surrogate mothers. One of the surrogate mothers offered only a wired surface, while the other was padded and covered with soft terry cloth. For some monkeys, one "mother" in each pair fed the infant monkey with a bottle embedded in its chest. With some monkeys, the terry-cloth mother did the feeding; with others, the wire mother did the feeding. In this way an infant monkey presented with two mothers could choose which mother to become attached to—wire versus cloth, feeding versus contact comfort.

There was little doubt about the results of this study; except for actual feeding time, an infant monkey spent much more time on the cloth mother, regardless of whether or not it provided milk. Clearly, not only was contact comfort as important as feeding, but it seemed to be the only thing that really mattered to the monkeys. Harlow's simple experiment dispelled the old "nutritional" theories in one fell swoop. In addition, new questions could be asked, and new methods similar to Harlow's surrogate mothers could be used to answer further questions about the development and maintenance of love in infancy. [From *The Study of Psychology,* Second Edition, edited by Joseph Rubinstein, pp. 108–109. Copyright © 1975 by the Dushkin Publishing Group, Inc., Guilford, Connecticut 06437.]

12. The paragraphs imply that parents should
    a. hold and touch their children

b. wear terry-cloth clothing
c. have monkeys feed their children
d. fasten a baby's bottle to a piece of wire

13. On the lines below, write the information you used to determine your answer to question 12.

____

____

____

____

14. The paragraphs imply that *surrogate* means a
a. monkey
b. mother
c. infant
d. substitute

E. THE COST OF COMPLIANCE

Goodyear Tire & Rubber Co. says it spent $30 million last year complying with Federal regulations. The tabulation:

Environmental costs (capital equipment, manpower, added fuel costs, miscellaneous)	$17.2 million
Occupational safety and health (capital equipment, manpower, miscellaneous)	$6.9 million
Motor vehicle safety standards (equipment and testing of tires and other products)	$3.4 million
Personnel and administration (manpower, accounting, reports, computer time, paper work, etc.)	$2.5 million
	Total $30 million

[*Newsweek* (December 15, 1975), p. 54.]

15. The paragraph implies that
a. complying with federal regulations costs companies a lot of money
b. complying with environmental regulations costs two and a half times as much as complying with occupational safety and health regulations
c. complying with motor vehicle regulations cost Goodyear Tire and Rubber Company $3.4 million
d. Goodyear Tire and Rubber Company spent $2.5 million dollars complying with personnel and administration regulations

16. Explain the reasoning you used in determining your answer(s) to question 15.

____

____

____

____

F. I DIDN'T STOP IN BALTIMORE

I woke up suddenly, feeling very wide awake, pulled the light cord, and sat straight up in bed.

"We'll be stopping in Baltimore," I announced loudly, in an authoritative voice. I looked around me. A private car, evidently. Good of the railroad people to supply those fruits, and all those flowers. The furniture looked a bit shoddy, but what can one expect these days? My wife was no doubt in the next stateroom. Where was the connecting door? I got up to explore.

The car was swaying heavily—the roadbed must be a disgrace. I supported myself on a table, and then a desk. Then there was a space of empty floor. I was halfway across it when the car gave a lurch, and I fell down. I sat on the floor for a bit, getting my bearings, then scrambled to my feet again, and opened a narrow green door. A locker, with my own clothes in it. I opened another door—a small bathroom.

Then I came to a much bigger door, and opened it, and leaned against the doorjamb. The swaying had stopped—the train, apparently, had halted. Outside was what I assumed was the Baltimore station—wide platform, dim lights, green tile. A whimpering noise, then silence, and no one to be seen. There was something hellishly grim about the place. Suddenly I was quite sure I didn't want to stop in Baltimore.

"We won't stop here," I said, again in a firm, authoritative voice. "Start up the train, and carry on."

I turned back toward my bed, and the big door closed behind me. I fell down twice on the way back—the crew must be pouring on the power, I thought—and getting into bed was like mounting a bucking horse. Safe in bed, I turned off the light, and was asleep in an instant.

This small episode did not happen on a private railroad car. (Who the hell did I think I was? Some ancient Belmont or

Vanderbilt?) It happened in my room on Floor 12, the Solid-Tumor Ward of the cancer clinic of the National Institutes of Health. My room, a room I'd been in for going on eight weeks, was the private car, and the corridor of the Solid-Tumor Ward was the Baltimore platform. But the falling down was real enough—the next morning I had the bruises to prove it.

I was in the Solid-Tumor Ward because NIH, for mysterious bureaucratic reasons, has ended the adult leukemia program, and the adult leukemics who are still about are taken care of in other wards. Leukemia is a sneaky disease—it attacks by indirection. It weakens the blood cells that fight infection, and then sends in surrogate diseases to finish off the victim.

In the two months I was in the Solid-Tumor Ward, my leukemia (or whatever it is—it is a most atypical disease) tried hard to finish me off. I had pneumonia; then an infection of the lower intestines; then a lung clot; then an edema of the lungs; then a second pneumonia; then two minor operations and a major operation; then another infection.

The major operation—opening my chest and snipping off a thumbnail-size bit of lung—was necessary because pneumonia can't be treated unless the doctors know what kind it is, and my second pneumonia stubbornly refused to identify itself. The bit of lung was given every known test—and the brilliant doctors at NIH know every known test—but it still refused to identify itself. Meanwhile the lethal "infiltrate" continued relentlessly to spread across both lungs, and my wife was told that the prognosis was "grim."

It was four days after the operation that I decided not to stop in Baltimore. The next day the able young doctor in charge of my case, Jack Macdonald, told me that he might be imagining things, but the X-rays of my lungs looked a bit better—certainly no worse. The day after, he said there was no doubt about it—the infiltrate was receding. Some days later, my battered old lungs were as close to normal as they will ever be.

Why? Jack Macdonald and the other doctors say frankly they don't know, though they all have a favorite guess. I have a favorite guess, too. My guess is that my decision not to stop at Baltimore had something to do with it. In a kind of fuzzy, hallucinated way, I knew when I announced the decision that it was a decision not to die.

Death is a word rarely mentioned in the NIH cancer clinic. But one is more aware of its presence in the Solid-Tumor Ward than in the now defunct leukemia ward. Leukemia is a sneakier disease than solid-tumor cancer, but it is also kinder at the end. Most leukemics drift into a quiet death, while the victims of a solid tumor can (although they by no means always do) suffer agonies before death comes.

All the rooms at NIH are double rooms, and almost all the patients (except those thought soon to die, which may be why I was alone on my private car) have roommates. Several of my roommates were terminal solid-tumor patients, who were given opium-based analgesics or painkillers at predetermined intervals, usually four hours. Almost always, the analgesic wore off too soon. To hear grown men, and brave men, whimpering, or howling, or pleading with a helpless nurse for another "shot" is not an experience likely soon to be forgotten.

As a result of that experience, I reached certain conclusions. NIH, like most hospitals, goes to great lengths to prevent suicide—patients are forbidden pills of their own, and the windows and even the rooftop solarium are firmly screened. It seems to me that a patient suffering beyond endurance should be given the option of ending his own life, and the means to do so should be supplied on request. An unquestionably terminal patient should be given another option. He should be given as much painkilling drug as he himself feels he needs. The drug probably ought to be heroin, which is estimated to be about four times as effective an analgesic as the synthetic painkillers now mostly in use. If a human being must die, it is surely better that he die in the illusion of painless pleasure—and heroin is very pleasurable—than in lonely agony.

Another conclusion is harder to define. Shakespeare, as usual, came closest, in the familiar cliché-quote from Hamlet: "There are more things in heaven and earth, Horatio, than are dreamt of in your philosophy." Perhaps my decision not to stop in Baltimore had nothing to do with my astonishing recovery. But there are mysteries, above all the mystery of the relationship of mind and body, that will never be explained, not by the most brilliant doctors, the wisest of scientists or philosophers.

For the rest, I hope to put back some (but not all) of the 43 pounds I have lost, to get a bit of rest, to get rid of the tail end of that second infection, and then again to examine in this space the more mundane mysteries of political Washington. ["I Didn't Stop in Baltimore," by Stewart Alsop. From *Newsweek* (March 11, 1974).]

17. The writer tells about being on a train in the Baltimore station. He was
    a. dreaming
    b. dying
    c. having an operation
    d. hallucinating

18. On the lines below, write the information you used to answer question 17.

____

____

____

____

____

____

19. Baltimore is a metaphor for
    a. a train trip

b. an operation
c. pneumonia
d. death

20. The writer makes an inference (draws a conclusion) based on his knowledge of the pain that some terminal cancer patients suffer. What are the two options that he says some cancer patients should have?

____

____

Task 22
Opinions

One reason for reading is to gain information you can use in solving problems, making decisions, or planning for future situations. Many of the questions an instructor asks about a reading assignment are meant to encourage you to use the information from your reading in these ways.

To answer such questions, you need to make inferences. You need to develop an idea or opinion that makes use of the information you know, from both your reading and your experience. In this module, such inferences are called *opinions.* An **opinion** is a conclusion that you have based on evidence but that you may not be able to prove absolutely.

An example should help you see how the process of forming an opinion works. Suppose that you are taking a business course and you read the paragraph below. According to the paragraph, the movement of families from the cities to the suburbs has affected the construction and manufacturing industries. The need for new buildings and facilities in the suburbs has increased the business of those industries. Thus, the paragraph implies that the migration of people from the cities to the suburbs is a good or positive trend.

> There has . . . been a marked migration of families from the cities to the suburbs. This trend has affected the construction industry, both in the building of homes and in the requisite facilities, such as shopping centers, service stations, medical buildings, schools, and hospitals. Those industries which manufacture the articles that go into the furnishing and equipping of these structures have shared in the increase of business in their areas. Many firms have moved their offices from the cities to the suburbs in order to be nearer to where their employees live and, in cases of expansion, to provide greater parking facilities for them and for the firms' customers. There has been a noteworthy growth of industrial parks in the suburban areas, apart from the residential sections, that has markedly affected many of the operational phases of industries. [Raymond E. Glos and Harold A. Baker, *Introduction to Business* (Cincinnati: South-Western Publishing Co., 1967), p. 42.]

However, your instructor may want you to develop your own opinion about the affect of the city-to-suburb migration. Suppose that your instructor asks, "What are the advantages and disadvantages to business, in general, of the migration of people from cities to suburbs?"

To answer the question, you could use the information in the paragraph to explain the advantages of the migration. According to the paragraph, construction and manufacturing companies have had an increase in business as a result of the migration. You might also know some other facts about the advantages of the migration. If so, you could include that information in your answer. But you must remember that the question is concerned only with advantages and disadvantages to business. You should not include as an advantage, for instance, that your children might have a larger yard to play in or perhaps cleaner air to breathe if you lived in a suburb.

The textbook paragraph does not discuss disadvantages of the migration. To explain the possible disadvantages, you must use information you know or can figure out.

You would probably decide that the migration is a disadvantage to businesses and industries located in the cities. But that opinion or judgment would be based on the fact that after the migration, fewer people would be living in the cities. Fewer people would mean less business for companies in the cities. Less business would mean less money or income for the companies. Less income would mean that owners would put off repairing their property and constructing new buildings. Although construction might increase in the suburbs, it would decline in the cities.

You would then answer the question by stating and explaining the advantages and disadvantages you determined from your reading and from your own information and reasoning. If you were asked to write your answer, perhaps in an essay examination, you might explain your opinion in the following way:

Question
What are the advantages and disadvantages to business, in general, from the migration of people from cities to suburbs?

Answer
The migration of people from cities to suburbs has resulted in both advantages and disadvantages to business in general. The movement of families to the suburbs has created a demand for new houses, offices, and other facilities. The construction companies and associated manufacturing industries have enjoyed an increase in business as a result of this demand. Suburban commercial establishments, such as clothing stores, have also had an increase in sales. However, the migration has been a disadvantage to businesses and industries located in the cities. With fewer people living in the cities, urban businesses have had a decline in sales and income. The lowered income has caused city businesses to put off property repairs and construction. Although the migration from cities to suburbs has increased business for the construction industry and for suburban commercial establishments, the increase has been at the expense of businesses and industries in the cities.

information from paragraph
advantage from your information
disadvantages from your information and experience
your opinion
answer explaine

Now suppose you read the following paragraphs in one of your textbooks. According to the paragraphs, children would benefit from learning during their school years about different jobs and how to prepare for them. As you read the paragraphs, think about answering the following question: What would be the advantages and disadvantages to children if they were required to learn during their early school years about different jobs and how to prepare for them?

WORK AND WELL-BEING

Many philosophers and writers see grave dangers in the changing nature of work and popular attitudes about it in terms of well-being, mental health, and even sanity. Camus felt that "Without work all life goes rotten, but when work is soulless life stifles and dies." The psychologist Erich Fromm sees the danger that man will "continue spending most of his energy on meaningless work," and that "completely automatized work" may lead to a "completely automatized life." Abraham Maslow believed that work can be psychotherapeutic, and that the proper management of the work-lives of human beings, and of the work environment, can improve the world as to the point of becoming the technique of a Utopian revolution.

If all this is true, then it may be that a first step toward solving the psychological problems of the working world is a massive educational program. From elementary school on, children should be given information about the different jobs required to operate society and how to prepare for these jobs. Such education could help to avoid structural unemployment, the oversupply of trained people in some areas and shortages in others. It could also help break down stereotypes associated with some vocations: for instance, that nursing is a field for women and truck-driving for men, that college graduates are "better" than technical school graduates because it is somehow more respectable to work with your head than with your head and hands together. [S. Bernard Rosenblatt, Robert L. Bonnington, and Belverd E. Needles, Jr., *Modern Business: A Systems Approach* (Boston: Houghton Mifflin Company, 1973), pp. 139–140. Copyright © 1973 by Houghton Mifflin Company. Used by permission.]

To answer the question, you would determine the advantages and disadvantages to children in learning about different jobs in their early school years. You would follow the steps we used in the example on pages 249–250. Like the example, the above paragraphs explain some of the advantages of learning about jobs. You can probably think of other advantages to include in your answer.

But what might be the disadvantages? Would something the children are now being taught have to be given up to make time for learning about jobs? Would the information the children were given in their early years be out of date by the time they were ready to choose an occupation?

On the lines below, write the information you would include in your answer. State the information in complete sentences. Then, write a paragraph in which you answer the question.

Question

What would be the advantages and disadvantages to children if they were required to learn, during their early school years, about different jobs and how to prepare for them?

1. Advantages

a. ______________________________________

____

b. ______________________________________

______________________________________ } *information from paragraphs*

c. ______________________________________

____

d. ______________________________________

______________________________________ } *your information*

2. Disadvantages

a. ______________________________________

____

b. ______________________________________

____

c. ______________________________________

____

d. ______________________________________

______________________________________ } *your information*

Answer ______________________________________

Perhaps you will want to discuss your answer with other students. Their answers may differ from yours. Your instructor may also want to read your answer.

The questions you are asked about reading assignments will not always involve advantages and disadvantages of a particular situation or event. For example, if you were studying to be a police officer, your instructor might ask you to explain the procedure you would use in handling a particular situation. In a sociology course, your instructor might ask you to suggest a solution for a particular social problem. In a teacher education course, you might be asked to work out a lesson to teach children a particular skill. In each case, your instructor will want your answer to show that you know the information explained in your reading assignments. But your instructor will also want your answer to show that you are able to form reasoned opinions about that information.

Sometimes you will need to answer such questions in class discussions. More often, you will be asked to write your answers, in a paragraph or short essay. In either case, you should be able to work out your answers to the questions by following the inference-making process you learned in this task.

Words and Terms to Know

opinion

Concepts to Remember

1. An opinion is a conclusion that you have based on evidence but that you may not be able to prove absolutely.
2. To form a reasoned opinion, you need to make inferences.
3. Forming a reasoned opinion involves using information you read and information you already know.

Assignments

1. Complete the worksheet at the end of this task according to your instructor's directions.
2. Your instructor will ask you to read one of the selections in Unit Three. After you have read the selection, your instructor will want you to answer a question based on the information in the reading. You should write your answer in a paragraph of five or more complete sentences.

NAME ______________________________ DATE ____________

Question ______________________________

Answer ______________________________

Task 22 **Worksheet**

NAME ______________________________ DATE ____________

Reading Practice

Read the paragraphs below. Answer the questions that follow the paragraphs. After you have answered the questions, label the information you used from your reading and the information you added from your own knowledge. Use the examples in the task as a guide in labeling your answers.

1. According to the information in the paragraphs below, many people are as well-off financially when they receive unemployment benefits as they are when they are working. If the number of unemployed people who are receiving financial benefits increases and if those benefits are paid out of taxes on workers, how will you be affected if you are working for your living?

> TO WORK OR NOT TO WORK
>
> One growing problem for both government and business is that the gap between the economic position of those who work and those who do not is growing steadily smaller. Many people have already discovered the ironic fact that they are better off financially when idle than busy. Those at the lower end of the wage scale are sometimes ahead drawing unemployment insurance and/or welfare than they are working for the legal minimum wage. All wages are subject to income tax withholding while unemployment payments are not. The unemployed do not have to pay for transportation, lunches or presentable clothing. And for increasing numbers in our society the old idea that work has a positive value in itself no longer has meaning. . . . [S. Bernard Rosenblatt, Robert L. Bonnington, and Belverd E. Needles, Jr., *Modern Business: A Systems Approach* (Boston: Houghton Mifflin Company, 1973), p. 139. Copyright © 1973 by Houghton Mifflin Company. Used by permission.]

Question If the number of unemployed people who are receiving financial benefits increases and if those benefits must be paid for out of taxes on the worker, how will you be affected if you are working for your living?

Answer ____

____

____

____

2. According to the paragraph below, a teacher can use games and stories to teach children how to process information. Suppose you are a teacher in a nursery school. How would you teach the children at least two different ways of classifying the clothing they wear?

> Based on an understanding of how children learn to process information, programs for preschool children use thinking games and stories. These games and stories involve activities like noting sequence of events (as in getting out of bed and getting dressed in the morning), noting likenesses and differences, and grouping objects that are alike or used together. Classification activities can be specifically planned, as in thinking games that require putting all the things that move in a group. Adults can help children in other activities, such as noting the similarities and differences in raw and cooked vegetables, or noting that the visiting rabbit and a cat are both animals. [Ruth Highberger and Carol Schram, *Child Development for Day Care Workers* (Boston: Houghton Mifflin Company, 1976), p. 127. Copyright © 1976 by Houghton Mifflin Company. Used by permission.]

Question How would you teach the children in a nursery school at least two different ways of classifying the clothing they wear?

Answer

3. According to the following paragraphs, several different plans for shorter work hours have been tried recently. If you were an employer, which of the plans would you prefer? Why? If you were a worker, which of the plans would you prefer? Why? Be sure to answer *all* the questions.

A SHORTER WORK TIME

One of organized labor's greatest victories was the eight-hour day. Today, as automation increases and the nature of work progressively changes, there is much thought about still shorter hours of flexible work weeks and various plans are being suggested and tried out. One of these is the so-called 4–40 plan, a work week consisting of four ten-hour days. Wittman has written that "A shorter workweek made possible by a longer workday—usually four 10-hour days instead of five 8-hour days—is becoming a reality for a greater number of workers and businesses in the United States."[1] In 1971 the Chrysler Corporation and the United Auto Workers planned a pilot program on the 4–40 basis.

There are other shorter work plans, including two weeks on and two weeks off, six months of work and six months of leisure, a three-day, thirty-six-hour work week, and a four-day, thirty-two-hour work week. By 1972, 400 employers had adopted some form of abbreviated work week on a test basis for the majority of their employees. [S. Bernard Rosenblatt, Robert L. Bonnington, and Belverd E. Needles, Jr., *Modern Business: A Systems Approach* (Boston: Houghton Mifflin Company, 1973), p. 137. Copyright © 1973 by Houghton Mifflin Company. Used by permission.]

[1]John Wittman, "The Compressed Week," *Manpower,* July 1971, p. 8.

Question If you were an employer, which of the shorter work plans would you prefer? Why? If you were a worker, which of the shorter work plans would you prefer? Why?

Answer ______

4. In theory, the United States is supposed to have a classless society. However, class differences do exist. According to the paragraphs below, differences in the work that people do contribute to class distinctions. What other factors do you think contribute to class differences in the United States?

IS A CLASSLESS SOCIETY POSSIBLE?

Social reformers and creators of fictional utopias often envision a society that is totally classless, with no differences in rank, no stratification whatever. Is this a possibility in a real as well as a philosophical sense? It is doubtful. Let us consider one type of contemporary community that was founded on the premise that it would remain classless.

The collective farm (kibbutz) system of Israel has been studied by Eva Rosenfeld, among others. At the time she made her observations, each kibbutz averaged about 200 inhabitants (there were a few exceptions)—small enough, one might assume, to make it possible to maintain an unstratified social system.

In the kibbutz system the means of production and all other property belong to the commune. Members who leave have no claim on it. An elected work committee assigns tasks to the kibbutz dwellers. Governance is provided by elected officials, who serve brief one- or two-year terms. The philosophical orientation of the kibbutz is: "From everyone according to his ability. To everyone according to his need." Accordingly, the manager of an important communal undertaking might live in smaller quarters and eat less well than some unskilled workers who need special food and housing. All commodities are distributed from a central point. Meals are taken in a common dining hall. Children are reared in communal children's homes.

Can such a system become stratified? It already has. Differentials in power and status exist. Managers have come to hold higher status than individuals whose work they direct. Persons with required skills or talents that are in short supply are at a premium, and this is apt to gain them high status. Additionally, the *vatikim,* kibbutz pioneers, constitute an aristocracy by seniority alone. Certain terms in the language bespeak a status system: *a yish hashoov* is "an important personality," whereas a *stam pkak* is just "an unskilled, movable worker." The kibbutz, then, is not unstratified.

Moreover, the kibbutzim constitute a rather small part of the nation's total population. Much of Israel is urbanized, and large segments of its people occupy class positions similar to those found in many modern societies. It is unlikely, in fact, that the utopian goal of classlessness can be achieved in any society today, when a complex division of labor is required to meet the needs of modern life. [From *Sociology: The Study of Human Interaction,* by David Dressler with Donald Carns, pp. 388–389. Copyright © 1969 by David Dressler. Copyright © 1973 by Alfred A. Knopf, Inc. Reprinted by permission of Alfred A. Knopf, Inc.]

Question What factors, in addition to differences in people's work, contribute to class differences in the United States?

Answer ______________________________

Task 23
Generalizations

Suppose that a new highway has just been built, near the town where you live. Within a few days after the highway opens, you begin to read articles in the newspapers about accidents on the highway. One article says that most of the accidents have happened near the entrance and exit ramps and that the accidents are caused by the design of the ramps. A second article says that the cars were going very fast and that the accidents were caused by drivers who were breaking the speed limit. A third article says that the accidents happened in rainy weather, when visibility was bad. According to that article, the accidents were caused by the weather. A fourth article says that a large number of the accidents involved a certain make of car. The accidents, according to that article, were caused by manufacturing faults in the cars.

What *is* the cause of the accidents? Which of the articles should you believe? Is one of the articles right about the cause that it states? Could more than one of the articles be right?

Before you decide what caused the accidents, you need to think about the explanations given in each of the articles. For example, does the first article prove, through the supporting data,* that most of the accidents happened near the highway ramps? Does the second article prove that the drivers were breaking the speed limit? Does the third article prove that the accidents happened in bad weather? Does the fourth article prove that there were manufacturing faults in the particular make of car?

After reading the articles closely, you find that the fourth one contains no proof that there were manufacturing faults in the cars. Therefore, you decide that manufacturing faults *may* be involved, but they are not a proven cause.

The other three articles contain information supporting the causes that are given. Those causes are the design of the ramps, speed, and bad weather. In fact, after you think about the evidence in the three articles, you realize that most of the accidents occurred when all three of the conditions were present. Therefore, you make the generalization that the accidents are caused by the design of the ramps, speed of the cars, and bad weather conditions.

Now suppose that someone asks you what you think are the causes of the accidents. You have made the generalization that the accidents are caused by the design of the ramps, the speed of the cars, and bad weather conditions. You can "argue" or support your generalization by using the information you chose from the different articles. You may also have other information, perhaps from your own observations while driving on a highway, that supports your generalization.

*The use of supporting data to explain an idea is explained in Task 13 of the *Ideas Module.*

However, there could be other causes. Although the fourth article did not prove that there were manufacturing faults in the cars, the article did prove, with facts, that many of the cars were a certain make. You would have to qualify, or limit, your generalization to admit that manufacturing faults could be a cause. Also, because there were some accidents when all three conditions were not present, you could not say that *all* the accidents were caused by the combination of the three factors.

You would need to state your generalization to allow for these exceptions. You could say, "The main causes of the highway accidents are the design of the ramps, speed, and bad weather conditions." Or you could say, "The evidence indicates that most of the highway accidents are caused by a combination of ramp design, speed, and weather."

A **generalization** is a broad idea, opinion, or conclusion that is based on a number of facts or ideas. You may often agree with the ideas in a particular article or book. However, you should agree only after you have examined and thought about opposing or differing views. Ideally, you will learn to make your *own* generalizations, rather than simply agreeing with the ideas in one article or another.

The chart below is based on the example of selecting information from four different articles about highway accidents. The chart should help you understand the process of selecting information from your reading, making your generalization, and explaining your generalization.

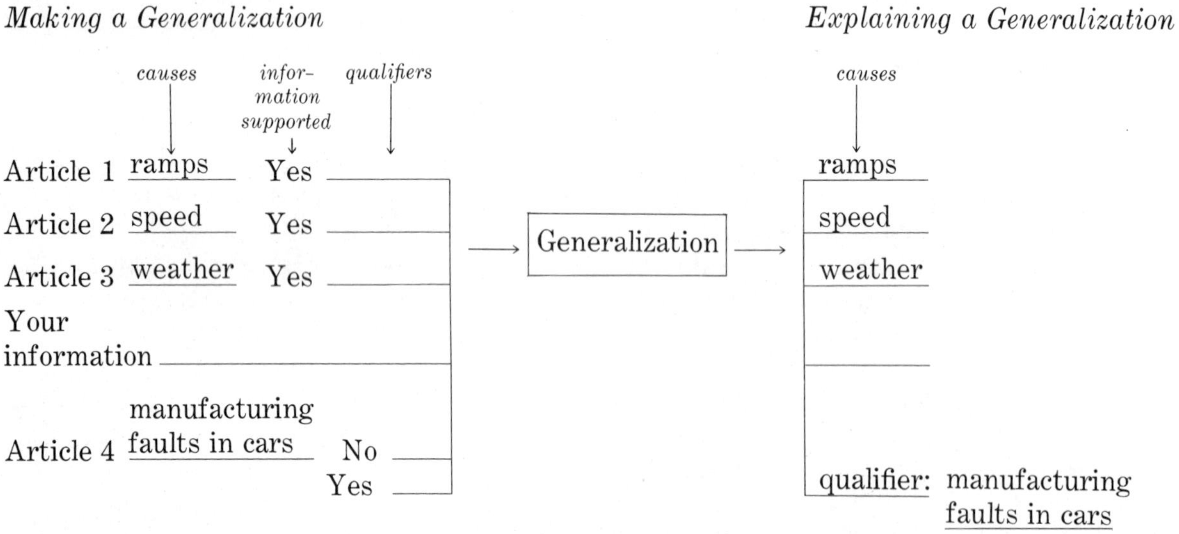

The articles that follow express different views about gun control and gun-control laws. You may already have an opinion about gun-control laws. However, you should not choose only the information that agrees with your opinion. Read the articles with an open mind. For example, suppose that you favor gun-control laws. Can you find information that supports the opinion that the laws are not working? If so, is there information that explains why the laws are not working? Or is there information that the laws *are* working? If so, what information explains why the laws are working? What advantages and disadvantages are there in gun-control laws? Are there ideas in the articles that are not supported and that you should reject? Should you qualify your acceptance of some of the ideas? Finally, by using some of the information in the articles and your own information, what generalization can you make about gun control?

Article 1 A Gun in Your Home

Every year thousands of Americans are killed—needlessly—by handguns. Even if you feel safer with one, you may have only an illusion of protection. Here are the shocking facts about the dangers of a gun in your home.

(1) It was all just too much for Gary Cohen, a Chicago boy of 13 whose mother died four years ago of cancer.

(2) Last June, his sister, Janice, 15, accidentally shot herself while handling a gun from her father's weapons collection. She was paralyzed from the chin down. Then, on November 9, after lonely months of brooding by his crippled daughter's hospital bedside, Gary's father, Philip, 38, gave up on life. He took one of the guns from his collection of pistols and rifles and committed suicide. Gary found him dead in the family bedroom, a note nearby telling of his misery.

(3) Three days later, while he was home alone from school—it was Veteran's Day, a holiday—Gary, too, was drawn to the deadly gun collection. The deeply troubled orphan took down another of his father's guns and shot himself in the head. Grieving over the dead youth, Gary's grandfather lamented, "A child doesn't see that there can be a future. He thinks the world disappears in one tragic act."

(4) For some 21,000 Americans each year, the world *does* disappear in one tragic act—a shattering blast from the barrel of a gun. The arsenal of firearms possessed by America's 50 million gun owners accounts for over 10,000 murders a year. Many of these are hot-tempered homicides which simply would not have occurred if guns were not so widely and quickly available. Our troubled nation also suffers 11,000 suicides a year and a "preponderant number" of these, according to U.S. Vital Statistics, are committed with firearms. Finally, there are the grisly gun accidents—averaging 2,600 a year—totally unnecessary, unpremeditated and pointless mishaps that leave their victims dead or maimed and often set off a tragic chain reaction—as in the case of Janice Cohen, her father and her 13-year-old brother. . . .

(5) The proliferation of handguns has now reached epidemic proportions. Although no one can accurately say how many pistols and revolvers are loose in America, accepted estimates put the figure above 30 million, and experts claim that each year around two million more handguns are added to that total. Nor can authorities determine just how many handguns are in the possession of street criminals or the organized underworld. What is known, and sadly deplored, is that millions of such weapons are kept by householders—many of them unlawfully—across the country. Guns are kept as protection, as sport weapons, war souvenirs or collectors' items such as the arms amassed by Gary Cohen's father. Many are hardly ever used or even touched. But for 2,600 Americans each year, one touch is enough to kill.

(6) It is a grim irony and a sobering fact that five years after the world was shocked by the murder of Senator Robert F. Kennedy (with a cheap handgun), this country is afflicted with more guns than ever before. What this boils down to is that every four minutes an American is killed or wounded with a handgun. Police say a new one is sold every 13 seconds. And used handguns—especially the inexpensive, pocket weapons dubbed "Saturday Night Specials"—are traded across the nation at the staggering rate of two a minute. Meanwhile, for all the talk, Washington is unable to stem the tidal wave of weapons. The critical question remains to be answered: *Why not?* Clearly most Americans want no more slaughter.

(7) According to both the Harris and Gallup pollsters, two-thirds of our citizens favor the registration of all firearms and the licensing of all gun owners. Strong preventative measures have been attempted by lawmakers such as Senators Edward Kennedy,

Birch Bayh and former Senator Joseph Tydings—measures that would ban the production, sale and possession of handguns. But they have met with little congressional success. The most significant step toward finding our way out of the firearms jungle was the Federal "Gun Control Act of 1968," enacted by Congress in the wake of the assassinations of Robert Kennedy and civil rights leader Martin Luther King, Jr.

(8) This law sought to (1) ban the interstate and mail-order traffic in weapons; (2) prevent sales to criminals, narcotics addicts and minors; and (3) dry up the flood of foreign-made Saturday Night Specials—some $16.4-million worth before the act's passage in 1968. But the law was found to contain gaping loopholes—loopholes which the gun merchants quickly discovered. While it prohibited the import of ready-to-fire Specials, it failed to ban the importation of the *parts* used in manufacturing the shoddy handguns. Thus, gun peddlers began to hire cheap labor (Cuban refugees in Miami, for example) to assemble Specials here at home from foreign parts they had imported.

(9) Despite the 1968 law, the gun dealers' cash registers scarcely missed a ring. U.S.-assembled Specials made here from Spanish, Italian and West German parts continued to flood the market. And, what was worse, other enterprising American gun manufacturers, thinking to take advantage of the new law, began producing their own brand of Specials from U.S. parts. By 1970, the increase of Specials on the streets exceeded the amount of the imports the '68 law had been designed to stop. . . .

(10) Further complicating the issue is the fact that attempts to curb crime by restricting the sale of the Saturday Night Special have in some cases backfired. New York police have reported that 75 percent of the handguns they have confiscated are not Specials at all, but "quality weapons." Of the 3,000 they seized last year, 98 percent were either stolen or acquired out-of-state. By now, even the politicians recognize what the police already knew: No self-respecting criminal carries a Special. It is too inaccurate, too undependable, too likely to be as dangerous to the shooter as to his target. And one final irony: The easily destructible Specials simply wear out and pass from circulation, while quality weapons last indefinitely.

(11) That pro-control politicians may be aiming at the wrong target provides anti-control elements with ready ammunition. The most substantial obstacle to stricter gun control is the nationwide sentiment generated by the National Rifle Association, a nonprofit—and tax-exempt—organization whose million or more members are hunters, sport shooters, gun collectors and dealers. The National Rifle Association is the nation's grassroots lobby against more gun controls. It champions stricter enforcement of current regulations and stands squarely behind the Second Amendment to the Constitution, the amendment which guarantees "the right of the people to keep and bear arms."

(12) What the NRA seldom talks about is the context in which that guarantee occurs. Here is the much-quoted amendment in its entirety: "A well-regulated militia being necessary to the security of a free state, the right of the people to keep and bear arms shall not be infringed." Clearly, what the founding fathers had in mind was the people's right to a citizens' militia for their common protection. It seems most unlikely that they were guaranteeing the right of individuals to commit mayhem with a gun. . . .

(13) All this adds up to a long, stormy battle, but probably little sweeping change. Certainly, before iron-fisted Federal mandates come out of Washington, there will have to be widespread public demand for states to adopt restrictive measures—as have New Jersey, New York, Massachusetts and California.

(14) Meanwhile, some local communities have already taken their own steps. Only last November, in Miami, the Dade County Commission passed three ordinances over the thundering protests of gun enthusiasts. One banned the Special. Another called for the licensing of all people involved in selling guns. The last, and most noteworthy, required the buyer to pass a firearms proficiency test on gun use, safety and laws

before acquiring a weapon.

(15) Though they may not be the answer, such local controls have already produced hopeful results. Philadelphia, back in 1965, adopted measures stronger than the 48-hour waiting period which the state required before a buyer could actually take possession of his handgun purchase. The city, in addition, made buyers obtain a permit, which meant furnishing fingerprints, a photograph, and the weapon's serial number. In one year, the permit plan weeded out almost 200 people with records of burglary, robbery, rape, addiction—plus 27 individuals who had been convicted of intent to kill and 96 others with police records for carrying concealed weapons. As the nation's rate of murder-by-firearms rose to 65 percent (of all murders), Philadelphia's inched up to only 44 percent. Toledo, once cast as the "gun capital" of the Midwest, instituted a plan similar to Philadelphia's. By 1970, its yearly handgun-murder rate had dropped eight percentage points. Louisville, Ky., experienced a ten percent reduction in armed robberies after requiring an eight-day waiting period for handgun purchase.

(16) All this is encouraging, but it alleviates only slightly the larger problem: the massive numbers of handguns still loose in the land. City and state controls can reduce the number of guns in criminal hands, but can't begin to resolve the problem of millions of lawful, if misguided, gun owners—ordinary householders who feel safer with a gun by their bedside. What these people need to know is that in the vast majority of instances a weapon offers only an illusion of protection, not the real thing.

(17) One of the gun lobby's favorite arguments is that in an emergency a gun may literally mean survival. There may be a point here, but it's not the point the lobby has in mind. Yes, survival *is* an issue where guns are concerned, but if we are to survive it will be *in spite* of our guns, not because of them. Everyday the newspapers bear out the frightening truth: Millions of guns in millions of homes are a threat to life—not to the life of some unseen enemy, but to the life of the people who own them. So if what you want is to protect yourself and your family, don't wait for stern measures to be handed down from Washington. Start your own gun-control program and start it now. If there's a gun in your home, turn it over to local authorities. Get rid of it, before it gets rid of you.

Article 2 Why Gun-Control Laws Don't Work

"The only effective way to cut down crime," says this distinguished legislator, "is to crack down on criminals."

(1) Let me say immediately that if I thought more gun-control laws would help diminish the tragic incidence of robberies, muggings, rapes and murders in the United States, I would be the first to vote for them. But I am convinced that making more such laws approaches the problem from the wrong direction.

(2) It is clear, I think, that gun legislation simply doesn't work. There are already some 20,000 state and local gun laws on the books, and they are no more effective than was the prohibition of alcoholic beverages in the 1920s. Our most recent attempt at federal gun legislation was the Gun Control Act of 1968, intended to control the interstate sale and transportation of firearms and the

Senator Barry Goldwater; reprinted with permission from the December 1975 *Reader's Digest,* pp. 183–184, 186, 188.

importation of uncertified firearms; it has done nothing to check the availability of weapons. It has been bolstered in every nook and cranny of the nation by local gun-control laws, yet the number of shooting homicides per year has climbed steadily since its enactment, while armed robberies have increased 60 percent.

(3) Some people, even some law-enforcement officials, contend that "crimes of passion" occur because a gun just happens to be present at the scene. I don't buy that. I can't equate guns with the murder rate, because if a person is angry enough to kill, he will kill with the first thing that comes to hand—a gun, a knife, an ice pick, a baseball bat.

(4) I believe our *only* hope of reducing crime in this country is to control not the weapon but the user. We must reverse the trend toward leniency and permissiveness in our courts—the plea bargaining, the pardons, the suspended sentences and unwarranted paroles—and make the lawbreaker pay for what he has done by spending time in jail. We have plenty of statutes against killing and maiming and threatening people with weapons. These can be made effective by strong enforcement and firm decisions from the bench. When a man knows that if he uses a potentially deadly object to rob or do harm to another person he is letting himself in for a mandatory, unparolable stretch behind bars, he will think twice about it.

(5) Of course, no matter what gun-control laws are enacted—including national registration—the dedicated crook can always get a weapon. So, some people ask, even if national registration of guns isn't completely airtight, isn't it worth trying? Sure, it would cause a little inconvenience to law-abiding gun owners. And it certainly wouldn't stop all criminals from obtaining guns. But it might stop a few, maybe quite a few. What's wrong with that?

(6) There are several answers. The first concerns enforcement. How are we going to persuade the bank robber or the street-corner stickup artist to register his means of criminal livelihood? Then there is the matter of expense. A study conducted eight years ago showed a cost to New York City of $72.87 to investigate and process one application for a pistol license. In mid-1970 dollars, the same procedure probably costs over $100. By extrapolation to the national scale, the cost to American taxpayers of investigating and registering the 40 to 50 million handguns might reach $4 billion or $5 billion. On top of that, keeping the process in operation year after year would require taxpayer financing of another sizable federal bureau. We ought to have far better prospects of success before we hobble ourselves with such appalling expenditures.

(7) Finally, there are legal aspects based on the much-discussed Second Amendment to the Bill of Rights, which proclaims that "A well regulated Militia, being necessary to the security of a free State, the right of the people to keep and bear Arms, shall not be infringed." The anti-gun faction argues that this right made sense in the days of British oppression but that it has no application today. I contend, on the other hand, that the Founding Fathers conceived of an armed citizenry as a necessary hedge against tyranny from within as well as from without, that they saw the right to keep and bear arms as basic and perpetual, the one thing that could spell the difference between freedom and servitude. Thus I deem most forms of gun control unconstitutional in intent.

(8) Well, then, I'm often asked, what kind of gun laws *are* you for? I reply that I am for laws of common sense. I am for laws that prohibit citizen access to machine guns, bazookas and other military devices. I am for laws that are educational in nature. I believe that before a person is permitted to buy a weapon he should be required to take a course that will teach him how to use it, to handle it safely and keep it safely about the house.

(9) Gun education, in fact, can actually reduce lawlessness in a community, as was demonstrated in an experiment conducted in Highland Park, Mich. City police launched a program to instruct merchants in the use of handguns. The idea was to help them protect themselves and their businesses from robbers, and it was given wide publicity. The store-robbery rate dropped from an average of 1.5 a day to none in four months.

(10) Where do we go from here? My answer

to this is based on the firm belief that we have a crime problem in this country, not a gun problem, and that we must meet the enemy on his own terms. We must start by making crime as unprofitable for him as we can. And we have to do this, I believe, by getting tough in the courts and corrections systems.

(11) A recent news story in Washington, D.C., reports that, of 184 persons convicted of gun possession in a six-month period, only 14 received a jail sentence. Forty-six other cases involved persons who had previously been convicted of a felony or possession of a gun. Although the maximum penalty for such repeaters in the District of Columbia is ten years in prison, half of these were not jailed at all. A study last year revealed that in New York City, which has about the most prohibitive gun legislation in the country, only one out of six people convicted of crimes involving weapons went to jail.

(12) This sorry state of affairs exists because too many judges and magistrates either don't know the law or are unwilling to apply it with appropriate vigor. It's time to demand either that they crack down on these criminals or be removed from office. It may even be time to review the whole system of judicial appointments, to stop weakening the cause of justice by putting men on the bench who may happen to be golfing partners of Congressmen and too often lack the brains and ability for the job. In Arizona today we elect our judges, and the system is working well, in part because we ask the American and local bar associations to consider candidates and make recommendations. In this way, over the last few years, we have replaced many weaklings with good jurists.

(13) We have long had all the criminal statutes we need to turn the tide against the crime wave. There is, however, one piece of proposed legislation that I am watching with particular interest. Introduced by Sen. James McClure (R., Idaho), it requires that any person convicted of a federal crime in which a gun is used serve five to ten years in jail automatically on top of whatever penalty he receives for the crime itself. A second conviction would result in an extra ten-year-to-life sentence. These sentences would be mandatory and could not be suspended. It is, in short, a "tough" bill. I think that this bill would serve as an excellent model for state legislation.

(14) And so it has in California which, last September, signed into law a similar bill requiring a mandatory jail sentence for any gun-related felony.

(15) Finally, it's important to remember that this is an area of great confusion; an area in which statistics can be juggled and distorted to support legislation that is liable to be expensive, counter-productive or useless. The issue touches upon the freedom and safety of all of us, whether we own firearms or not. The debate over gun control is an adjunct to the war against crime, and that war must be fought with all the intelligence and tenacity we can bring to it.

Article 3 Gun Control: Neat, Plausible and Wrong!

Gun control advocates corrode constitutional freedoms while burdening taxpayers with greater bureaucratic expense.

(1) If one studies the history of mankind's major calamities one must eventually reach the conclusion that most of them were engineered by individuals or groups whose good intentions and high purposes were above question. Within their own conceptual framework, their actions were both moral and in the best interests of some social or

Gary G. Vance, *Guns & Ammo* Magazine (October, 1974), pp. 34–35.

political grouping. The failure of such well-intentioned enterprises is that they are invariably short-sighted, selfish and simplistic. They are born more of passion than of wisdom. In the name of justice and societal welfare both Communism and Fascism have perpetrated some of the most heinous, brutal and dehumanizing acts known to man, all with good intentions.

(2) The damage issuing from such good intentions is not confined to sweeping political movements. Around my home in Southeast Alaska there are still a few of the original totems carved and colored by the Tlingit and Haida Indians native to this area. The totems were a means of recording family or tribal history and they represent an art form that I consider singularly magnificent. There were once many such totems on the islands where the Indians lived but most were burned by early missionaries because they were thought to be pagan and godless. More good intentions.

(3) When the U.S. Constitution was amended to make the manufacture, sale and consumption of alcoholic beverages illegal, the advocates of the amendment surely had our best interests at heart. The issue was simple. Some people drank too much which resulted in wasted lives and ravaged families. Make the alcohol illegal and the problem would be solved. Only things did not work out as they had planned; bootlegging became big business. Alcohol was everywhere, much of it being scarcely better than poison. Prices skyrocketed. And, most important of all, that great social experiment resulted in the establishment of an organized criminal empire that flourishes even today. So much for good intentions.

(4) The history of mankind's survival is one narrow escape after another from the ministrations of some misguided zealot and his particular recipe for the common good. This is not to say there have not been events and individuals that have done much to correct inequities in human affairs. The decision of the U.S. to plunge into the mad war in Europe in 1942 was a necessary step to rekindle the lights which were winking out under Nazi domination of that sad continent. However, that whole grim chapter in history need never have happened. It was born of the good intentions of all the political leaders who sought to appease and conciliate the criminals that had seized power in Germany. A firmer and less well-intentioned approach to Hitler's government may have changed the entire history of the world much for the better.

(5) Today we are threatened by still another cadre of politicians who are convinced that they alone know what is best for us all. I am personally appalled by the plans they are making. The gun control issue is a classic example of how these well-intentioned hustlers promote injustice, infringe on human rights and move us ever further down the road toward the practice of empire. And make no mistake that the practice of empire is what these gentlemen have in mind. They all staunchly proclaim their belief in the concept of government by the people but they enjoy their power as a personal attribute, they are convinced that they personally know what is best for you and me, they are determined to impose their will to the fullest extent possible, and most of them are frightfully naive and shortsighted opportunists. Let's see what happens when you and I, law-abiding citizens, are deprived of our right to own handguns of any sort and are forced to register long guns with a government bureau.

1. A lucrative black market in handguns will spring up, with little delay, across the entire nation, centering primarily on the major cities. Huge sums will be spent on a law enforcement effort that will, at best, be no more effective than present efforts in controlling the criminal use of guns. Handguns will still be widely available to anyone who may want one for a quick stick-up or to back up other illegal activities. They will also be available to any blowhard who feels he needs one to bolster his sagging ego. All he has to do is pay the black market price.
2. Crime rates will show no significant slackening and may well increase as the average citizen becomes more

vulnerable. The causes of crime in the U.S. have nothing to do with the availability of legitimately owned guns.

3. The record-keeping costs for long guns will multiply as another federal bureaucracy becomes entrenched and begins to grow fat and sloppy. The bureaucrats will seek ever newer controls and restrictions to justify more expansion and broader powers. Record-keeping will become an end in itself.
4. Little information useful in the solving of crimes will be generated by all of those expensive records. This is borne out by other cases of registration both here and abroad.
5. Red tape harassment of law-abiding gun owners will grow out of proportion to any rational purpose. The shooting sports will go into a decline resulting in sharply reduced revenue for game conservation purposes. (By far the greatest amount spent for conservation comes from the pocket of the shooters and hunters of this nation; recently around $160 million a year.)
6. Game habitat and control will deteriorate and game animals, as well as non-game animals, will die off in great numbers further insuring the decline of hunting in particular and the shooting sports in general.
7. A readily available listing of arms in the hands of private citizens will be created which internal enemies could conceivably use in a case of armed confrontation. Couldn't happen in the U.S., you say? The naive trust of a complacent citizenry is the foundation upon which totalitarian governments are built. The framers of the Constitution fully intended that personal arms should *not* be taken from the private citizen. Gun control advocates will argue that such reasoning is obsolete, pointing to huge standing armies and nuclear hardware. But they fail to explain away the increasing trend toward kidnapping, terrorism and guerrilla warfare as instruments of social change. An armed citizenry is just as important now as it ever was.

(6) In summary, the crime problem will remain unchanged and possibly grow worse; taxes will be increased or funds diverted from other programs (probably wildlife conservation) to pay for the new bureaus; our national wildlife resources will decline and we will grow individually and collectively more vulnerable to the tyrants known to exist everywhere, in every nation, throughout history.

(7) Meanwhile, those well-intentioned fellows that started the whole thing will express "deep personal concern" over the worsening situation. They will draw up even more restrictive measures to "sew up the loopholes" in their earlier efforts. They will even order "funding of special task forces and study groups to come to grips with the problem." You have heard their siren speeches and witnessed their posing before. By that time the battle will be lost.

(8) H. L. Mencken once wrote, "There is always an easy solution to every human problem . . . neat, plausible, and wrong." Strict gun controls simply feel right to those crusading politicians seeking an easy scapegoat to complex social problems. Guns are loud, dangerous, expensive and unnecessary in their estimation. Many people get along fine without them so obviously they are not needed. Arms represent a source of power in the hands of private citizens and in the gun control politician's mind such power is a threat to his own.

(9) The outlawing of guns is strangely like the outlawing of books. The beginnings of tyranny can invariably be traced to episodes of attempted thought-control through the banning of certain books. And just as tyrants seek to control our thoughts, they must seek to control our actions. It is the mind and will of a free people, seeking to determine their own outcomes, that is the enemy of the empire builders. What difference is there between the tyrant who decides to dispose of certain books because he believes the common man cannot be trusted

to judge them wisely and the politician who advocates the banning of guns because he believes the common man cannot be trusted to use them wisely? Attempts to pass laws legalizing the seizure and control of guns or books must be met with unfailing resistance wherever such attempts are encountered. I am not interested in how nobly conceived attempts at control may be. I am only interested in the end result. The road to hell, it's said, is paved with good intentions.

Perhaps you were surprised to learn, as you read the articles, that we already have a great many gun-control laws. Article 1 refers to the Gun Control Act of 1968 (paragraph 7) and also to local or city laws (paragraphs 14 and 15). Article 2 also refers to the Gun Control Act of 1968 (paragraph 2) and to "20,000 state and local gun laws" that have been passed (paragraph 2). Article 3 does not mention any laws. As you may have noticed, the article refers only to such laws being planned by politicians. Although the article was published in 1974, it seems to be out of date.

The intent of the laws is to reduce the number of deaths caused by guns. Therefore, you should examine the information that tells you whether the laws are helping to achieve that goal. If you look at the figures in paragraph 4 of article 1, you will find that there are 21,000 deaths each year from guns. In paragraph 15 of the same article, the author says that the *rate* of increase in murders by guns has not been as great in Philadelphia, which has a gun law, as in the nation as a whole. But the paragraph does not say that the number of murders in Philadelphia has gone down. Instead, it says that the *percent* of murders by guns went down. In article 2, the statement (paragraph 2) that the number of homicides has increased is not supported with statistics. Consequently, you would not want to accept that statement as a fact. In article 3, the claim is made that gun laws will not decrease but may even increase crime (paragraph 5, item 2). However, the statement, like many of the claims made in the article, is not supported with facts or other evidence. In fact, the article lacks both accurate information about gun laws that have been passed and support for the ideas that are expressed. For these reasons, the article is not a good source. You will want to base your generalization on the information in articles 1 and 2.

So far, even though the first two articles express different views about gun control, you have found some information that is the same in both articles. Both articles say that we already have federal, state, and local gun laws. They also say that the laws have not resulted in a decrease in the number of deaths by guns. However, each article states different reasons for the failure of the laws. Article 1 says (paragraphs 8 and 9) that gun merchants took advantage of loopholes in the ban against Saturday Night Specials, which was part of the 1968 Gun Law. Paragraph 10 points out that criminals were not affected by the law because criminals do not use Saturday Night Specials. Article 2 says that enforcement of gun laws is the problem. First, criminals won't give up their guns (paragraph 6). Second, enforcement is very expensive (paragraph 6). Third, gun laws may not be legal, since the Bill of Rights guarantees a person the right to bear arms (paragraph 7). The article also says (paragraph 4 and paragraphs 10 through 12) that the judges are either not enforcing the laws we already have or are not handing down stiff enough sentences for breaking the laws.

Perhaps you could make a generalization about why gun-control laws are not working, based on some or all of the reasons you have now found in the articles. You might say, for example, "Gun-control laws do not work because merchants find loopholes in the laws." You could support your generalization by using the information you have found in the articles.

However, there are other generalizations you could make from the information in the articles. Are there any laws mentioned that have provisions in them that seem to be effective? Is enforcement the problem? Is education of gun owners effective? Is the Second Amendment to the Bill of Rights still needed in a society that has police, national guard, and an army?

Read the articles again. Choose information on which you can base your own generalization. Write the information on the following page. Add any information you have from reading other articles or from your own information. Then, state the generalization you have made. When you have finished, ask your instructor to check your work. After your instructor approves your generalization and the information you used, write a paragraph of six to ten sentences in which you state and explain your generalization.

NAME ______________________ DATE ____________

Information from Gun-Control Articles ______________________

Information from Other Articles and/or Experiences ______________________

Generalization

Explanation of Generalization

Words and Terms to Know

generalization

Concepts to Remember

1. A generalization is a broad idea, opinion, or conclusion that is based on a number of facts or ideas.
2. Before making a generalization, you should examine and think about opposing or differing views that are expressed in your reading materials.

Assignments

1. Complete the worksheet at the end of this task according to your instructor's directions.
2. Your instructor will ask you to read a set of articles in Unit Three. Select information from the articles, add any facts or information you have about the topic, and make a generalization from your information. Write a paragraph of six to ten sentences in which you state and support your generalization by using information from the articles and your own information.

NAME ________________________________ DATE ____________

Information from Articles and Other Sources ________________________________

Generalization ________________________________

Explanation of Generalization ________________________________

Task 23 **Worksheet**

NAME ______________________________ DATE ____________

Reading Practice

Read the articles that follow. Select information from the articles and make a generalization based on that information and other information you have about the subject. Write the information you have used on the lines below. Then, write your generalization. Ask your instructor to check your work.

Information from Articles and Other Sources ______________________________

Generalization ______________________________

A. THE OTHER YOU

What if our society uses new-found technologies of "genetic engineering" to interfere with the biological nature of human beings? Might that not be disastrous?

What about cloning, for instance?

Cloning is a term originally used in connection with nonsexual reproduction of plants and very simple animals. Now it is coming into use in connection with higher animals, since biologists are finding ways of starting with an individual cell of a grown animal and inducing it to multiply into another grown animal.

Each cell in your body, you see, has a full complement of all the genes that control your inherited characteristics. It has everything of this sort that there was in the original fertilized egg-cell out of which you developed. The cells in your body now devote themselves to specialized activities and no longer grow and differentiate—but what if such a cell, from skin or liver, could be restored to the environment of the egg-cell? Would it not begin to grow and differentiate once more, and finally form a second individual with your genes? Another you, so to speak? It has been done in frogs and can undoubtedly be done in human beings.

But is cloning a safe thing to unleash on society? Might it not be used for destructive purposes? For instance, might not some ruling group decide to clone their submissive, downtrodden peasantry, and thus produce endless hordes of semi-robots who will slave to keep a few in luxury and who may even serve as endless ranks of soldiers designed to conquer the rest of the world?

A dreadful thought, but an unnecessary fear. For one thing, there is no need to clone for the purpose. The ordinary method of reproduction produces all the human beings that are needed and as rapidly as is needed. Right now, the ordinary method is producing so many people as to put civilization in danger of imminent destruction. What more can cloning do?

Secondly, unskilled semi-robots cannot be successfully pitted against the skilled users of machines, either on farms, in factories or in armies. Any nation, depending on downtrodden masses, will find itself an easy mark for exploitation by a less populous but more skilled and versatile society. This has happened in the past often enough.

But even if we forget about slave-hordes, what about the cloning of a relatively few individuals? There are rich people who could afford the expense, or politicians who could have the influence for it, or the gifted who could undergo it by popular demand. There can then be two of a particular banker or governor or scientist—or three—or a thousand.

Might this not create a kind of privileged caste, who would reproduce themselves in greater and greater numbers, and who would gradually take over the world?

Before we grow concerned about this, we must ask whether there will really be any great demand for cloning. Would *you* want to be cloned? The new individual formed from your cell will have your genes and therefore your appearance and, possibly, talents, but *he will not be you.* The clone will be, at best, merely your identical twin. Identical twins share the same genetic pattern, but they each have their own individuality and are separate persons.

Cloning is *not* a pathway to immortality, then, because *your* consciousness does *not* survive in your clone, any more than it would in your identical twin if you had one.

In fact, your clone would be far less than your identical twin. What shapes and forms a personality is not genes alone, but all the environment to which it is exposed. Identical twins grow up in identical surroundings, in the same family, and under each other's influence. A clone of yourself, perhaps thirty or forty years younger, would grow up in a different world altogether and would be shaped by influences that would be sure to make him less and less like you as he grows older.

He may even earn your jealousy. After all, you are old and he is young. You may once have been poor and struggled to become well-to-do, but he will be well-to-do from the start. The mere fact that you won't be able to view it as a child, but as another competing and better-advantaged *you,* may accentuate the jealousy.

No! I imagine that, after some initial experiments, the demand for cloning will be virtually nonexistent.

But suppose it isn't a matter of your desires, but of society's demands? I, for instance, have published 158 books so far, but I am growing old. If there were a desperate world demand for me to write 500 more books, I would have to be cloned. The other me, or group of me's, could continue. Or could they?

The clones will not grow up my way. They won't be driven to write, as I was, out of a need to escape from the slums—unless you provide each with slums to escape from. Unlike me, they will all have a mark to shoot at—the original me. I could do as I please, but they will be doomed to imitate me and they may very well refuse. How many of my clones will have to be supported and fed and kept out of trouble in order to find one who will be able to write like me, and will want to?

It won't be worth society's trouble, I assure you. [Isaac Asimov, "The Other You," *The American Way* (March, 1975), pp. 9–10. Copyright © 1975 by *The American Way.* Reprinted by permission of the author.]

B. GENETIC ENGINEERING

Scientists are now able to do strange things with cells and genes. For example, one group of scientists took out the nucleus of a fertilized frog egg and substituted the nucleus of a regular frog cell. This made it possible to rear "clones" of frogs. A clone is a group of genetically identical creatures.

Theoretically, the technique could be applied to humans. By tinkering with primitive human cells, perhaps by modifying the genetic material in the sperm and the ovum, scientists might be able to produce a human being of high mentality with a superb body—and then, if the fertilized ovum could be induced to grow outside the uterus, clone it to produce an army of such individuals.

None of this can be done as yet, but we are getting frighteningly close. So close, in fact, that scientists who are involved in genetic-engineering research recently declared a moratorium on certain research projects until they can hold an international meeting to discuss the possible end results of their research. Who, for example, will decide what characteristics a "superperson" should have?

As with nuclear fission, there is in genetic engineering great potential for good but equally great potential for harm. By manipulating cell nuclei we might be able to wipe out such conditions as mongolism and mental retardation, such diseases as diabetes and even cancer. We might also—say, by changing the characteristics of the bacteria currently being used in research—produce an epidemic of lethal disease that could kill millions of people. We might make the "Andromeda Strain" a reality.

Genetic engineering is an idea whose time may have come before we have the ethical-philosophical knowledge and understanding to deal with it safely. We could be like five-year-old children given dynamite to play with. In this area I make no predictions; I simply hope we don't blow ourselves up. [William A. Nolen, "The Next One Hundred Years," *McCall's* (April, 1976), pp. 138, 140. Reprinted by permission of the author's agent, Lurton Blassingame. Copyright © 1976 The McCall Publishing Company.]

Readings **Unit Three**

In this unit, you will find a collection of articles and excerpts from books. Your instructor will want you to read some of them and use the reading skills you have learned in this module.

Reading 1 The Bandanna

Modern cowboys seem to be giving up the bandanna handkerchief. Perhaps the moving pictures have made it tawdry. Yet there was a time when this article was almost as necessary to a cowboy's equipment as a rope, and it served for purposes almost as varied. The prevailing color of the bandanna was red, but blues and blacks were common, and of course silk bandannas were prized above those made of cotton.

When the cowboy got up in the morning and went down to the water hole to wash his face he used his bandanna for a towel. Then he tied it around his neck, letting the fold hang down in front, thus appearing rather nattily dressed for breakfast. After he had roped out his bronc and tried to bridle him he probably found that the horse had to be blindfolded before he could do anything with him. The bandanna was what he used to blindfold the horse with. Mounted, the cowboy removed the blind from the horse and put it again around his own neck. Perhaps he rode only a short distance before he spied a big calf that should be branded. He roped the calf; then if he did not have a "piggin string"—a short rope used for tying down animals—he tied the calf's legs together with the bandanna and thus kept the calf fast while he branded it.

In the summertime the cowboy adjusted the bandanna to protect his neck from the sun. He often wore gloves too, for he liked to present neat hands and neck. If the hot sun was in his face, he adjusted the bandanna in front of him, tying it so that the fold would hang over his cheeks, nose and mouth like a mask. If his business was with a dust-raising herd of cattle, the bandanna adjusted in the same way made a respirator; in blizzardly weather it likewise protected his face and ears. In the swift, unhalting work required in the pen the cowboy could, without losing time, grab a fold of the bandanna loosely hung about his neck and wipe away the blinding sweat. In the pen, too, the bandanna served as a rag for holding the hot handles of branding irons.

Many a cowboy has spread his bandanna, perhaps none too clean itself, over dirty, muddy water and used it as a strainer to drink through; sometimes he used it as a cup towel, which he called a "drying rag." If the bandanna was dirty, it was probably not so dirty as the other apparel of the cowboy, for when he came to a hole of water, he was wont to dismount and wash out his handkerchief, letting it dry while he rode along, holding it in his hand or spread over his hat. Often he wore it under his hat in order to help keep his head cool. At other times, in the face of a fierce gale, he used it to tie down his hat.

The bandanna made a good sling for a broken arm; it made a good bandage for a blood wound. Early Irish settlers on the Nueces River used to believe that a bandanna handkerchief that had been worn by a drowned man would, if cast into a stream above the sunken body, float until it came over the body and then sink, thus locating it. Many a cowboy out on the lonely plains has been buried with a clean bandanna spread over his face to keep the dirt, or the coarse blanket on which the dirt was poured, from touching it. The bandanna has been used to hang men with. Rustlers used to "wave" strangers around with it, as a warning against nearer approach, though the hat was more commonly used for signaling. Like the Mexican sombrero or the four-gallon Stetson, the bandanna could not be made too large.

When the cowboys of the West make their final parade on the grassy shores of Paradise, the guidon that leads them should be a bandanna handkerchief. It deserves to be called the flag of the range country.

Reading 2 The Basis of Capital

In remote parts of Alaska, some trappers and traders still make their living by trapping fur-bearing animals for skins to trade for money or goods. These men need little more than their clothing, traps, guns, and perhaps a horse, a few dogs, or a jeep. Yet simple as this equipment is, it illustrates the essential characteristics of business capital.

Every business, whatever its size or activity, must raise capital, produce goods or services, sell the goods or services, and dispose of the proceeds of sale. The Alaskan hunter must have, or borrow, enough money to buy his first outfit. He then traps animals and sells or trades them, and disposes of the proceeds in any of several ways. He may use most of the proceeds to buy more traps and equipment, or he may divert most of the proceeds to buy food, clothing, and housing for himself. He has to use some of the proceeds to live on, but he must also plan for the replacement of broken traps, horses that die, and hunting boots that wear out.

The problems of capital which the hunter faces are basically similar to those of IBM and General Motors: there are differences of magnitude and of physical characteristics, but not of fundamental character. It is the size and variety of operations of the large public corporation that makes its financial problems more intricate than those of the simple hunter.

S. Bernard Rosenblatt, Robert L. Bonnington, and Belverd E. Needles, Jr., *Modern Business: A Systems Approach* (Boston: Houghton Mifflin Company, 1973), p. 143.

Reading 3 The Industrial Revolution Begins

The French nation's destruction of the monarchy and substitution of a republic is an outstanding example of a political revolution. In this chapter another type of revolution will be discussed, a revolution caused by the substitution of machinery for hand labor in many manufacturing processes. These new machines changed conditions in the handicraft trades so radically and multiplied output so enormously that the accelerating consequences of the Industrial Revolution still dominate modern civilization. The use of the term "revolution" to describe a change that began in the eighteenth century and is still transforming society in new and more dynamic ways is confusing, but the label has been hallowed by long usage and is valid if applied to the world economy over the past two centuries. The revolution began in the manufacture of textiles in England in the late eighteenth century.

For reasons not yet fully understood, the eighteenth century brought an unusual increase of population to the European countries. This growth can be explained in part by improved living conditions, stricter sanitation, and cheaper food. Between 1750 and 1800, the English population rose from 6 to 9 million and the French from 19 to 26 million. The same years saw a rise in the general standard of comfort. Sugar, choco-

Robert Edwin Herzstein, *Western Civilization,* Vol. 2 (Boston: Houghton Mifflin Company, 1975), pp. 490–491.

late, coffee, tea, furs, and silks came to be looked upon as necessities in the homes of the well-to-do, while the poor were enabled to vary their diet with new vegetables like potatoes and carrots and to afford cotton and linen clothing. The normal consequence of this increased demand was a marked quickening in trade, especially colonial trade, and an acceleration of business life. Anvils rang, and spinning-wheels hummed to a swifter tune. Roads and canals were extended and improved so that goods might travel with greater dispatch, and sailing ships bound for distant markets crowded on more sail in the hope of a fleeter passage.

Rising demand meant greater profits, and the urge to speed production led manufacturers to experiment with new methods. When English foundry-owners discovered that they could not fill their orders for iron because sufficient wood to smelt the ore was lacking, they found a way to use coke instead. This meant more business for the mine-owners, but they in turn were handicapped by water in the mines, until the problem was solved with a steam-driven pump invented by Thomas Newcomen and improved by James Watt.

Similarly when spinning and weaving by hand proved too slow and costly a method of producing cotton fabrics for an expanding market, an improved loom was constructed by John Kay in 1733, and a swifter method of spinning was devised by James Hargreaves in 1764. Five years later, Richard Arkwright invented a still better spinning frame, only to see it superseded within ten years by Samuel Crompton's "mule," a machine run by one worker which could equal the output of two hundred hand-spinners.

Reading 4 *from* Death in Miami Beach

At Key West, a few days before Christmas, I visited the turtle slaughterhouse. It is one of the few tourist attractions on this spot of island, "North Havana," raised far out into the sea off the coast of Florida. Visitors take their kiddies by the hand and lead them to see the nice turtles.

Before being killed and canned, the turtles swim in dense kraals, bumping each other in the murky water, armor clashing, dully lurching against the high pens. Later, trussed on a plank dock, they lie unblinking in the sun, their flippers pierced and tied. The tough leather of their skin does not disguise their present helplessness and pain. They wear thick, sun-hardened accumulations of blood at their wounds. Barbados turtles, as large as children, they belong to a species which has been eliminated locally by ardent harvesting of the waters near Key West, but the commercial tradition still brings them here to be slaughtered. Crucified like thieves, they breathe in little sighs, they gulp, they wait.

At a further stage, in the room where the actual slaughtering occurs, the butchers stride through gore in heavy boots. The visitor must proceed on a catwalk; a misstep will plunge him into a slow river of entrails and blood. Because it was near Christmastime, the owners of the plant had installed a speaker system for musical divertissement of the butchers, and while the turtles dried under the sun or lay exposed to the butchers' knives, Christmas bells tolled out, electronically amplified, *God Rest Ye Merry, Gentlemen,* or the Bing Crosby recording of *Adeste Fideles.*

Herbert Gold, *The Age of Happy Problems* (New York: The Dial Press, 1962).

Reading 5 The Man Who Drew the Boundaries of a New Nation's Capital

[Washington, D.C.] visitors looking at maps of the nation's capital may wonder why the District of Columbia is a perfect square plunked down astride the Potomac River. Who put this square precisely where it lies between Virginia and Maryland?

The story of the man who had key responsibility for fixing the exact location of Washington began in an African village on the far side of the Atlantic about the year 1698. At that time in West Africa certain powerful rulers of large areas often sent out military forces to subdue weaker neighboring inland peoples and to bring back captives. One such prisoner of war was a slender youth named Bannka, son of a chief.

The black ruler who held Bannka sold him, along with other captives, to a white slave trader on the sea coast. Bannka was surely frightened at his first sight of a sailing ship gliding over the water, then stopping as if by magic. Even more terrifying, his captors put iron chains on his legs and made him lie down spoon-fashion between two other men, strangers perhaps whose language he could not speak. The space where he lay was so low he could not sit upright, and it stank.

Somehow Bannka survived a two-month voyage across the Atlantic. (Five out of six Africans died or killed themselves before their captors got them onto an auction block in the North American colonies.) Nevertheless, the captain who had bought him did not think Bannka was worth much. He was too skinny—and too defiant. Accordingly the captain put a low price on him—a price so low that a most unusual bidder could afford him.

Bannka's buyer was a woman named Molly Welsh who had managed to acquire a tobacco farm of her own and by herself had raised good enough crops to pay for Bannka and one other slave as well. Molly Welsh had a special feeling about slavery. She herself had been a virtual slave, although white, as an indentured servant for seven years, brought to America as a convicted criminal. Before that, in England, she had worked on a farm. One day the cow she was milking had kicked over the milk pail. When her employer discovered the pail was empty, he accused her of stealing the milk and had her tried for theft. The court found her guilty.

Usually the punishment for theft was death. But Molly Welsh "called for the Book"—that is, she called for the Bible and read a passage from it, proving that she was literate. At that time English law provided that prisoners who could read need not be hanged. So it was that Molly Welsh found herself not on some gallows in England but alive in Maryland and free after working off her indentured servitude.

Molly Welsh not only bought Bannka; she also freed him and married him, even though he proudly refused to give up his own religion. One of their children, Mary, took her father's name as a surname which, with a slight change in spelling, became Banneky. In due course Mary Banneky did just what her mother Molly Welsh had done. She married a man from Africa who had been a slave. Both Mary and her newly freed husband used her surname and passed it along to their children, one of whom was Benjamin. When his name was written down it came out Benjamin Bannaker or Banneker, and so it remained.

With help from his grandmother and from Quaker neighbors, Benjamin Banneker learned to read. He went on to master mathematics by himself. By the year 1753 he had become a celebrity in the part of Maryland where he farmed his grandmother Mol-

Franklin Folsom, "The Man Who Drew the Boundaries of a New Nation's Capital," *Mainliner* (August, 1975), pp. 35–36.

ly's land. Neighbors black and white came from miles around to marvel at an accurate clock he had built almost entirely of wood, although the only time pieces he had ever seen were sundials and watches.

Banneker continued his studies and became a proficient astronomer. By 1776 he had acquired the knowledge he would later put to use in an annual publication called *Banneker's Almanac* which included accurate data about the movements of heavenly bodies, together with observations about life. One of his bits of wisdom was surely meant as democratic encouragement for his black fellows, most of whom were slaves and who knew little if anything of their ancestry: "There is nothing that is less in our power and less our own than our birth, and therefore of all pretenses a man takes hold of to value and prefer himself to others, that of his birth appears the most groundless; and the truth is, a man does seldom insist upon it, but for want of another merit."

One of the white neighbors who understood Banneker's abilities was Major Andrew Ellicott, the best surveyor in the colonies. The creative collaboration of these two men brings us to that square piece of land along the Potomac River.

After the Revolution Congress decided that a new nation should have an entirely new capital city, and at the recommendation of President George Washington the site chosen lay close to the busy seaport of Alexandria, Virginia. Both Virginia and Maryland donated the land, a square area exactly ten miles on each side which came to be known as the District of Columbia, and construction could begin once a competent surveyor had defined the city's borders.

Major Ellicott undertook the survey, but before he could send assistants into the woods dragging the chains used for measuring, he had to have a place from which all measurements would start. Only an astronomer could make this delicate determination, and Ellicott knew the man for the job. He asked Benjamin Banneker to serve as his scientific assistant.

By observing the stars and correlating their movements with times shown by an accurate clock, Banneker could fix a definite point on the face of the earth and describe its location so that it could be found whenever needed by any surveyor. With his knowledge of mathematics he could also check all measurements made by the chains which had an annoying way of expanding and contracting with changes in temperature. Finally, he could check all computations brought in from the field by the crews that worked with rod and chain.

As Silvio A. Bedini tells the story in his *Life of Benjamin Banneker,* the self-taught astronomer lived day and night throughout the winter of 1790–91 in a tent which became the very center of the surveying operation. A hole in its roof made it an observatory through which Banneker with his instruments could keep track of the stars. The clock by which he timed his observations had to be carefully protected from vibrations that might be caused even by footsteps, so Banneker placed it not on a table but on a large, solid tree stump over which the tent had been raised. Surrounding the delicate timepiece, thermometers gave warning of temperature changes which might set it running a shade too fast or too slow. All this equipment and much more Benjamin Banneker used and cared for during the determination of the exact boundary of the District of Columbia.

Finally, on April 15, 1791, the Commissioners of the District and other dignitaries assembled to place a marker on Jones Point on the west side of the Potomac River. From this marker the square outline of the nation's capital was to be laid out. A large throng watched while members of the Masonic Lodge hung a plumb bob over the marker stone as a symbol of rectitude. On the stone the Freemasons laid a square, symbol of virtue, and a level symbolizing equality.

There was no equality that day for the man who more than anyone else had done the highly skilled work of deciding exactly where the marker stone should be placed. Not one single account of the event in newspapers up and down the coast mentioned the name of Benjamin Banneker. . . .

Reading 6 Single Man in 1776 Could Have Survived for a Year on Less Than $1,000 in 1976 Dollars

A single man in 1776 could get by on less than $1,000 a year in 1976 dollars. And to live at subsistence level in New England, an average family of six needed about $1,700 in the country and about $2,200 in town, according to a report in *Money* magazine.

National Enquirer August 31, 1976, p. 51. Adapted from *Money* Magazine, July, 1976.

On the average, about $1,100 went for food, $450 for clothing, $180 to $375 for housing, $185 for medical expenses and schooling, $100 for taxes, firewood and other expenses, reports *Money.*

A family with $3,500 a year could maintain itself in some comfort—and according to one church record a family with $10,000 could live "in a genteel manner and yearly lay up something for posterity."

Reading 7 The Bad-Paper Vets

Although some attention has been given to the plight of Vietnam veterans returning to "a society that just wants to forget them" (and we can thank the establishment media for producing the attitude in society that their own cliché describes), not much is known about the "bad-paper" vets—those veterans discharged from the military with less-than-honorable discharges. Bad-paper vets face the same economic and psychological oppression honorably discharged vets have faced, but they are also burdened with a lifelong stigma that serves to prolong and amplify those problems.

There are four types of less-than-honorable discharges: general, undesirable, bad conduct, and dishonorable. (The military have also used discharge coding systems secretly to discredit even honorable discharges. Millions of veterans unknowingly carry those hidden, derogatory codes on their discharge papers, so that many veterans never learn the real reason why they were turned down for a job or bank credit.) More than a million vets have less-than-honorable discharges, according to Defense Department figures, and well over half of them were discharged during the Vietnam era. Significantly, the number of bad-papers issued since the end of hostilities in Vietnam has increased rather than declined. More bad-paper vets were created in 1974 than in any other year since the Pentagon began keeping records twenty-five years ago.

The upsurge in bad-paper discharges coincides with military attempts to reduce troop levels, pruning down to the "new, all-volunteer Army." This could lead one to conclude that the bad-paper discharge is being used by the military to weed out what it considers dead weight in order to make room for more dedicated volunteers. Many young people are waiting to enlist, now that the war is over and jobs are scarce.

When the war demanded more men for front-line combat, the military instituted

Gary Anderson, *The Progressive* (February, 1976), p. 9. Reprinted by permission from *The Progressive,* 408 West Gorham Street, Madison, Wisconsin 53703.

programs to provide human cannon fodder. They temporarily lowered their qualifications to admit volunteers and draftees who previously would not have been admitted, and now would not be, because of low IQ or lack of aptitude. Now that the military can be choosy about recruits, it seems happy to get rid of these people, at least the ones who survived.

The majority of bad-papers are general and undesirable discharges. These are awarded administratively, without court martial and with little opportunity for the soldier to enter a defense. They are awarded not for crimes committed but for such vague reasons as "unsuitability" and "unfitness," catchalls for a wide range of behavior that careerists may wish to call deviant, from homosexuality to obesity, from bed-wetting to questioning authority, and for emotional, psychological, and political reactions to the peculiar kind of life our military system imposes on people.

The services claim that general discharges are not punitive, but studies have shown that most employers not only would turn down vets with punitive discharges, but would be negatively influenced by general discharges as well. Local, state, and Federal governments seem to be the most prejudiced employers, excluding persons from civil service jobs on the basis of less-than-honorable discharges. In most cases, bad-paper vets are also ineligible for unemployment compensation and GI benefits. It is no wonder, then, that many bad-paper vets turn to crime, drugs, and suicide. About 25 per cent of the California penal institutional inmates, and 35 per cent of the inmates in Newark, New Jersey, are bad-paper vets. The bad-paper discharge is punitive in nature, and it punishes the veteran for the rest of his or her life.

The image of the bad-paper vet as an inadequate human being and a high risk for employment is perpetuated by discriminatory laws and hiring practices, and by the determined efforts of the military. Since the bad-paper vets are not organized, or even visible, they have become a new outcast group that can be exploited, just as blacks, women, farmworkers, and other oppressed minorities have historically been exploited in America.

Reading 8 Assimilation

When two or more cultural groups living in the same locality are in the process of uniting and becoming a single cultural group, the form of interaction taking place is termed assimilation. This process is marked by the gradual disappearance of some cultural differences distinguishing the groups and is a product of prolonged cooperation between or among them.

We in the United States are a people who have received and assimilated cultural elements from many lands. Our culture, which has its distinctive characteristics today, has borrowed from the cultures of the American Indian and the immigrants from many lands who came and still come to our shores. A full measure of the cultures of incoming Poles, Russians, Britons, Italians, Germans, and many others has been incorporated into our way of life. Afro-Americans have contributed elements of their original African cultures. The progenitors of the American in Minnesota gave us elements of Swedish culture. The ancestors of the American in Pennsylvania contributed elements of Hungarian culture.

And just as we "Americans" have taken over many cultural elements from other groups, so have newer arrivals to this land borrowed aspects of the culture they found here. Assimilation is a two-way process.

But this does not mean that one group exchanges all of its cultural characteristics for an entirely different set of cultural characteristics. Immigrants to America do not enter a figurative melting pot and emerge "100 percent Americans," each exactly like every other individual in this country, in every respect culturally identical. Realistically considered, ours is not one culture, but a mosaic of a number of cultural patterns. There is indeed a recognizable, identifiable, overall culture that we may call "American." It is shared by most of the people who have lived here for some time. But there are other, subsidiary cultures—those of identifiable groups that, while sharing the overall culture, retain some aspects of life styles that are distinct from what we think of as "our own." Scandinavians, Chinese, Irish, Afro-Americans, English, Mexicans, French, Dutch, and Puerto Ricans are among these groups. All these have certain of their own ways of behaving and believing, even though they have assimilated the greater part of the "100 percent American" culture. There are, in fact, different American cultural identities: there is a Yankee type, and there are "hillbillies" whose particular cultural traits are identifiable. Catholics, as a religious group, have their distinctive cultural characteristics, as have Jews and Moslems. American Indians, numerically a tiny minority in this country, cannot be considered fully assimilated into the culture of the land they once owned exclusively, for they maintain their cultural identity to a marked degree.

So it is that what we call an American, meaning a native of the United States, is a product of assimilation, but of a partial assimilation only. Cultural persistencies have played and continue to play a strategic role in our way of life. Our modes of speech, recreation, eating, farming, manufacturing, burying our dead, singing, and dancing have been partly shaped by various ethnic, nationality, religious, and other groups.

The African continent offers contemporary examples of assimilation in progress. Where white men have come in and industrialized a region, they have assumed the dominant role, even when constituting a minority of the population. They need cheap labor, hence they teach the black man to mind and tend machines. But the black African usually goes beyond that, incorporating other elements of the Caucasian culture into his own life-ways. He does this even though the white man offers resistance. Thus, on the Rhodesian Copperbelt, native blacks leave their villages to take work in the cities. They join unions, participate in strikes—activities quite unknown to them before. Some attend the white man's school. Some read newspapers and books, use radio, and attend movies. Family life has undergone some change, influenced by the culture the white man brought with him. Some assimilation, then, has already occurred. And it is a two-way proposition. The white man is influenced by the black man as the black man is influenced by the white man. The white man learns to communicate with the black man, to use his labor effectively, to sell to him at retail. To date, however, the assimilation has been largely in one direction; the black African is borrowing more of the white man's culture than the white man is borrowing of his.

Reading 9 The Hundred Days

When Franklin Delano Roosevelt gave his inaugural speech on March 4, 1933, America was in a state of chaos, and it was obvious something drastic had to be done. From leftist radicals to ultraconservatives, Americans were hopeful that the new president would bring about much needed government intervention. "This nation asks for action,

Robert Kelley, *The Shaping of the American Past,* © 1975, pp. 759–760. Reprinted by permission of Prentice-Hall, Inc., Englewood Cliffs, New Jersey.

and action now," Roosevelt said. "Our greatest primary task is to put people to work. . . . We must act, and act quickly." During the first Hundred Days of his administration, fifteen major bills were passed and signed into law.

Thousands of banks had failed; depositors everywhere had taken out their savings, fearing a national disaster. An estimated $1,212,000,000 had been withdrawn from circulation. The day after his inauguration, Roosevelt declared a nationwide, four-day bank holiday so that the banks could be investigated. Only those that were sound could reopen. Congress quickly passed an emergency bank bill and placed an embargo on the export of gold. Most Americans supported the decree with enthusiasm, and many helped those who were caught without cash: churches took IOUs in collection plates; theaters accepted personal checks at the box-office; companies paid employees in scrip acceptable to stores and redeemable by banks; and stores accepted food produce as payment for merchandise. People having deposits in banks that could not open had small consolation in the Internal Revenue Service's announcement that they could claim their deposits as bad debts on income tax returns.

Roosevelt's kindliness and warmth of feeling toward the public were perhaps best revealed in his radio "fireside chats." He felt it important that there be a direct, open, and honest relationship between his administration and the American people, so he kept them abreast of the various stages of his policymaking. This was also revealed in his frequent press conferences. In his easy rapport with the nation, noted the humorist Will Rogers, the president could take a complicated subject like banking and make everyone understand it, even the bankers. Many of the New Deal programs were organized for the benefit of the unemployed, dispossessed, and underprivileged, who responded with an affection and loyalty seldom given a president.

Drastic measures were needed to alleviate the plight of farmers suffering from poverty, foreclosures, overproduction of food, and the downward spiral of food prices. On March 16, Roosevelt asked Congress to pass the Agricultural Adjustment Act. The bill provided federal payments to producers of seven basic commodities in return for their reducing production. Following its enactment, $100 million in benefits was paid by the government to cotton farmers who plowed under a total of 10 million acres of surplus cotton crop. Americans were horrified when the Agricultural Adjustment Administration destroyed millions of pigs. Eleanor Roosevelt telephoned the AAA administrator and asked why pigs were being dumped into the Mississippi River while thousands of people in the nation were starving. It was largely due to Mrs. Roosevelt's intervention that food surplus was distributed thereafter to the needy.

The conservation of national resources was a goal cherished by Roosevelt, and he requested Congress on March 21 to authorize a Civilian Corps Reforestation Youth Rehabilitation Movement, retitled Civilian Conservation Corps in July. By June more than 300,000 youths between the ages of eighteen and twenty-five were working in more than a thousand forest camps. They, and legions of other workers who later joined the CCC, constructed dams and bridges, built reservoirs, planted trees and shrubbery, erected fire towers, cleaned beaches, and eradicated plant diseases. Each recruit was paid thirty dollars a month, twenty-five of which was either sent to his family or placed in an account until his term of enlistment was up. So enjoyable was the work that many remained to settle in the areas where they worked. Others, in later years, looked back on the time with nostalgia. "I feel almost as if I owned that land," said one CCC veteran.

A gigantic undertaking, involving 40,000 square miles of land along the Tennessee River, was the program of the Tennessee Valley Authority. Signed into law on May 18, the bill called for the construction of twenty dams and of power plants to provide inexpensive electrical power. The government's program also included flood control, conservation, and employment of a large labor force, almost all of which was recruited from the area.

While signing the National Industrial Recovery Act (NRA) on June 16, Roosevelt beamingly told the congressmen clustered around him that "history will undoubtedly record the National Industrial Recovery Act as the most important and far-reaching legislation ever enacted by the American Congress." The president's past association with the nation's "business brains" convinced him that too many executives were selfishly out for their own interests, mindless of the economic plight of others. The purpose of the NRA was both to stimulate industry and to get thousands of the unemployed back on decent payrolls. The law allowed businessmen to draw up codes of fair business practices, enabling them to raise prices by limiting production, but only if they paid employees wages at or above a certain minimum, limited working hours to a stated maximum, and recognized workers' rights to organize unions and bargain collectively over wages and hours. The law also greatly reduced child labor.

The laws enacted during the first Hundred Days of Roosevelt's administration did not solve the nation's problems. Nor did they create a socialist state, as many feared. They did, however, give temporary relief to the plight of many American people and create an environment in which it was possible to work out reforms. Americans realized that only a progressive involvement by the federal government could bring about the economic and social well-being of the nation.

Reading 10 National and Regional Preferences for Foods

One of the strongest influences on food habits is the nationality of the family group. Sometimes the use of certain national foods is very firmly entrenched and a person will go to great lengths to secure them. If they are impossible to get, he may become very unhappy. For example, students from the Far East who come to America to study and have to eat in American restaurants complain that it is difficult to get an adequate amount of rice or that it is not cooked to their liking. In other countries—for instance, Greece and Italy—food means bread, and all other foods are a complement to bread. To American Indians, food meant corn. It would be interesting to speculate which food of a given nationality group would be the last one to disappear when its families were being acculturated.

Although regional lines are fast disappearing in America because of rapid transportation and wider distribution of food, nevertheless, each region of the country may still harbor a fondness for certain foods typical of that area. This fact is exemplified by the New Englander who still has a strong taste for seafood, the Southerner who likes hot breads, and the West Coast resident who likes salads. The extensive mobility of families in this country is helping to spread these regional preferences. The homemaker who has picked up some ideas about food in Texas may introduce them to neighbors in Illinois or in Oregon or wherever she may reside. The result is that many families today have eating patterns that reflect the foods of many different parts of the country and, especially in urban areas, of other countries.

Reading 11 Old-Style Occupations That Still Pay

Jerry Marx, 37, has grown accustomed to having doors slammed in his face when he appears at midmorning upon suburban Los Angeles thresholds in his full working regalia—top hat, tails and pin-stripe pants, with a red bandanna knotted around his neck. Yet this is the traditional costume of European chimney sweeps, and a chimney sweep is just what Jerry Marx is. Marx . . . is one of a small number of people who still manage to earn a living in the U.S. working full time at jobs that have become obsolete, or at least obsolescent, since the advent of such things as the cotton gin and the internal combustion engine. They do things the hard way, using timeless methods that antedate the Industrial Revolution. Those whom *Money* talked to vary widely in age, personal background, geographic location, motivation and size of income. But all are complete individualists, and all say that they have found great fulfillment by doing old things in old ways.

FARRIER

A blacksmith, by definition, fashions almost anything out of iron. A farrier works with the same metal and most of the same tools—but only to shoe horses. Rod Gordon, 29, of Little Mountains Farm in Albemarle County, Va. is a farrier. The son of a farmer turned real estate appraiser, Gordon . . . is darkly handsome and, at six feet three inches and a sinewy 175 pounds, badly shaped—for a farrier. "Most farriers are shorter and stockier," he says. "It's easier for them to work hunched over under horses all day." After two years at the University of Tennessee, Gordon found himself at loose ends, without a career in sight. He traveled—among other places, to California, Hawaii and the Virgin Islands—but "after I saw a bit of the world, I decided that the place I really loved was right back here."

Although he had never felt any particular affinity with horses, one day he saw a farmer shoeing and "something clicked." He went to Martinsville, Va. to study the farrier's craft under one "Smoky" Ward. It turned out to be more complicated than he had expected. "Anyone can nail a shoe on a hoof," he says. "But a good farrier must study every horse he works with—how its weight is distributed, how its legs are shaped and its gravity—the relationship of the horizontal bones to the vertical bones."

Reward? "The average is probably \$7,000 to \$8,000 a year," he says, "but one can easily make \$15,000 to \$16,000, and if you get in with some big thoroughbred stables, you can make up to \$25,000 to \$30,000." Money aside, Rod Gordon likes the life. "You get in your van in the morning," he says, "and you drive along country roads and you see a lot of pretty things and you work with fine animals."

STONE CARVER

In Washington, the Episcopal Cathedral Church of St. Peter and St. Paul (popularly called the National Cathedral) has been abuilding off and on since 1907 and is now scheduled for completion in 1980—if sufficient additional money can be raised. Whether working on a scaffold 100 feet up on a spire or wielding his mallet and chisel down on the ground on one of the more than 500 gargoyles that will eventually adorn the Gothic structure, Malcolm Harlow, 39 . . . has a sense of mission. Of his seven fellow stone carvers—most of them older men, Europeans who learned their art as boyhood apprentices in the old countries—Harlow says: "These are the last of the great technicians. I have learned from them, and I feel that I can help preserve some of what's going to be lost when they are gone."

Champ Clark, "Old-Style Occupations that Still Pay," reprinted from the July 1976 issue of *Money* Magazine by special permission;

Harlow was a professional sculptor before he was a stone carver. Born in Northampton, Mass., he had graduated from the Maryland Institute of Art and set up his own studio when he heard that the cathedral was in desperate quest of carvers. "They had a need," he says, "and I had a need." Harlow finds a sculptor's freedom of expression in his gargoyles. No two are alike, and "we just make them up as we go along. The cathedral wants them to reflect the world in which we live. We are discouraged from copying traditional works from reference books." Thus Harlow's grotesque little creatures wear tattoo symbols, thumb their noses at the world and, in one case, sport musical notes as facial decorations. That one was suggested by an attractive young woman who happened to drop by the workshop. Harlow makes $10.10 an hour for a 40-hour week throughout the year. At the rate the cathedral has been going, he should be busy for a long while.

STAINED GLASS DESIGNER

The Yellow Pages of most telephone directories have long listings under "Glass—Stained & Leaded." But there are stained glassmen and stained glassmen. Gerry Hiemer, 42, of Clifton, N.J. . . . is an uncommon practitioner who still applies the all-but-lost arts and techniques of the 9th century to his present-day vocation. A skilled stained glass artisan can make up to $20,000 a year. Hiemer, the head of a company with 15 employees that grosses $400,000 annually, is the grandson of a Munich stained glass designer and the son of one who started in Munich and set up studios in the Philippines, Tokyo and Mexico City before settling in Columbus, Ohio, where Gerry was born. Except for making the glass, most of which is imported from Europe, Hiemer's firm does everything with stained glass, from research and design through color selection, fabrication and installation. Gerry Hiemer is proficient at all of it.

Hiemer deals almost exclusively with ecclesiastical windows and, within that category, with the Roman Catholic Church. Hiemer, himself a Catholic, lives and works with Christian epics ranging from the story of the Resurrection to the obscure legend of St. Kevin of Dublin. His work appears throughout the U.S. and in such places as San Salvador and Kingston, Jamaica; he now has two projects under way in Newfoundland.

Hiemer's artistry often calls for difficult research. One church wished to show the venerated Madonna of each and every North, Central and South American nation. Some leftist governments refused to answer Hiemer's letters. In other cases, bishops offered to cooperate only at the cost of generous donations. But Hiemer got the job done.

BUTLER

Nearly 15 years ago, social arbiter Amy Vanderbilt remarked: "It is a rare household these days that boasts of a butler, that well-trained English-style servant whose duties are quite circumscribed and who is chief-of-staff in an establishment." It is even rarer today; few families can afford the $8,000 to $10,000 a year in wages plus room and board that a butler typically commands. Joaquin Bano, 49, has been in service since he was 18 years old and is now majordomo for the James Van Alens of Newport, R.I., Manhattan, Long Island and St. Croix. Van Alen is, among many other things, the originator and enthusiastic promotor of the sudden-death scoring system in tennis.

The son of a Spanish railroad conductor, Bano . . . began his career in time-honored style as a footman, a sort of butler's aide who is charged with such menial tasks as washing windows, polishing shoes and carrying wood to fireplaces. Bano graduated to butler for the Duke of Real Agrado upon the death of the incumbent. Bano moved to the U.S. eight years ago and today, for the Van Alens, performs such traditional functions of butlery as answering the telephone, polishing the silver and keeping the keys to the wine cellar (the word "butler" derives from the Middle English *buteler,* or bottle carrier). He is in command of others on the household staff—excluding, by tradition, the cook, who has her own domain. That is perhaps just as well, since the cook is Bano's wife, Esperanza.

BOOKBINDER

Edward Gray Parrot II, 27, of Hancock, Maine, near Bar Harbor, is a thoughtful, slender young man in a printer's apron who clearly cares more about a book's covering than its contents. A physician's son, Parrot . . . received the best that liberal education can offer: he went to prep school at Middlesex and majored in English literature at Harvard. At college he worked part time in the famed Houghton Rare Books Library. While others might only have devoured the literary wisdom of the past, Parrot came to develop a deep appreciation of "what those 18th-century bookbinders had in mind" in trying to make their own works as beautiful and enduring as the words they enclosed.

From that discovery, Parrot's path led naturally to an unpaid bookbinding apprenticeship under Arno Werner ("the best in the country") in Pittsfield, Mass., thence to a bookbinding school in Ascona, Switzerland and finally to the roomy Maine farmhouse where he lives with his wife and three small children. There he plies his trade with needle and thread, fine leather and immense patience, and relaxes in his small book-lined study.

His is hardly a mass production vocation, and the financial returns so far have been meager. Yet he contemplates his future with confidence. Says Parrot: "If a person has talent, is willing to work hard and establishes a reputation, he can expect to gross from $22,000 to $30,000 a year and to net from $18,000 to $23,000. This is not to say he'll ever get rich, but he'll find a lot of satisfaction."

ORNAMENTAL BLACKSMITH

Ivan Bailey, 31 . . . of Savannah, Ga. sometimes calls himself an "artsmith." Yet he is in reality a blacksmith, using the traditional (and often antique) tools of that hardy calling to work with iron. His forge produces highly original, exquisitely traced handwrought griffins and roses and sunflowers, tiny sea creatures on gates and fire-screens and a multitude of other ornamented objects. (He has tried reproductions but finds little satisfaction in the work.)

A native of Oregon, Bailey attended Portland State University, got his masters in fine arts at the University of Georgia, then spent a year studying under Professor Fritz Ulrich, a master artsmith, in Aachen, Germany. Because he insists on working with authentic tools and equipment, costs run high—$16,000 just to set up his shop, Bailey's Forge—but once his initial investments are paid off, he expects to net upwards of $12,000 a year.

Bailey's enjoyment in his work has an almost therapeutic effect. In casual conversation, Ivan Bailey stammers. Yet when he speaks of the art of the blacksmith, the words flow clean and pure. "There is something almost magical," he says, "about pulling the white hot iron out of the fire and shaping it on the anvil and turning it into something beautiful."

QUILL PEN MAKER

Every lawyer appearing before the Supreme Court of the U.S. finds on the table before him a pure-white ten-inch quill pen fashioned according to precise specifications laid down by Chief Justice John Marshall (1801–35). The pens (which the attorneys may take home as souvenirs) are made by a salty 77-year-old named Lewis Glaser, of Charlottesville, Va.

Raised in a Chicago orphanage, Glaser . . . was sent one summer to a Wisconsin farm, where he "played with the dog and fed the geese." That experience led, years later, to raising geese in Connecticut. One day Dwight Eisenhower, then president of Columbia University, paid a ceremonial visit to Yale—and Glaser was on hand to see the great man. He found himself standing near Mamie Eisenhower, fell into conversation with her and wound up promising to send the Eisenhowers some goose livers. Ike evidently liked the stuff. After he became President he asked Glaser to make two quill pens for his White House desk. At the President's suggestion, Glaser started making quill pens full time because, in Ike's words, "it might help give our young people a better sense of American history."

His overhead is low—merely the rent for his second-floor studio and the annual cost of 1,200 pounds of snow white feathers taken from about 50,000 purebred Embden geese and imported from Israel or France. But the profits are tidy: starting work at five each morning, Glaser turns out some 50,000 pens a year, and though he gives away 1,500 a year to the Supreme Court, he sells many of the rest at $15 for a matched pair in a pewter inkwell. Lewis Glaser's hands are ordinarily palsied. Yet when he sits down to work with his tiny penknife, the gift of a friend whose initials—D. D. E.—are engraved on the blade, those same hands are as swift and sure as darting birds.

CHIMNEY SWEEP

Mustached and a lean six feet two in his traditional European trappings, Jerry Marx . . . has been fascinated by chimney sweeps since he was in the service in Germany in the late 1950s and became friends with a man who came from a long line of sweeps. Back in the U.S. in a beauty-supply business, he "started reading books, contacting people in fireplace equipment, working on my own fireplace, improvising my tools." Where most modern chimney cleaners use high-powered vacuums that "only take off what's already loose," Marx uses brushes of his own design (he later found out that his brushes were similar to those used for centuries in England). He works "from the bottom up, because it's cleaner that way. You have to go into every fireplace. I've never liked heights, but in 99% of the houses, I go up on the roof. With some houses and roofs, it's too dangerous. And if I don't have to, I don't." Jerry Marx makes $20,000 to $30,000 a year—not bad for someone with an occupation that's obsolete.

Reading 12 Occupational Profile

As industries continue to grow, changes will take place in the Nation's occupational structure. Jobs will become more complex and specialized offering an even greater number of occupational choices to persons planning a career. By first studying the outlook for broad occupational groups, the task can be made more manageable. (See chart 4.)

Among the broad occupational groups, white-collar jobs have grown most rapidly. In 1974, white-collar workers—professional, managerial, clerical, and sales—outnumbered blue-collar workers—craftworkers, operatives, and laborers by almost 12 million. (See chart 5.)

Through the mid-1980's, we can expect a continuation of the rapid growth of white-collar and service occupations, a slower-than-average growth of blue-collar occupations, and a further decline of farm workers.

Occupational Outlook Handbook, 1976–1977 Edition, U.S. Department of Labor, Bureau of Labor Statistics.

The rapid growth expected for white-collar and service workers reflects continuous expansion of the service-producing industries, which employ a relatively large proportion of these workers. The growing demand for workers to perform research and development, to provide education and health services, and to process the increasing amount of paperwork throughout all types of enterprises, also will be significant in the growth of white-collar jobs. The slower-than-average growth of blue-collar and farm workers reflects the expanding use of labor-saving equipment in our Nation's industries and the relatively slow growth of the goods-producing industries that employ large proportions of blue-collar workers. (See chart 6.)

The following sections describe in greater detail the changes that are expected to occur among the broad occupational groups through the mid-1980's.

Professional and technical workers, the third largest occupational group in 1974,

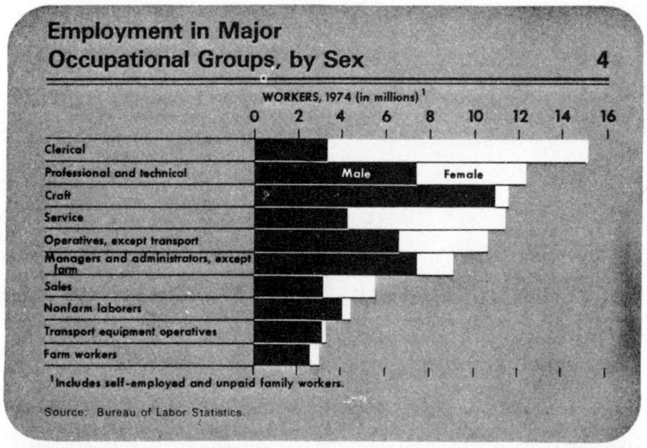

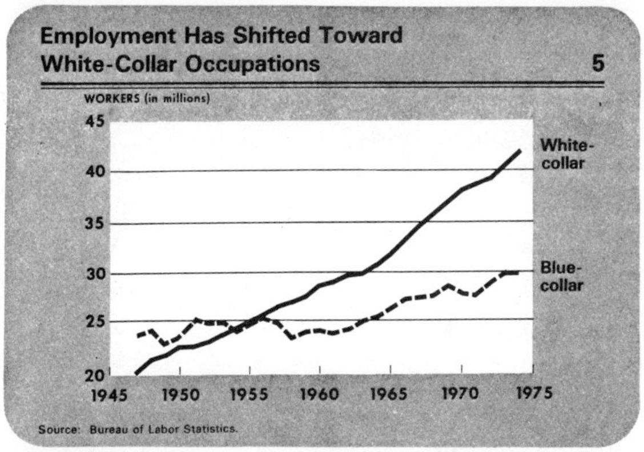

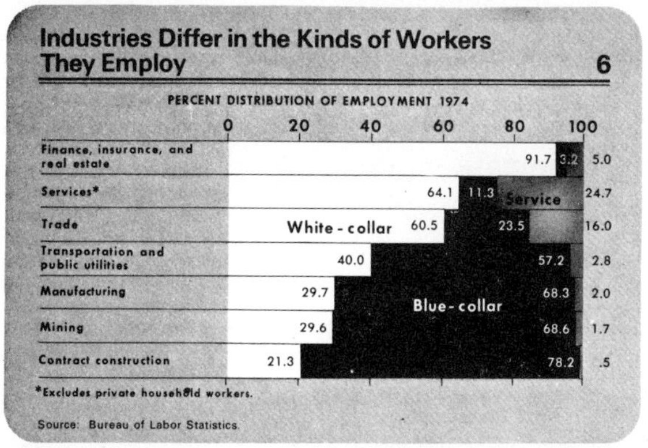

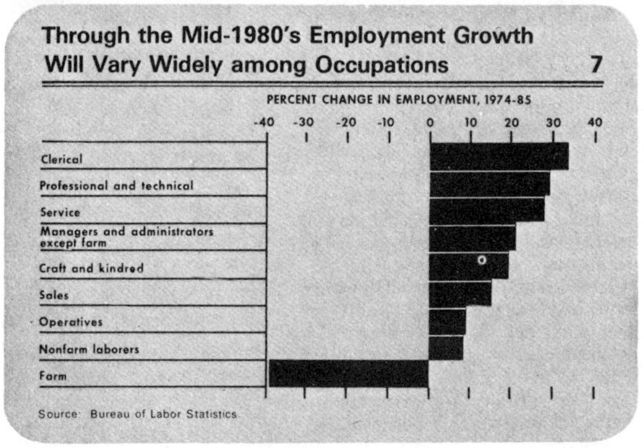

at 12.3 million, include such highly trained personnel as teachers, dentists, accountants, and clergy.

Professional occupations will grow by about 30 percent between 1974 and 1985—second only to clerical occupations in terms of growth rate. (See chart 7.) Professional workers in this area will be in great demand as the Nation makes greater efforts in transportation, energy production, rebuilding the cities, and enhancing the beauty of the land. The quest for scientific and technical knowledge is bound to grow, raising the demand for workers in scientific and technical specialties. The late 1970's and early 1980's will see a continuing emphasis on the social sciences and medical services.

Managers and administrators totaled about 8.9 million in 1974. As in the past, requirements for salaried managers are likely to continue to increase rapidly because of the growing dependence of business organizations and government agencies on management specialists. On the other hand, the number of self-employed managers is expected to continue to decline as the trend toward larger businesses continues to restrict growth of the total number of firms, and as supermarkets continue to replace small groceries and general stores. Overall, the number of managers will increase about as fast as the average for other occupations.

Clerical workers, numbering 15 million made up the largest group of workers in 1974. They are expected to be the fastest growing group during the 1974–85 period—increasing about one-third. Included in this category are workers who operate computers and office machines, keep records, take dictation, and type. . . . Many new clerical positions are expected to open up as industries employing large numbers of clerical workers continue to expand. The demand will be strong for those qualified to handle jobs created by electronic data processing operations.

Sales workers, accounting for about 5.4 million workers in 1974, are found primarily in retail stores, manufacturing and wholesale firms, insurance companies, real estate agencies, as well as offering goods door-to-door. Salesworkers are expected to increase about 16 percent between 1974 and 1985. Salesworker employment will grow as population growth and business expansion increase the demand for a wide range of goods and services.

Craft workers, numbering about 11.5 million in 1974, include a wide variety of occupations such as carpenters, tool and diemakers, instrument makers, all-round machinists, electricians, and typesetters. Industrial growth and increasing business activity will spur the growth of craft occupations through the mid-1980's. However, technological developments will tend to limit the expansion of this group. Employment of craft workers is expected to increase about as fast as the average for all occupations, rising to nearly 20 percent by 1985.

Operatives made up the second largest major occupational group in 1974, with about 13.9 million workers engaged in such activities as assembling goods in factories; driving trucks, buses, and taxis and operating machinery.

Employment of operatives is expected to increase about 9 percent by 1985, more slowly than the average for other occupations. Technological advances will reduce employment for some types of semiskilled occupations. Increases in production, as well as the trend toward motor truck transportation of freight, are expected to be major factors contributing to the overall employment increase.

Laborers (excluding those in farming and mining), numbered nearly 4.4 million workers in 1974. They move, lift, and carry materials and tools in the Nation's work places. Employment of laborers is expected to increase only about 9 percent between 1974 and 1985 in spite of the rises in manufacturing and construction, where most are employed. Increased demand is expected to be offset by rising productivity resulting from continued substitution of mechanical equipment for manual labor.

Service workers, including men and women who maintain law and order, assist professional nurses in hospitals, give haircuts and beauty treatments, serve food, and clean and care for our homes, totaled about 11.4 million in 1974. This diverse group is expected to increase 28 percent between 1974 and 1985. Some of the main factors that are expected to increase requirements for these occupations are the rising demand for hospital and other medical care; the greater need for protective services as urbanization continues and cities become more crowded; and the more frequent use of restaurants, beauty salons, and other services as income levels rise and an increasing number of housewives take jobs outside the home. The employment of private household workers, however, will continue to fall despite a rise in demand for their services. Fewer persons will accept household employment because of low wages and the strenuous nature of the work.

Farm workers—including farmers, farm managers, laborers, and supervisors—numbered nearly 3.1 million in 1974. The demand for food products, both at home and for export, will continue to grow rapidly. Farm employment, however, will decline through the mid-1980's as farm technology continues to improve.

JOB OPENINGS

In considering careers, young people should not eliminate an occupation just because it will not be among the fastest growing. Although growth is an indicator of future job outlook, it is not the only factor. More jobs will be created between 1974 and 1985 from deaths, retirements, and other labor force separations than from employment growth. (See chart 8.) Replacement needs will be particularly significant in occupations which have a large proportion of older workers. Furthermore, an occupation with many

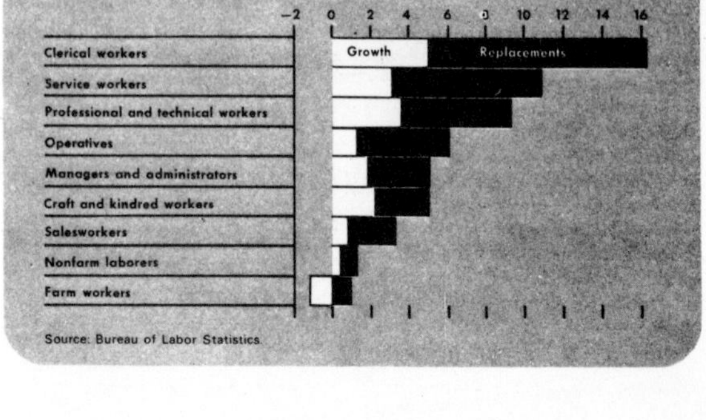

workers, even though it may have little prospects for growth, may offer more openings than a fast-growing, small one. For example, among the major occupational groups, openings for operatives resulting from growth and replacements combined will be greater than for craftsmen, although the rate of growth in the employment of craftsmen will be considerably more rapid than the rate of growth for operatives.

OUTLOOK AND EDUCATION

Numerous opportunities for employment will be available for skilled jobseekers during the years ahead. Employers are seeking people who have higher levels of education because many jobs are more complex and require greater skill. Furthermore, employment growth generally will be faster in those occupations requiring the most education and training. For example, employment in clerical and professional and technical jobs will grow faster than in all other occupational groups.

A high school education has become standard for American workers. Thus, a high school graduate is in a better competitive position in the job market than a nongraduate.

Although training beyond high school has been the standard for some time for many professional occupations, other areas of work also require more than a high school diploma. As new, automated equipment is introduced on a wider scale in offices, banks, insurance companies, and government operations, skill requirements are rising for clerical and other jobs. Employers increasingly are demanding better trained workers to operate complicated machinery. In many areas of sales work, developments in machine design, use of new materials, and the complexity of equipment are making greater technical knowledge a requirement. Because many occupations are becoming increasingly complex and technical, specific occupational training such as that obtained through apprenticeship, junior and community colleges, and post-high school vocational education courses is becoming more and more important to young people preparing for successful careers.

Young persons who do not get good preparation for work will find the going more difficult in the years ahead. Employers will be more likely to hire workers who have at least a high school diploma. Furthermore, present experience shows that the less education and training a worker has, the less chance he has for a steady job. (See chart 9.)

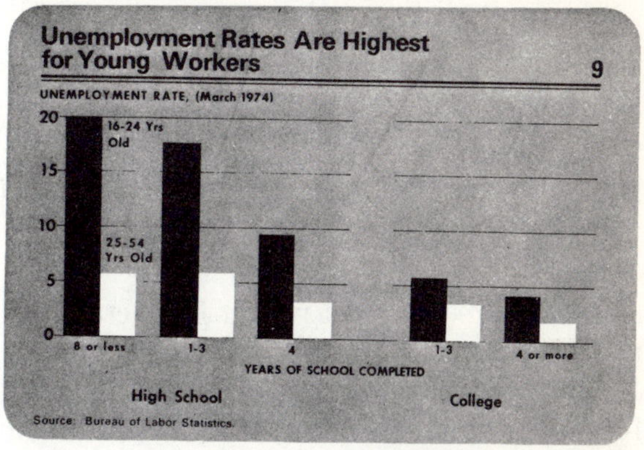

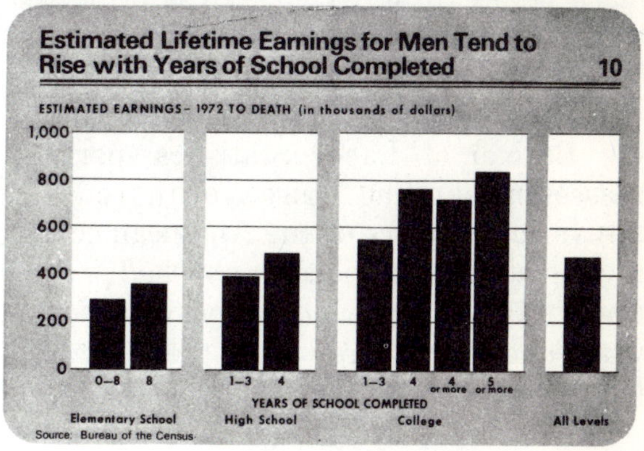

In addition to its importance in competing for jobs, education makes a difference in lifetime income. According to the most recently available data, men who had college degrees could expect to earn about $760,000 in their lifetimes, or nearly two and three quarters times the $280,000 likely to be earned by workers who had less than 8 years of schooling, nearly twice the amount earned by workers who had 1 to 3 years of high school, and more than 1½ times as much as high school graduates. Clearly the completion of high school pays a dividend. A worker who had only 1 to 3 years of high school could expect to earn only about $45,000 more than workers who had an elementary school education, but a high school graduate could look forward to a $135,000 lifetime income advantage over an individual completing elementary school. (See chart 10.)

In summary, young people who have acquired skills and a good basic education will have a better chance for interesting work, good wages, and steady employment. Getting as much education and training as one's abilities and circumstances permit should therefore be a top priority for today's youth.

Reading 13 The U.S. Labor Force in 1990: New Projections

According to the most recent projections of the U.S. Department of Labor's Bureau of Labor Statistics, the Nation's civilian labor force is estimated to pass the 100.0 million mark before 1980. By 1990, it is projected that nearly 114 million persons will be in the labor force, up from 92.6 million in 1975.

These estimates were derived as part of the Bureau of Labor Statistics' periodic reassessment of the future growth trends of the various sectors of the American economy. Relative to previously published projections, the new projections envision a somewhat more rapid growth of the American labor force.

MORE WOMEN WORKERS PROJECTED

The primary reason for the upward revision in the Bureau's labor force projections is that more women are projected to enter the labor force than previously anticipated. Rates of labor force participation for women have risen very rapidly in the past few years and, although the pace of this increase is projected to taper off very gradually, nearly 12 million more women are estimated to be added to the work force between 1975 and 1990. . . . By 1990, somewhat more than 1 out of every 2 women, 16 years of age and over, are projected to be in the labor force.

Most of the projected growth in the female labor force is estimated to be among women age 25 to 54. Participation rates for women in this group, which averaged about 55 percent in 1975, are projected to rise to the 60 to 65 percent range by 1990.

SLOWER GROWTH FOR MEN

Labor force growth for men in the 1975 to 1990 period is estimated to be slower than that for women. The male labor force is projected to grow from 55.6 million to 65.2 million over the 15-year period with the bulk of this 9.6 million increase occurring among men age 25 to 54. . . . Although males are estimated to continue to make up the largest part of the labor force, their participation is projected to continue its slow, long-term decline. By 1990, the overall participation rate for males is projected to be about 77 percent compared with 79 percent in 1975.

THE EFFECT OF THE BABY BOOM

The increase in the size of the labor force to 1990 will also reflect the complete absorption of the post–World War II baby boom. As the large numbers of persons born from the mid-1940's to the early 1960's move into the prime age labor force, a greater proportion of the civilian labor force is estimated to be composed of prime age workers. In 1975, workers age 25 to 54 represented 61 percent of the work force; in 1990, this proportion is estimated to increase to 69 percent. . . . By 1990, therefore, the labor force is estimated to be more experienced and presumably more productive.

News, September 15, 1976 (Washington, D.C.: U.S. Department of Labor, Bureau of Labor Statistics).

PROJECTIONS BY MAJOR AGE GROUPS

When the labor force is divided into the youth labor force, age 16 to 24, the prime age labor force, age 25 to 54, and the older labor force, age 55 and over, the projections to 1990 appear as follows:

The *youth labor force* is estimated to continue to grow in the late seventies, but at a much slower rate relative to the increase posted during the late 1960's and early 1970's. During the eighties, the size of the youth labor force is projected to decline, reflecting the sharp drop in births in the sixties. By 1990, the youth labor force is projected to total 21.0 million, about 1.3 million lower than in 1975.

The *prime age labor force* is estimated to grow rapidly to 1990, reflecting both the aging of the post–World War II baby boom as well as the greater proclivity of women to enter the job market. The size of the labor force age 25–54 is projected to be 78.6 million in 1990, up from 56.2 million in 1975.

The *older labor force* is estimated to rise slightly in the late seventies, level off in the early eighties, and then decline during the late eighties. The growth of this group's labor force is estimated to be held back by the projected continuation of the trend toward early retirement. In addition, during the second half of the 1980's there will be a slowdown in the growth of this group's population, reflecting the drop in the birth rate during the 1930's. Thus by 1990, the group's labor force is estimated to total 14.3 million, only slightly larger than in 1975.

Reading 14 Educational Attainment of Workers, March 1976

The average educational level of the labor force, as measured by years of school completed, continued its gradual rise during the past year. In March 1976, nearly 3 out of 4 employed persons were high school graduates. One-third of the employed had completed at least 1 year of college, and half of these were college graduates. These proportions were substantially lower for unemployed workers, but even among the unemployed over half had completed high school and almost one-fifth had completed 1 year of college or more. (See table 1.) The median educational attainment of the labor force was 12.6 years for the employed and 12.2 years for the unemployed.

A somewhat larger proportion of women than men in the labor force had graduated from high school (75 percent versus 71 percent). However, more of the men than of the women were college graduates (18 percent versus 14 percent). Smaller proportions of black[1] workers than of white workers had completed either high school or college. Black workers had completed an average of 12.3 years of school compared with 12.6 years for whites. Two-thirds of black women workers had finished high school compared to less than half of the black men. . . . This report analyzes the relationship between education and labor force activity in March 1976 and examines trends in education attainment and in occupations of college graduates over the past 10 years.

Special Labor Force Report 193, U.S. Department of Labor, Bureau of Labor Statistics.

LABOR FORCE ACTIVITY IN 1976

The extent of formal education is highly correlated with participation and success in

[1]Data for all persons other than whites are used to represent data for blacks, because the latter constitute about nine-tenths of all persons other than whites in the United States.

Table 1. Employment status of the population by sex, race, and educational attainment, March 1976 [Numbers in thousands]

Years of School Completed, Sex, and Race	*Total, 16 Years and Over*	*Labor Force*					*Not in Labor Force*
		Total			*Unemployed*		
		Number	*Percent of Population*	*Employed*	*Number*	*Percent of Labor Force*	
BOTH SEXES							
Total	153,180	93,063	60.8	85,533	7,530	8.1	60,117
Elementary: Less than 8 years[1]	13,659	4,855	35.5	4,384	471	9.7	8,803
8 years	12,558	5,068	40.4	4,565	503	9.9	7,490
High school: 1 to 3 years	30,478	15,890	52.1	13,732	2,157	13.6	14,588
4 years	55,222	37,005	67.0	33,980	3,025	8.2	18,218
College: 1 to 3 years	21,912	14,889	68.0	13,944	945	6.3	7,023
4 years or more	19,352	15,355	79.3	14,926	429	2.8	3,996
Median school years completed	12.4	12.6	—	12.6	12.2	—	11.8
MEN							
Total	72,346	55,246	76.4	50,924	4,322	7.8	17,100
Elementary: Less than 8 years[1]	6,844	3,426	50.1	3,106	319	9.3	3,419
8 years	5,908	3,329	56.4	3,006	323	9.7	2,579
High school: 1 to 3 years	14,119	9,427	66.8	8,152	1,275	13.5	4,692
4 years	23,344	20,153	86.3	18,548	1,605	8.0	3,191
College: 1 to 3 years	10,890	8,863	81.4	8,308	556	6.3	2,026
4 years or more	11,241	10,048	89.4	9,803	245	2.4	1,193
Median school years completed	12.4	12.6	—	12.6	12.2	—	10.6
WOMEN							
Total	80,834	37,817	46.8	34,609	3,208	8.5	43,017
Elementary: Less than 8 years[1]	6,814	1,430	21.0	1,278	152	10.6	5,384
8 years	6,650	1,739	26.1	1,559	180	10.3	4,911
High school: 1 to 3 years	16,359	6,463	39.5	5,580	883	13.7	9,896
4 years	31,878	16,852	52.9	15,432	1,420	8.4	15,027
College: 1 to 3 years	11,023	6,026	54.7	5,637	389	6.5	4,997
4 years or more	8,110	5,307	65.4	5,123	184	3.5	2,803
Median school years completed	12.3	12.6	—	12.6	12.3	—	12.1
WHITE							
Total	134,985	82,450	61.1	76,309	6,142	7.4	52,535
Elementary: Less than 8 years[1]	10,407	3,620	34.8	3,254	364	10.1	6,788
8 years	11,149	4,448	39.9	4,022	426	9.6	6,702
High school: 1 to 3 years	25,719	13,507	52.5	11,802	1,705	12.6	12,212
4 years	49,867	33,189	66.6	30,711	2,478	7.5	16,678
College: 1 to 3 years	19,941	13,533	67.9	12,758	775	5.7	6,409
4 years or more	17,901	14,154	79.1	13,762	393	2.8	3,747
Median school years completed	12.4	12.6	—	12.6	12.2	—	12.0

[1]Includes persons reporting no school years completed.

Table 1 (continued)

Years of School Completed Sex, and Race	Total, 16 Years and Over	Labor Force: Total: Number	Labor Force: Total: Percent of Population	Labor Force: Employed	Labor Force: Unemployed: Number	Labor Force: Unemployed: Percent of Labor Force	Not in Labor Force
BLACK AND OTHER							
Total	18,195	10,612	58.3	9,224	1,389	13.1	7,583
Elementary: Less than 8 years[1]	3,251	1,236	38.0	1,130	106	8.6	2,015
8 years	1,408	620	44.1	543	77	12.4	788
High school: 1 to 3 years	4,759	2,383	50.1	1,931	452	19.0	2,376
4 years	5,356	3,816	71.2	3,269	547	14.3	1,540
College: 1 to 3 years	1,971	1,357	68.8	1,187	170	12.5	614
4 years or more	1,450	1,201	82.8	1,165	36	3.0	249
Median school years completed	11.8	12.3	—	12.3	12.1	—	10.2

[1]Includes persons reporting no school years completed.

the labor force. In March 1976, only 36 percent of the persons with less than 8 years of schooling were working or looking for work compared with 67 percent of those with 4 years of high school and 79 percent of all college graduates. (See table 2.) For both men and women, whites and blacks, labor force participation rates among adults tend to increase with increasing amounts of formal schooling. While this relationship is evident even among men of prime working age, it is particularly pronounced among women. To illustrate, among men 25 to 54 years old, labor force rates range from the low to mid-eighties for those with less than an elementary school education to over 95 percent for college graduates. Among women in the comparable age groups, participation ranged from about 40 percent for the least educated to over 70 percent for those who were college graduates.

Unemployment rates in March 1976 were highest for workers with only 1 to 3 years of high school (13.6 percent), and lowest for college graduates (2.8 percent). (See table 3.) Persons who did not have any high school education whatsoever fared a little better in the job market than high school dropouts. However, the principal reason for this apparent anomaly is that, on average, persons without any high school education are much older and presumably have more job experience and seniority. For comparable age groups, there was a fairly persistent reduction in unemployment rates with each additional level of education.

The overall drop in the unemployment rate from March 1975 to March 1976 was accompanied by declines for most of the educational groups. The largest decreases were among persons who had not graduated from high school—those who had suffered the greatest increases in unemployment between 1974 and 1975. The unemployment rate dropped most sharply for those with less than 8 years of schooling. For college graduates, the unemployment rate did not change over the year but remained appreciably lower than the rates for workers with less formal education.

Table 2. Labor force participation rates of the population, by age, sex, and educational attainment, March 1976

Sex and Age	Total	Elementary: Less than 8 years[1]	Elementary: 8 Years	High School: 1 to 3 Years	High School: 4 Years	College: 1 to 3 Years	College: 4 Years or More
MEN							
Total, 16 years old and over	76.4	53.0	56.4	66.8	86.3	81.4	89.4
16 to 19 years	53.6	42.4	41.7	48.1	72.7	48.8	(2)
Major activity school	34.8	(2)	15.9	36.7	34.3	32.9	—
Major activity other	88.3	64.4	76.3	85.5	94.6	89.8	(2)
20 to 24 years	82.5	85.5	92.8	87.4	91.4	69.4	81.6
Major activity school	35.4	(2)	(2)	(2)	33.0	36.1	36.0
Major activity other	94.7	79.9	94.4	91.7	95.3	95.4	97.8
25 to 34 years	94.9	85.3	89.9	91.7	96.8	94.8	95.5
35 to 44 years	95.3	86.6	90.1	94.0	96.6	97.1	98.1
45 to 54 years	90.8	76.7	87.2	87.6	93.8	93.9	97.0
55 to 64 years	74.4	63.2	68.0	75.0	78.4	81.9	84.2
65 years and over	20.6	14.2	16.0	21.2	24.9	32.4	35.9
WOMEN							
Total, 16 years old and over	46.8	23.5	26.1	39.5	52.9	54.7	65.4
16 to 19 years	46.1	24.6	25.9	40.0	61.8	48.2	(2)
Major activity school	31.2	(2)	16.9	32.4	27.2	35.7	(2)
Major activity other	70.6	31.1	35.3	63.5	80.6	79.3	(2)
20 to 24 years	63.5	33.5	33.5	40.4	66.9	64.0	85.3
Major activity school	34.6	(2)	(2)	(2)	27.3	36.7	30.7
Major activity other	68.0	33.5	33.0	41.0	68.4	80.1	91.5
25 to 34 years	56.8	38.4	41.8	45.9	54.6	60.9	71.3
35 to 44 years	58.1	39.5	42.2	55.7	59.2	60.2	71.8
45 to 54 years	54.4	42.9	45.6	47.9	57.1	58.2	70.5
55 to 64 years	41.9	33.7	36.7	36.5	44.9	50.8	57.5
65 years and over	8.5	5.4	6.7	9.9	11.2	9.9	14.2

[1]Includes persons reporting no school years completed. [2]Percent not shown where base is less than 75,000.

Table 3. Unemployment rates of workers by educational attainment, sex, race, and age, March 1975 and March 1976

Years of School Completed, Race, and Sex	1975: Total, 16 Years and Over	1975: 16 to 24 Years	1975: 25 to 54 Years	1975: 55 Years and Over	1976: Total, 16 Years and Over	1976: 16 to 24 Years	1976: 25 to 54 Years	1976: 55 Years and Over
BOTH SEXES								
Total	9.2	17.1	7.1	5.3	8.1	15.5	5.9	5.6
Elementary: Less than 8 years[1]	12.4	30.4	13.3	7.7	9.7	20.3	9.0	8.8
8 years	11.3	31.2	11.6	6.7	9.9	29.2	8.1	7.7
High school: 1 to 3 years	15.2	24.6	11.1	5.9	13.6	22.6	9.0	6.0
4 years	9.1	16.1	7.1	5.5	8.2	14.8	6.2	5.1
College: 1 to 3 years	6.9	10.8	5.7	3.3	6.3	9.1	4.4	4.4
4 years or more	2.9	6.4	2.5	1.7	2.8	6.4	2.4	2.0

[1]Includes persons reporting no school years completed.

Table 3 (continued)

Years of School Completed, Race, and Sex	1975 Total, 16 Years and Over	1975 16 to 24 Years	1975 25 to 54 Years	1975 55 Years and Over	1976 Total, 16 Years and Over	1976 16 to 24 Years	1976 25 to 54 Years	1976 55 Years and Over
MEN								
Total	9.0	18.2	6.8	5.4	7.8	16.2	5.4	5.8
Elementary: Less than 8 years[1]	12.7	29.8	13.5	8.0	9.3	19.0	8.2	9.5
8 years	11.4	33.5	10.8	7.1	9.7	26.3	7.9	8.0
High school: 1 to 3 years	14.7	24.2	10.9	5.3	13.5	23.2	8.6	6.3
4 years	9.1	17.3	6.8	5.9	8.0	15.3	5.8	5.2
College: 1 to 3 years	6.6	11.7	5.2	2.4	6.3	9.7	5.3	4.5
4 years or more	2.5	6.9	2.2	1.8	2.4	5.4	2.2	2.3
WOMEN								
Total	9.5	15.9	7.8	5.3	8.5	14.7	6.6	5.1
Elementary: Less than 8 years[1]	11.7	32.6	12.7	6.9	10.6	23.8	11.3	7.3
8 years	11.2	27.0	13.1	6.1	10.3	35.6	8.8	7.3
High school: 1 to 3 years	15.9	25.1	11.6	5.4	13.7	21.7	9.7	5.7
4 years	9.1	14.7	7.5	5.0	8.4	14.2	6.7	4.9
College: 1 to 3 years	7.4	9.8	6.5	4.9	6.5	8.4	5.7	4.1
4 years or more	3.6	6.0	3.3	1.6	3.5	7.2	3.0	1.2
WHITE								
Total	8.5	15.6	6.6	5.1	7.4	14.1	5.4	5.3
Elementary: Less than 8 years[1]	11.9	27.6	12.9	7.1	10.1	21.1	9.3	9.3
8 years	10.8	28.9	11.4	6.6	9.6	28.1	7.6	7.8
High school: 1 to 3 years	14.0	22.3	10.4	5.7	12.6	20.7	8.5	5.7
4 years	8.4	14.4	6.8	5.5	7.5	13.7	5.6	4.9
College: 1 to 3 years	6.6	10.6	5.3	3.0	5.7	7.8	5.0	4.2
4 years or more	2.8	6.1	2.5	1.8	2.8	6.3	2.4	1.9
BLACK AND OTHER								
Total	14.7	29.6	10.8	7.2	13.1	25.9	9.5	7.5
Elementary: Less than 8 years	13.6	39.0	14.3	8.9	8.7	(2)	8.3	7.6
8 years	15.3	43.2	13.1	7.0	12.4	(2)	11.1	6.2
High school: 1 to 3 years	22.0	39.8	14.7	7.4	19.0	34.4	11.7	8.4
4 years	15.2	28.5	10.5	4.0	14.3	23.5	11.2	8.1
College: 1 to 3 years	10.1	13.5	8.9	(2)	12.5	20.8	9.3	(2)
4 years or more	4.0	10.2	3.3	—	3.0	7.3	2.5	1.3

[1]Includes persons reporting no school years completed. [2]Percent not shown where base is less than 75,000.

CHANGES IN EDUCATIONAL ATTAINMENT—1966 TO 1976

The educational attainment of the labor force has increased steadily over the last 10 years, from a median of 12.2 years in 1966 to 12.6 years in 1976. Along with a general increase in the proportion of men and women workers who are high school or college graduates, there has also been a very significant narrowing of the educational attainment gap between whites and blacks. As shown in table 4, the proportion of workers who are high school graduates has increased more among men than among women, so that in 1976 the average educational attain-

Table 4. Educational attainment of the labor force by sex and race, March 1966 and March 1976

Item	*Both Sexes*	*Men*	*Women*	*White*	*Black*
Percent of labor force who graduated from high school:					
1966	58.9	56.1	63.9	61.5	37.8
1976	72.3	70.7	74.5	73.8	60.1
Percent of labor force who graduated from college:					
1966	11.8	12.8	9.9	12.5	5.8
1976	16.5	18.2	14.0	17.2	11.3
Median years of school completed:					
1966	12.2	12.2	12.3	12.3	10.5
1976	12.6	12.6	12.6	12.6	12.3

ment of men and women was the same.

Equality between the sexes has not, however, been reached in terms of the proportions with a college degree. As was the case in 1966, relatively more men than women workers had completed college in March 1976. However, there are indications that the gap is narrowing. Among persons 25 to 34 years old, most of whom have completed their formal education, the rise in the past decade in the proportion with a college degree was faster for women than for men. The difference between whites and blacks in the proportion of workers with college degrees has narrowed slightly over the decade, as the percent of black workers who graduated from college nearby doubled in the last 10 years. Although the median educational attainment of blacks still lags behind that of whites, the difference was considerably less in 1976 than in 1966.

Several factors account for the educational upgrading of the labor force. There has been a general increase in educational opportunities coupled with both private and government programs to encourage completion of high school. Another factor is that as older workers with less education leave the labor force, they are replaced by younger, more educated workers.

EDUCATION AND OCCUPATION

The general increase in educational attainment over the last 10 years has been pervasive across the occupational spectrum. The proportion of workers who are high school graduates has gone up by at least 10 percentage points in nearly all occupational groups, for both men and women. Among men, these changes have been especially pronounced among blue-collar, service, and farm workers. And, although the numbers involved are relatively small, there have been dramatic increases in the proportions of workers outside the white-collar groups who have some college training. For instance, in March 1976, 18 percent of male craft workers and at least 10 percent of other blue-collar workers had 1 year of college or more, proportions double those of a decade ago.

In the past 10 years the number of working women with college degrees has doubled and the number of employed male college graduates has increased by two-thirds. However, the proportion of college graduates working in professional positions has declined substantially, a decline which was much more pronounced for women than for men. In March 1966, 60 percent of the

Table 5. Occupation of employed persons, by educational attainment and sex, March 1976 [Percent distribution]

Occupation and Sex	Total Employed, 16 Years and Over (thousands)	Elementary: 8 Years or Less[1]	High School: 1 to 3 Years	High School: 4 Years	College: 1 to 3 Years	College: 4 Years or More
MEN						
All occupational groups, total:						
Number (in thousands)	50,924	6,112	8,152	18,548	8,308	9,803
Percent	100.0	100.0	100.0	100.0	100.0	100.0
Professional, technical, and kindred workers	15.4	.9	1.8	5.7	16.3	53.3
Manager and administrators, except farm	14.2	6.6	6.6	12.8	20.0	23.0
Sales workers	6.1	1.6	4.1	5.4	9.8	8.8
Clerical and kindred workers	6.3	2.7	4.7	7.8	9.3	4.7
Craft and kindred workers	20.5	23.6	24.0	28.0	17.8	3.8
Operatives, except transport	11.3	19.1	16.4	13.9	6.9	1.2
Transport equipment operatives	5.7	9.5	9.3	6.9	3.0	.6
Laborers, except farm	7.1	12.2	12.7	7.3	4.7	.8
Service workers, including private household	9.1	11.6	15.1	8.5	10.0	2.5
Farm workers	4.2	12.3	5.3	3.7	2.1	1.3
WOMEN						
All occupational groups, total:						
Number (in thousands)	34,609	2,837	5,580	15,432	5,637	5,123
Percent	100.0	100.0	100.0	100.0	100.0	100.0
Professional, technical, and kindred workers	16.2	.8	2.3	6.0	18.7	67.8
Managers and administrators, except farm	5.7	2.8	3.4	5.9	7.0	7.9
Sales workers	6.6	4.6	8.2	7.2	7.6	2.8
Clerical and kindred workers	35.1	8.0	19.1	47.9	46.7	16.0
Craft and kindred workers	1.4	1.6	2.2	1.6	1.1	.4
Operatives, except transport	11.4	33.8	21.1	10.2	2.9	1.2
Transport equipment operatives	.6	.5	1.2	.7	.4	.1
Laborers, except farm	1.1	2.2	2.3	.9	.6	.2
Private household workers	3.2	12.5	7.8	1.6	1.0	.2
Service workers, except private household	17.8	30.4	31.1	17.2	13.4	3.3
Farm workers	.9	2.6	1.3	.8	.5	.3

[1]Includes persons reporting no school years completed.

men and 80 percent of the women with college degrees had professional jobs. By March 1976, these proportions had dropped to 53 percent and 68 percent, respectively. (See table 5.) For men, the drop reflected smaller proportions of college graduates in engineering and medical and health fields. For women, nearly four-fifths of the decline was accounted for by the smaller proportion in teaching. For both men and women college graduates, the proportion in service occupations increased somewhat; for women the proportion in clerical jobs rose substantially. The proportion of women college graduates in managerial jobs doubled over the past 10 years to 8 percent, but remained much lower than the unchanged 23 percent for men.

Reading 15 Students, Graduates, and Dropouts in the Labor Market, October 1975

The recent recession affected young workers severely. Among youth 16 to 24 years of age, the number holding jobs declined sharply between October 1974 and October 1975. Also, the proportion unemployed rose for youth both in and out of school.[1]

There were nearly 22 million youth 16 to 24 years old in the job market in October 1975. For the 70 percent who were no longer in school, employment dropped by more than 750,000 over the year. Among those in school—a population group that increased significantly between October 1974 and October 1975—the number employed was about the same as a year earlier. The year-to-year increase in unemployment was significantly greater for out-of-school youth—jumping from 10.8 to 14.9 percent—than for students—rising from 13.1 to 15.0 percent. (See table 1.)

Enrolled in school. School enrollment increased by 800,000 over the year among all youth 16 to 24 years of age, a greater rise than the population increase for this group. Evidently, many youths responded to the difficult job situation by continuing or resuming their education.

Anne McDougall Young, reprinted from June, 1976 *Monthly Labor Review* with supplementary tables (Washington, D.C.: U.S. Department of Labor, Bureau of Labor Statistics), pp. 37–41.

[1]This report is based on supplementary questions in the October 1975 Current Population Survey, conducted and tabulated for the Bureau of Labor Statistics by the Bureau of the Census. Data relate to persons 16 to 24 years of age in the civilian noninstitutional population in the calendar week ending Oct. 18, 1975.

Sampling variability may be relatively large in cases where the numbers are small. Small estimates, or small differences between estimates, should be interpreted with caution.

The most recent report in this series was published in the *Monthly Labor Review* in August 1975 and reprinted with additional tabular data and explanatory notes as Special Labor Force Report 180.

Among male students, the proportion who were in the labor force declined slightly, particularly among those 20 to 24 years old. (See table 2.) For white men, the decline was a reversal of a pattern of gradually rising labor force participation rates during the past decade, while the rate for black[2] men, which has fluctuated considerably over the decade, fell below the 1965 level. In contrast, among both white and black female students, labor force participation rates have risen steadily and were 16- and 10-percentage points higher, respectively, than in 1965.

College enrollment of 16- to 24-year-olds expanded over the year by 600,000, twice as large an increase as in the previous 1-year period. Nearly all of the rise was among full-time students and was somewhat greater for women. Nevertheless, among all college students, the proportion enrolled full time has declined slightly over the past decade, slipping from 86 percent in 1965 to 84 percent in 1975.

In recent years, community colleges have provided for the education of an increasing proportion of college students, from 17 percent of all undergraduates in 1966, when data on this subject were first collected, to 29 percent in 1975.[3] Two-thirds of the over-the-year increase in undergraduate enrollment was among students in 2-year colleges. This group accounted for 43

[2]Data for all persons other than white are used to represent data for blacks, since the latter constitute about nine-tenths of all persons other than white in the United States.

[3]The increase is understated in that some of the undergraduates in 1966 were 14–15 or 25–34 years old; it was not possible to disaggregate these age groups. See *Characteristics of Students and their Colleges, October 1966,* Series P–20, No. 183 (Bureau of the Census, 1969), table 1; and *School Enrollment—Social and Economic Characteristics of Students: October 1974,* Series P–20, No. 286 (Bureau of the Census, 1975), table 24.

percent of all first- and second-year students enrolled in college in 1975.

Compared to their counterparts in 4-year schools, 2-year college students tend to come from lower income families, are somewhat older, and proportionally more of them are married. As a result of these financial pressures, community college students 16 to 24 years old had substantially higher labor force participation rates in October 1975 than similar students in 4-year schools.

	Total	*Enrolled Full Time*	*Enrolled Part Time*
2-year colleges:			
Students	1,810	1,294	516
In labor force	1,152	705	447
Labor force participation rate	63.6	54.5	86.6
First 2 years of 4-year colleges:			
Students	2,364	2,187	177
In labor force	818	670	148
Labor force participation rate	34.6	30.6	83.6

Table 1. Employment status of persons 16 to 24 years old, by school enrollment status, educational attainment, sex, and race, October 1974 and 1975 [Numbers in thousands]

	Civilian Non-institutional Population		*Civilian Labor Force*									
			Number		*Percent of Population*		*Employed*		*Unemployed: Number*		*Unemployed: Percent of Labor Force*	
Characteristics	*1974*	*1975*	*1974*	*1975*	*1974*	*1975*	*1974*	*1975*	*1974*	*1975*	*1974*	*1975*
Total, 16 to 24 years old	33,968	34,700	21,818	21,833	64.2	62.9	19,306	18,564	2,514	3,268	11.5	15.0
Enrolled in school	14,482	15,284	6,562	6,730	45.3	44.0	5,702	5,716	862	1,012	13.1	15.0
16 to 19 years	10,666	11,163	4,434	4,551	41.6	40.8	3,750	3,772	684	778	15.4	17.1
20 to 24 years	3,816	4,121	2,128	2,179	55.8	52.9	1,952	1,944	178	234	8.4	10.7
Men	7,648	8,085	3,605	3,598	47.1	44.5	3,162	3,061	445	536	12.3	14.9
Women	6,835	7,198	2,958	3,130	43.3	43.5	2,544	2,655	417	476	14.1	15.2
White	12,405	13,077	5,912	6,096	47.7	46.6	5,236	5,241	677	855	11.5	14.0
Black and other[1]	2,077	2,207	651	633	31.3	28.7	469	478	182	156	28.0	24.6
Elementary and high school	7,862	8,063	3,311	3,279	42.1	40.6	2,759	2,641	552	636	16.7	19.4
Men	4,094	4,270	1,831	1,801	44.7	42.2	1,557	1,464	274	336	15.0	18.7
Women	3,768	3,793	1,480	1,478	39.3	39.0	1,202	1,177	278	300	18.8	20.3
White	6,549	6,710	2,972	2,997	45.4	44.7	2,538	2,450	434	546	14.6	18.2
Black and other	1,313	1,350	339	283	25.8	21.0	221	192	118	92	34.8	32.5
College	6,620	7,221	3,252	3,448	49.1	47.7	2,942	3,074	310	376	9.5	10.9
Men	3,554	3,816	1,772	1,796	49.9	47.1	1,600	1,597	172	201	9.7	11.2
Full time	3,021	3,245	1,286	1,283	42.6	39.6	1,132	1,126	154	158	12.0	12.3
Part time	533	571	486	513	91.2	90.0	468	471	18	43	3.7	8.4

[1]Persons identified as black or Negro make up 89 percent of the population other than white. The remaining 11 percent are mostly American Indians and persons of Asian origin.

Table 1 (continued)

			Civilian Labor Force									
									Unemployed			
	Civilian Non-institutional Population		*Number*		*Percent of Population*		*Employed*		*Number*		*Percent of Labor Force*	
Characteristics	*1974*	*1975*	*1974*	*1975*	*1974*	*1975*	*1974*	*1975*	*1974*	*1975*	*1974*	*1975*
Women	3,066	3,405	1,480	1,652	48.3	48.5	1,342	1,477	138	175	9.3	10.6
Full time	2,506	2,813	998	1,156	39.8	41.1	889	1,008	109	149	10.9	12.9
Part time	560	592	482	496	86.1	83.8	453	469	29	26	6.0	5.2
White	5,857	6,366	2,942	3,101	50.2	48.7	2,694	2,792	248	310	8.4	10.0
Men	3,162	3,434	1,603	1,644	50.7	47.9	1,461	1,471	142	176	8.9	10.7
Women	2,695	2,932	1,339	1,457	49.7	49.7	1,233	1,321	106	134	7.9	9.2
Black and other	763	856	310	350	40.6	40.9	249	284	62	63	20.0	18.0
Men	392	382	169	153	43.1	40.1	140	128	30	23	17.8	15.0
Women	371	474	141	197	38.0	41.6	109	156	32	40	22.7	20.3
Not enrolled in school	19,486	19,416	15,256	15,103	78.2	77.8	13,604	12,848	1,652	2,256	10.8	14.9
High school graduates, no college	10,350	10,366	8,371	8,379	80.9	80.8	7,553	7,238	818	1,141	9.8	13.6
Men	4,477	4,568	4,256	4,319	95.1	94.5	3,869	3,730	387	589	9.1	13.6
Women	5,871	5,798	4,112	4,060	70.0	70.0	3,683	3,508	429	552	10.4	13.6
White	9,078	9,124	7,354	7,417	81.0	81.3	6,717	6,508	637	909	8.7	12.3
Black and other	1,270	1,242	1,014	962	79.8	77.5	835	730	179	232	17.7	24.1
High school dropouts	4,847	4,824	3,108	2,969	64.1	61.5	2,514	2,219	594	750	19.1	25.3
Men	2,343	2,247	2,028	1,898	86.6	84.5	1,701	1,477	327	421	16.1	22.2
Women	2,504	2,577	1,080	1,071	43.1	41.6	813	742	267	329	24.7	30.7
16 to 19 years	2,079	2,001	1,380	1,230	66.4	61.5	1,042	862	338	368	24.5	29.9
20 to 24 years	2,769	2,822	1,728	1,740	62.4	61.7	1,472	1,358	256	382	14.8	22.0
White	3,866	3,742	2,525	2,382	65.3	63.7	2,115	1,840	410	542	16.2	22.8
Black and other	982	1,082	582	588	59.3	54.3	398	380	184	208	31.6	35.4
College graduates	1,452	1,373	1,339	1,290	92.2	94.0	1,272	1,183	67	107	5.0	8.3
Men	673	635	655	615	97.3	96.9	621	555	34	60	5.2	9.8
Women	779	738	684	675	87.8	91.5	651	628	33	47	4.8	7.0
White	1,313	1,275	1,219	1,208	92.8	94.7	1,167	1,107	52	101	4.3	8.4
Black and other	140	99	121	81	86.4	81.8	105	76	16	5	13.2	6.2
College, 1 to 3 years	2,837	2,851	2,438	2,465	85.9	86.5	2,265	2,207	173	258	7.1	10.5
Men	1,367	1,388	1,311	1,316	95.9	94.8	1,226	1,183	85	133	6.5	10.1
Women	1,470	1,463	1,127	1,149	76.7	78.5	1,039	1,024	88	125	7.8	10.9
White	2,537	2,527	2,195	2,209	86.5	87.4	2,055	2,003	140	206	6.4	9.3
Black and other	300	324	244	256	81.3	79.0	210	204	34	52	13.9	20.3

[1]Persons identified as black or Negro make up 89 percent of the population other than white. The remaining 11 percent are mostly American Indians and persons of Asian origin.

The overall increase in the student labor force in recent years reflects the emerging pattern of school and work, rather than first school, then work, more common when a smaller proportion of youth went to college.

Table 2. Labor force participation rate[1] of persons 16 to 24 years old enrolled in school, by sex and race, selected years, October 1965–October 1975

	Men				*Women*			
Year and Race	*16–24*	*16 and 17*	*18 and 19*	*20–24*	*16–24*	*16 and 17*	*18 and 19*	*20–24*
All persons:								
1965	39.8	37.2	36.2	49.0	28.9	26.0	29.0	39.6
1970	42.9	38.9	41.2	51.2	38.0	33.5	37.7	50.5
1973	47.4	44.2	45.5	54.7	40.9	38.0	38.1	50.3
1974	47.1	43.4	44.5	55.5	43.3	39.2	39.5	56.2
1975	44.5	41.7	42.0	51.2	43.5	38.9	41.1	55.1
White:								
1965	40.5	38.0	36.6	49.2	30.0	27.2	30.2	39.8
1970	44.5	41.1	42.3	52.1	40.0	35.5	39.4	51.9
1973	50.0	47.9	47.7	55.2	43.8	42.0	39.6	51.6
1974	49.2	46.3	46.1	56.3	45.9	42.7	41.6	57.2
1975	47.2	46.0	43.8	51.9	45.9	42.2	43.1	56.2
Black and other:								
1965	33.3	31.1	32.0	(2)	20.3	17.4	18.8	(2)
1970	29.2	23.9	31.5	41.2	25.3	20.4	26.9	38.9
1973	30.1	21.8	30.4	50.0	23.5	14.8	28.9	41.2
1974	34.8	26.8	34.7	50.7	27.6	18.7	29.2	49.0
1975	27.0	16.9	31.8	44.5	30.3	20.7	31.0	48.7

[1]Labor force as percent of civilian noninstitutional population.
[2]Percent not shown where base was less than 100,000.

The steady increase in the labor force participation rate of women college students seems to be related to the increasing proportion of women enrolled in 2-year rather than 4-year colleges, rising from 18 percent in 1966 to 29 percent in 1975. Also, the proportion of women enrolled who were 20 to 24 years old rose over the decade, probably reflecting the increased desire of many women to gain the education required for a job with career potential. On the other hand, the proportion of men enrolled in 2-year colleges rose less sharply and the proportion of all male college students 20 to 24 years old remained unchanged over the decade.

The increased number of students in the labor force at a time of relative job scarcity was reflected in the large over-the-year rise in unemployment rates for students of all ages.[4] Among 20- to 24-year-olds, the unemployment rate in October 1975 was close to double the rate in 1973 at the beginning of the recession. All of the 1974–75 increase in unemployment was among white students; the unemployment rate for black students was not significantly different from the very high rate of a year earlier.

Further evidence of the recession was the rise in average duration of unemployment among students, particularly among those 20 to 24 years old. Among unemployed students, the proportion looking for work for a total of 15 weeks or more rose by a third over the year for 16- to 19-year-olds, and more than doubled for those 20 to 24.

Not enrolled in school. Over 15 million out-of-school youth were in the labor force in October 1975, about the same as in 1974. However, the number with jobs dropped by 755,000, while the number unemployed rose by 600,000 to 2.3 million, almost double the level in October 1973. The labor force participation rate declined among blacks while remaining largely unchanged among whites.

Age for age, unemployment rates in October 1975 for youth not in school were generally higher than for those in school.

	Students	*Not in School*
16 to 24 years	*15.0*	*14.9*
16 and 17	*18.3*	*36.6*
18 and 19	*14.9*	*18.8*
20 and 21	*11.7*	*15.6*
22 to 24	*9.6*	*11.1*

The fact that the overall unemployment rates for the two groups were the same, in spite of the differences evident within each age group, reflects the concentration of students in the younger age brackets where unemployment is always greater; for example, the proportion of 16- and 17-year-olds among students in the labor force was 10 times higher than among nonstudents.

In spite of the sharp rise in unemployment over the past 2 years, the educational attainment distribution of unemployed out-of-school youth remained virtually unchanged. Somewhat over one-third had not graduated from high school, one-half had completed no more than high school, and the

[4]See also, Janice Neipert Hedges, "Youth unemployment in the 1974–75 recession," *Monthly Labor Review,* January 1976, pp. 49–56.

Table 3. School enrollment and labor force status of 1975 high school graduates and 1974–75 school dropouts,[1] by sex and race, October 1975 [Numbers in thousands]

Characteristics	Civilian Noninstitutional Population	Civilian labor force: Number	Civilian labor force: Percent of Population	Civilian labor force: Employed	Unemployed: Number	Unemployed: Percent of Labor Force	Not In Labor Force
Total 1975 high school graduates	3,186	1,917	60.2	1,588	329	17.2	1,269
Men	1,513	974	64.4	816	158	16.2	539
Women	1,673	943	56.4	772	171	18.1	730
White	2,823	1,736	61.5	1,474	262	15.1	1,087
Black and other	362	179	49.4	113	66	36.9	183
Enrolled in college	1,615	641	39.7	566	75	11.7	974
Men	796	318	39.9	285	33	10.4	478
Full time	722	263	36.4	236	27	10.3	459
Part time	74	55	(2)	49	6	(2)	19
White	722	298	41.3	266	32	10.7	424
Black and other	74	20	(2)	19	1	(2)	54
Women	819	323	39.4	281	42	13.0	496
Full time	770	282	36.6	244	38	13.5	488
Part time	49	41	(2)	37	4	(2)	8
White	724	300	41.4	265	35	11.7	424
Black and other	93	21	22.6	15	6	(2)	72
Not enrolled in college	1,571	1,276	81.2	1,022	254	19.9	295
Men	717	656	91.5	531	125	19.1	61
Women	854	620	72.6	491	129	20.8	234
Single	686	522	76.1	418	104	19.9	164
Married and other marital status[3]	167	97	58.1	72	25	25.8	70
White	1,377	1,138	82.6	943	195	17.1	239
Black and other	195	138	70.8	79	59	42.8	57
Total 1974–75 high school dropouts[4]	727	455	62.6	300	155	34.1	272
Men	361	297	82.3	195	102	34.3	64
Women	366	158	43.2	105	53	33.5	208
Single	229	108	47.2	70	38	35.2	121
Married and other marital status[3]	137	50	36.5	35	15	(2)	87
White	579	369	63.7	266	103	27.9	210
Black and other	151	88	58.3	34	54	61.4	63

[1] 16 to 24 years old.
[2] Percent not shown where base is less than 75,000.
[3] Includes widowed, divorced, and separated women.
[4] Persons who dropped out of school between October 1974 and October 1975. In addition, 93,000 persons 14 and 15 years old dropped out of school.

remainder had completed 1 year of college or more. As would be expected, the unemployment rate was highest among school dropouts—25.3 percent—and was lowest among college graduates—8.3 percent.

Among the unemployed youth who had completed high school, 29 percent had looked for work continuously for at least 15 weeks, while for those who had dropped out of school before graduation from high school, the proportion was 20 percent—substantially higher than a year earlier. The proportion of unemployed white youth who were out of work 15 weeks or longer almost doubled over the year, reaching the already high level for black youths.

Among 16- to 24-year-old jobseekers, both those who had graduated from high school and those who had not, the proportions reporting they had lost their job or had been temporarily laid off increased between October 1974 and October 1975.

	Total	*Lost Job or Laid Off*	*Quit Job*	*Left School*	*Other*
High school graduates:					
1974	100	31	26	17	26
1975	100	47	15	16	21
Dropouts:					
1974	100	35	22	14	30
1975	100	44	13	13	30

In 1975, a much smaller proportion of the jobless youth than in 1974 reported voluntarily leaving former jobs, not surprising since all workers tend to remain on their job when unemployment levels rise and new job prospects decrease. The proportions looking for work because they had just finished school or for other reasons such as wanting a temporary job, financial needs, or discharge from the Armed Forces, did not change significantly over the year.

Recent graduates and dropouts. About 3.2 million persons graduated from high school in 1975 and, subsequently, 51 percent enrolled in college last October. (See table 3.) This proportion was close to the 1970 percentage, after falling below the 50-percent mark in recent years. The increase in college enrollment was concentrated among whites; the percentage of blacks who enrolled in college was not significantly different from the comparable figure a year earlier. Labor force participation and unemployment among the college entrants were about the same as in 1974.

Among the 1975 high school graduates who did not go on to college, the number and proportion in the labor force was about the same as in 1974. Unemployment rates for this group were not significantly higher than a year earlier.

Eighty thousand fewer youth 16 to 24 years of age left school without receiving a high school diploma in the year ended in October 1975 than during the previous year, with men accounting for all of the decrease. Labor force participation rates were generally lower and unemployment rates higher among dropouts than among the year's high school graduates not in college. The overall unemployment rate for recent school dropouts was 34.1 percent in October 1975.

Reading 16 Families and the Rise of Working Wives—An Overview

Families in which not only the husband but also the wife, and possibly some other family member, are in the labor force (multiworker families) are a major—and growing—segment of American society. In 1975, nearly half of all husband-wife families had 2 workers or more and about two-fifths of all children under age 18 were in such families. As the numbers and proportions of these families continue to rise, their impact on the economy in terms of higher family income and consumption will increase as well.

This article examines past and current trends in the growth of families with two workers or more. It discusses such subjects as the influence of trends in fertility on the growth of these families, the relation between husbands' and wives' occupations, and some of the impact of the recession and inflation on these families.

EARLY TRENDS

Until recently, husbands have usually been the sole producers of earned income for their families, whether the income was derived from their own farms or businesses or from their labors in a factory. Wives, on the other hand, had contributed to the families' economic well-being largely through home production tasks.

From the colonial era into the 19th century, a small proportion of wives earned money operating taverns, inns, and shops; working in the needle trades and in cottage industries; and operating primary schools.[1] As early as 1820, they were employed in at least 75 kinds of manufacturing establishments. By the 1830's, women were employed in a great variety of occupations including shoebinding, typesetting, bookbinding, saddling, brushmaking, tailoring, whipmaking, and many other trades. The census of 1850 enumerated nearly 175 industries in which women were employed.[2]

With the onset of the industrial revolution in the 19th century, a transformation occurred in the economic position of women and in the character and conditions of their work. Many of their unpaid services had been transformed into paid employment and much of their work had been moved from the home to the factory and workshop, thereby increasing their range of possible employment.[3] These growing opportunities were not ignored; the proportion of wives who made contributions to their families' economic welfare in the form of money earnings began to rise. Small though it was, this change in the role of wives can be illustrated by the proportions of wives that were gainfully employed in the following selected years:[4]

Year	*Percent Gainfully Employed*
1890 (est.)	4.6
1900	5.6
1910	10.7
1920	9.0

Howard Hayghe, reprinted from May 1976 *Monthly Labor Review* with corrections (Washington, D.C.: U.S. Department of Labor, Bureau of Labor Statistics), pp. 12–15.

[1]See Edith Abbott, *Women in Industry, A Study in American Economic History* (Appleton and Co., 1910), reprinted by Arno Press, 1969.

[2]Helen L. Sumner, "Report on the Condition of Women and Child Wage Earners in the U.S.," *History of Women in Industry in the U.S.,* Vol. 9, p. 17.

[3]Sumner, "Report on the Condition of Women," p. 11.

[4]J. A. Hill, *Women in Gainful Occupations 1810 to 1890,* Census Monographs IX, p. 76. It should be noted that "gainfully employed" as used here is not really comparable to "employment" as currently defined. A person who was gainfully employed was someone 10 years or over in an occupation in which he earned money or its equivalent or produced a marketable good. The primary purpose of gainful worker statistics was to produce a count of occupations, not the employment status of persons. It seems likely that the number of employed wives was undercounted while the number of employed husbands was probably too high. For further details, see *Historical Statistics of the United States—Colonial Times to 1957* (U.S. Department of Commerce, Bureau of the Census, 1960), p. 68.

From 1900 to 1910, the proportion of working wives almost doubled. Most wives apparently worked to supplement the earnings of their husbands. Data from a 1920 survey of women wage earners in four cities (Butte, Mont.; Passaic, N.J.; Jacksonville, Fla.; and Wilkes-Barre, Pa.)[5] show that about 85 percent of the working wives in the study had husbands who also were employed. In March 1975, this proportion was *almost exactly* the same. The contribution of working wives in terms of money to their families appears to have been substantial. A study of workers employed primarily in the shoe industry in Manchester, N.H., in 1919 and 1920 showed that wives contributed an average of 26 percent of their families' wage and salary income.[6] It is startling to note that in March 1975, the earnings of working wives were about the same proportion of family income as in 1920.

Between 1920 and 1950, the proportion of employed wives—and hence the proportion of families with two workers or more—rose from 9 to 22 percent. Economic, social, and technological changes had an impact on the employment of wives. Many consumer goods and labor-saving devices became available, substantially decreasing the amount of time needed for housework as well as the variety of tasks involved. Also, World War II brought millions of wives into the work force to meet the demands of war production.

TRENDS FROM 1950 TO 1975

Over the 25-year period, 1950–75, the proportion of employed wives continued its rapid growth. Consequently the proportion of multiworker families advanced from 36 out of 100 families to 49 out of 100 in 1975. (See table 1.)

Data on multiworker families by age are not available. However, using wives' labor force participation rates by age as a proxy for the proportion of multiworker families, it appears that the growth of these families from 1950 to 1975 has been uneven, beginning among middle-aged families and continuing among progressively younger groups. (See table 2.) Thus, between 1950 and 1955, the labor force rates of women 35 to 44 and 45 to 64—women who were past the most fertile childbearing ages and whose own children were largely grown—rose by 5.2 and 7.2 percentage points, respectively, while the rates for women 20 to 24 and 25 to 34—the prime childbearing ages—rose less. By the last half of the 1960's, declining birth rates and the onset of the highest inflation to date in this century were among the factors helping to bring about a shift in this pattern: the labor force participation rates of wives under age 35 were rising at a more rapid clip than the rates of older wives.

Labor force participation on the part of wives is a measure of the growth of multiworker families. Family members other than the wife have not contributed much to the increasing proportion of multiworker families. As of March 1975, in only 16 percent of multiworker families was there an additional worker who was not the wife but rather a son, daughter, or other family member related to the husband by blood or marriage. The proportion has declined sharply since 1955. (See table 3). Offsetting somewhat the declining proportion of multiworker families where the wife was *not* the additional worker was an increase in the proportion of families where both the wife and at least one other family member were in the labor force. This proportion rose from 12.3 percent in 1950 to 17.4 percent in 1975.

Wives work or look for work for a multiplicity of reasons. The most recent Bureau of Labor Statistics survey[7] detailing the reasons why wives work was conducted for the year 1963, when only about a third of all wives were employed. This study showed that 42 percent worked because of financial necessity, 19 percent for personal satisfaction, 17 percent to earn extra money, and the

[5]Agnes L. Peterson, "What the Wage Earning Woman Contributes to Family Support," Bulletin 75 (U.S. Department of Labor, Women's Bureau, 1929), p. 14.

[6]See *The Share of Wage Earning Women in Family Support,* Bulletin 30 (U.S. Department of Labor, Women's Bureau, 1923), p. 77.

[7]Carl Rosenfeld and Vera C. Perrella, "Why women start and stop working: A study in mobility," *Monthly Labor Review,* September 1965, pp. 1077–82. Reprinted with additional tabular material as Special Labor Force Report 59.

Table 1. Trends in the proportion of husband-wife families with 2 workers or more and the labor force participation rates of wives, March 1950–March 1975 [In percent]

Year (March to March)	Proportion of Families with 2 Workers or More	Labor Force Participation Rate of Wives	Year	Proportion of Families with 2 Workers or More	Labor Force Participation Rate of Wives	Year	Proportion of Families with 2 Workers or More	Labor Force Participation Rate of Wives
1950	36.1	23.8	1961	40.3	32.7	1968	44.1	38.3
1955[1]	36.2	27.7	1962	39.8	32.7	1969	45.1	39.6
1956	37.9	29.0	1963	41.0	33.7	1970	46.2	40.8
1957	38.3[2]	29.6	1964	41.8	34.4	1971	46.0	40.8
1958	37.8	30.2	1965	41.6	34.7	1972	46.7	41.5
1959	38.8	30.9	1966	42.5	35.4	1973	47.3	42.2
1960	38.3	30.5	1967	43.9	36.8	1974	48.0	43.0
						1975	48.7	44.4

[1]The reference month for 1955 is April. [2]Estimated.

Table 2. Percentage point changes in labor force participation rates of wives 16 to 64 years old for 5-year intervals, 1950–75

Period (March to March)	16 to 19 Years	20 to 24 Years	25 to 34 Years	35 to 44 Years	45 to 64 Years
1950–55[1]	−4.2	0.9	2.2	5.2	7.2
1955–60	2.8	0.6	1.7	2.5	5.2
1960–65	1.7	5.6	4.4	4.4	4.8
1965–70	9.0	11.8	7.2	6.6	5.1
1970–75	9.6	9.7	9.0	4.9	0.0

[1]The reference month for 1955 is April.
Note: Data for years prior to 1967 include persons 14 years old and over; in accordance with the change introduced in 1967, data for subsequent years include only persons 16 years old and over.

Table 3. Families with 2 workers or more by relationship of additional worker(s) to husband, 1955–75 [Percent distribution]

Month and Year	Families with 2 Workers or More (in thousands)	Where Additional Worker Was— Total	Not Wife	Wife Only	Wife and Other Member(s)
April 1955	13,608	100.0	28.0	59.7	12.3
March 1960	15,068	100.0	25.8	59.8	14.4
March 1965	17,322	100.0	22.2	62.4	15.4
March 1970	20,517	100.0	17.5	65.0	17.5
March 1975	22,881	100.0	16.2	66.4	17.4

remainder for a variety of other reasons. These proportions might differ significantly if the survey were taken today because many more married women are working and, on average, they tend to be younger, about 39 years old compared with 42 years in 1963.

Race. For both blacks[8] and whites, the proportion of multiworker families has increased since 1965,[9] but the increase has been more rapid among whites. The proportion of white families with two workers or more has increased by about one-fifth whereas the rise among the black families was much smaller. As a result, the differences in the proportions have narrowed:

	Black	White	Percentage Point Difference
1965	51.2	40.7	10.5
1970	54.6	45.4	9.2
1975	53.7	48.4	5.3

These developments have paralleled labor force participation patterns of black and white wives—the labor force participation rates of white wives, although smaller than those of black wives, have risen faster over this period.[10]

[8]Prior to 1975, data for nonwhites are used to represent data for blacks.
[9]Data by race were first tabulated in 1965 in the Current Population Survey's Marital and Family series.
[10]Howard Hayghe, "Marital and family characteristics of workers, March 1974," *Monthly Labor Review,* January 1975, pp. 60–64.

The Inferences Module Tasks **Unit Four**

Task 21: Implied meanings

You should be able to determine the implied meanings in the readings assigned by your instructor.

Task 22: Opinions

You should be able to form a reasoned opinion to answer a question that is based on the information in a reading selection. You should be able to state and support your opinion by using both the information in a reading selection and your own information.

Task 23: Generalizations

You should be able to make a generalization that is based on information in two or more readings and your own information. You should be able to state and support your generalization by using information from the readings and your own information.

EFGHIJ—M—798